Hill Harper is the author of the *New York Times* bestseller *The Conversation,* which was an Essence Book Club Pick; the bestseller *Letters to a Young Brother,* which won two NAACP awards and was named a Best Book for Young Adults by the American Library Association in 2007; and the *New York Times* bestseller *Letters to a Young Sister.* For three consecutive years, Hill was named Outstanding Actor in a Drama Series by the NAACP Image Awards for his role on *CSI: NY.* Harper currently stars on the USA Network's hit drama *Covert Affairs.* His numerous other credits include *For Colored Girls, The Skulls, He Got Game, Lackawanna Blues,* and *The Sopranos.* He graduated magna cum laude with a BA from Brown University and cum laude with a JD from Harvard Law School. He also holds a master's degree from Harvard's Kennedy School of Government. Named one of *People* magazine's Sexiest Men Alive, he lives in Los Angeles.

HILL HARPER

Letters to an
INCARCERATED BROTHER

*Encouragement, Hope, and Healing for
Inmates and Their Loved Ones*

AVERY
an imprint of Penguin Random House
New York

an imprint of Penguin Random House LLC
375 Hudson Street
New York, New York 10014

Previously published in hardcover by Gotham Books
First trade paperback edition, April 2014
Copyright © 2013 by Uncle Frank, Inc.

Most Avery books are available at special quantity discounts for bulk purchase for sales promotions, premiums, fund-raising, and educational needs. Special books or book excerpts also can be created to fit specific needs. For details, write SpecialMarkets@penguinrandomhouse.com.

ISBN 978-1-59240-871-9

Printed in India

16th Printing

Book design by Spring Hoteling

Out of suffering have emerged the strongest souls; the most massive characters are seared with scars.

—Kahlil Gibran

CONTENTS

PART 4
BECOMING AN ACTIVE
ARCHITECT OF YOUR LIFE

PART 5
ADDENDUM

Dear:

Hill Harper my name is Brian I'AM 16 years old. And I'AM IN Jail I can't use a computer so I can't E-mail you. I wrote these to some place in NeyYork And I hope and pray the fax these letter to you are give it to you someway. Because I really want to talk to you about a lot of stuff. Hill I just finishe reading your book Letters to a young Brother it was the Best book I ever read in my life and I mean that. So if PENguiN INC give you these letter I would like to have your home address. So we can correspond back and forth to each other. Like you said in your book many young people don't have a role model I didn't have one thats why I'AM in Jail but I have one now and his name is Hill Harper. I really hope PENguiN INC give you these letter first class. And if you DO get it. Can you please write me back. I read in your book that you play in CSi:Ny I like that show and I also like csi:miami but I Do like youre show a little better. and I also read you weNt to school

Barack obama if you can
tell him I said hellow. If I was
at home I would vote him president
if I was older. I'AM only 16
years old. I tell you why I'AM
in jail and how much time I
have if you write me back.
or if you even get my
letter which I hope you Do.
well thats ever thing for write
Now hope you write back.

                    your friend and Brother

INTRODUCTION
by Hill Harper

"There is no doubt that if young white people were incarcerated at the same rates as young black people, the issue would be a national emergency."

—Dr. Cornel West, Foreword, *The New Jim Crow*

This was a book I had to write. After the publication of my first book, *Letters to a Young Brother*, I began receiving an increasing number of moving letters from inmates who had read it. With each letter I thought more about our broken systems of incarceration and our collective lack of political will to change something that is deeply flawed. It seems political debate has become more and more preoccupied with power maintenance, with few real solutions ever contemplated, let alone offered. The great issues of poverty, race, civil rights, exploited workers, or access to quality public education seem abandoned.

Meanwhile, millions of young men and women graduate from the streets and matriculate to prison rather than to college. About 2.24 million people in this country are now being held in federal and state prisons or local jails[1]—more than one-quarter of the world's total of eight million prisoners.[2] Another 4.8 million are under parole supervision or probation.[3] In thirty years, our prison population has quintupled.[4] We aren't experiencing a mass incarceration crisis, this is a hyper incarceration crisis.

No mind, because we rarely see these people, do we? *Wrong.* We distract ourselves from thinking about it by discussing the high price of fighting crime, or we bitterly debate the efficacy of helping others by means of expensive social programs. We try not to think too much about "the immigrant problem." When you can't do anything about it, it's better to lock away pain and poverty behind walls or push them to the outskirts of our boutique cities. Or like Chicago, tolerate young Black men killing one another at twice the rate of deaths of the war in Iraq. Or Washington, DC, where a mind-boggling three out of every four young Black men end up escalating through its penal system.

In "The Caging of America," Adam Gopnik writes, "Mass incarceration on a scale almost unexampled in human history is a fundamental fact of our country today—perhaps *the* fundamental fact, as slavery was the fundamental fact of 1850. In truth, there are more black men in the grip of the criminal-justice system—in prison, on probation, or on parole—than were in slavery then."

Apparently, all the proposed solutions for our social problems have become "business models." Which would cost taxpayers less: government-funded incarceration like that of the past or the increasing privatization of the present? How can we lower the "debt margin" of having to feed these "unpleasant" people whom we've sent to prison? Perhaps they can make up for it by working at jobs below minimum wage. There's an "elephant in the room" that is becoming more and more obtrusive—our system of incarceration. I, for one, am incapable of ignoring it.

So are others. In Michelle Alexander's awe-inspiring study, *The New Jim Crow*, she provides a chilling thesis: When you're locked up, you're locked out of the American mainstream and trapped within America's latest caste system. If this were equally a threat to all citizens, it would be terrifying enough (and something would have already been done about it). But that's far from the case. The target populations of our prison system are highly skewed toward three groups of citizens: Black males, low-income people in urban environments, and immigrants. African-Americans are at the top of the list, with an astonishing prison rate that is seven times higher than the imprisonment rate for white, non-Hispanic Americans. In fact, at this point, this country has locked up a *larger percentage* of its Black population than South Africa did during the worst years of apartheid.[5] How did it happen? Alexander makes the case that the burgeoning incarceration of Blacks and other minorities is actually a reemergence of old Jim Crow.

The Jim Crow laws were state and local laws in the United States enacted in the South about a year after the Civil War ended and endured until 1965. Their purpose was to establish de jure (law-based) segregation of the races in every public institution or facility of the former Confederacy. The establishment of the so-called separate-but-equal rule separated African-Americans from the white population starting in 1890, formalizing inferior economic, social, and educational conditions for Blacks. Northern segregation differed in that it was de facto (by common practice), perpetuated by housing, bank lending, and job discrimination. In the 1950s, school segregation was declared unconstitutional. The remaining Jim Crow laws were struck down by the Civil Rights Act of 1964 and the Voting Rights Act of 1965. Jim Crow, however, has endured in the form of the prison industrial complex.

The term *prison industrial complex* is an attempt to sum up the various strategies used by our system of incarceration to enslave and eliminate various populations in our country—and, as a side benefit, to create pools of cheap labor. As scholar and sixties activist Angela Davis bluntly put it: "Jails and prisons are designed to break human beings, to convert the population into specimens in a zoo—obedient to our keepers, but dangerous to each other." Such virulent criticisms of the current prison system have revealed that dirty living conditions, unpalatable food, and unchecked violence in prison have a manipulative purpose. They are there to break the will of incarcerated men and women and to ensure that a large percentage (more than half) will return again as a source of labor, often within months of being released.

The profit-making strategies of incarceration go virtually unchecked when private companies such as the Corrections Corporation of America or the GEO Group run them. Companies such as these are controlled by few government regulations. About 16 percent of federal prisoners (33,830) and nearly 7 percent of state prisoners (94,365) are housed in private facilities, even though their existence has never been statistically justified.[6] In 2001, a study by the Bureau of Justice Assistance concluded that the supposed savings involved in privatizing prisons had "simply not materialized."[7] When money was saved, it was done by reducing staff, strangling education programs, or cutting medical services.

Meanwhile, in less than thirty years, our prison population has mushroomed—six to ten times higher than the prison populations of any other industrialized nation in the entire world.[8] At the same time, our crime rates have dropped below the international average. Yet as far back as 1973, the

National Advisory Commission on Criminal Justice Standards and Goals clearly disproved the myth that decreasing crime rates have anything to do with increasing incarceration and announced that *prisons unmistakably create crime* rather than prevent it.[9] In our cities, out-of-control incarceration has infected poorer neighborhoods like a plague. There are more than 1.7 million children in the United States with one parent—usually their father—locked up.[10] Single-parent households put severe economic strain on the remaining parent, who must support her children financially and be their homemaker at the same time. They also make it more likely that children will drift into defiant, disobedient frames of mind. Many know that, statistically, they as well are slated for incarceration.

However, swollen prison populations are not just the result of drug arrests or longer sentencing. They're also caused by the way such inmates are "rehabilitated." Quite often, a prisoner is released with no resources and little planning and placed in a halfway house from which he is given a certain time period to find a job or be sent back to jail. Federal and state governments across the country have spent billions of dollars on halfway houses, despite statistics that prove they sometimes make it more likely that offenders will return.

As dire as these problems are, there is hope and there are solutions. I, along with countless others, watched, filled with inspiration, as newly elected Pope Francis washed and kissed the feet of inmates, expressing to one prisoner, "Washing your feet means I am at your service. . . . And I do it with my heart." Others serving and providing solutions include Catherine Rohr, an ex–venture capitalist who founded a nonprofit group called Defy Ventures with bankers and other financial managers. Using $800,000 in donations and $60,000 of Rohr's own money, they created an internship program that helps ex-cons succeed as entrepreneurs, income earners, fathers, and even role models for their communities.[11] Why is this so successful? In my opinion, it's because Defy educates and brings together two disparate social groups. The covert segregation of the new Jim Crow alienates the incarcerated from society. Rohr and others like her are grafting them back in. Other old and new strategies are proving just as effective. Founded in 1972, the Safer Foundation of Illinois has offered job-finding services that have reduced recidivism rates to 13 percent for their participants in a state whose recidivism rate overall is 52 percent. Mayor Cory Booker of Newark, New Jersey, sees his Office of Reentry and job-placement programs for the recently incarcerated as a way of helping Newark's economic renewal. In a state with a 50 percent recidivism rate, he's managed to lower the rate of re-arrest after nine months to 29 percent.[12]

Such statistics have inspired me to get more involved with the problem of incarceration in this country, but I suppose my reason for writing this book also has a deeper emotional component. In part, my own identity as a Black man compelled me to create it for my brothers and sisters. *Letters to an Incarcerated Brother* is an attempt to reach out to those who make up our mostly concealed incarcerated population, to speak to as many as possible against the apathy of contemporary American ideas and attitudes about the subject. This book seeks systemic change by providing advice and inspiration in the face of debilitating challenges along with encouraging words for restoring a sense of self-worth.

I want to demonstrate the transformative value of education and pathways to bring it to our prisons. I want to show how every one of us can create a detailed plan of reform and self-improvement and follow it to the letter. I want us all to blueprint the steps leading from whatever burdens we may be living with to a successful life as equal Americans. I want to offer books, manuals, and organizations that will agree to educate our prison population about the legal aspects of their incarceration and stand behind them with information as they face the parole board or teach them how to file a grievance with full knowledge of the consequences and risks.

I want to offer examples of those who rose from the mire in which they were trapped but also reveal the manipulations of the prison industrial complex to produce and hold on to cheap laborers. I want all of us to feel the suffering of families torn apart and plunged deeper into poverty by the absence of a locked-up parent. I want us to understand how their child's incarceration curtails the basic rights of mothers, forcing them to travel hundreds of miles and to pay thousands of dollars for expensive and required prepay collect-call services just to stay in contact with an incarcerated loved one. I want everyone to know that longer prison terms make it more likely that the next generation will end up suffering the same or a greater form of oppression. I want to reveal the housing, employment, counseling, training, recovery, and medical services available after parole and highlight methods to beat the odds and avoid returning. I want us to understand that, until the current prison system is reformed, we are *all* Incarcerated Brothers.

Finally, this book isn't just for the incarcerated. There are many people living in prisons not made of iron bars whom I hope this book will help free.

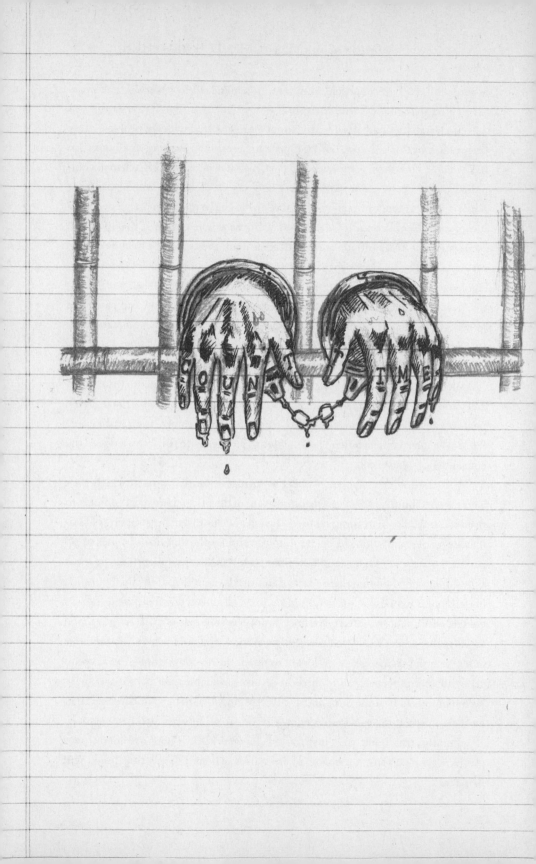

PART 1

RECONNECTING

THE WRONG BLUEPRINT

Hill,

whats good homie, you get my first letter?
i wrote you that kite weeks ago and this is
the second i sent you since being in county
fam. Been laying in the bitch forever waiting
to see how long they gonna ship me away for.
Bullshit court appointed attorney told me to cop
instead of going to trial. Said there are no wins
for a nigga like me with any jury they pick. i
just wanna get this shit ova with. i swear to
God it fuckin wearin on me. i jus wanna start
my bid eventhough its still fucked i had to
plead guilty for some shit i aint do jus cuz the
system is stacked against me. im tired going
back and forth to court sleepin on cold floors
why they try to break us down before we go
to court. And fuck peanut butter with no jelly
sandwiches and stale bologna.
i bet you dont even remember who i am. Do
you Hill Harper? i was 16 when we forst started
talkin. Told you about my life my big bro vern,
my girl Yvette and how my moms was killed. not
that her life was worth much anyway seeing

how my drunk ass pop would always beat the shit out of her. Even worse after she dies his ass takes off with some skank ass bitch and they stick us with my aunt who only takes us cuz we got nowhere else to go. Then vern who was really more like my dad then my bro gets locked up for 15-30 for bullshit possession charge. Even after all that started working for minimum wage at walmart and sticking my face in books instead of pussy. i was gonna be a graphic designer and i just learned that Yvette was going to have my son. i read your book twice and listened to what you wrote me. i really wanted to believe you. FUCK GOOD IT DID ME THOUGH. Now im up shit creek and cant afford a paddle so i suggest you stop preaching like you no everything or like you got the formula to cure all ills. Your shit dont work. its broken. You and me come from two different worlds homie. You know as much about being in my situation as i know how to sit in hamocks. i bet your ass be sittin in hamocks.

—your locked up nigga

LETTER 1

Aftermarket

First comes thought; then organization of that thought, into ideas and plans; then transformation of those plans into reality. The beginning, as you will observe, is in your imagination.

—Napoleon Hill, *Think and Grow Rich*

Dear Brotha,

Yes, I got your letters, and let me first say I'm sorry. I'm sorry it's taken me so long to respond, and I'm sorry that you had to write me more than once. I know there's no good excuse for not answering your first letter in a timely fashion, even just saying, "Hey, I got your letter." But I didn't, and I apologize.

The truth is—damn, this is hard to admit—the truth is, I didn't know what to say. So I tried to pretend that if I just ignored it, the problem would disappear.

Not to say you're a problem, but your letter to me certainly was. See, I'm somebody who wants to believe I can solve any problem—that if I don't know an answer, I'll find it eventually. But because of your letters, it's clear, my kind of thinking is just my BS ego talking. The truth is, your letters messed me up a little and brought me to my knees, literally and figuratively, because I have no clue how to answer them. No idea how to help you. I mean, I've never even spent one night in a prison, what am I supposed to say? I feel a weird mix of guilt, anger, and helplessness. Which I thought was crazy, 'cause I don't even know you. Why should it bother me so much? But that's bullshit, too, cause in a way, *I do know you.*

And those aren't the only reasons I didn't write back at first. There was another. Your trying to hold *me* responsible for what's going on with you pissed me off. I'll be blunt about it, Brotha: *It's your life, not mine.* Yet I do believe that "we are bound together in a single garment of destiny," as Dr. King said. So maybe my being pissed off at your letter was just my cover for the guilt I felt, because in a way you and I are actually inextricably linked. Your future is linked to mine, and mine to yours.

You're probably saying, "What the hell does all that mean, Hill?" What it means is that if I'm truly serious about helping you, then I will never be successful unless you are. And, ironically, you won't be successful unless I am. You and I, my friend, are inextricably linked in a single ragged and torn garment of destiny.

Those were the reasons your letter sat in the inbox on my desk as if somebody else was gonna magically come along and write you back. Then your second letter came, rightfully giving me hell for not answering. Yet all I could think about, again, was how could I respond to you when I have no idea what it feels like to be incarcerated—even for one night?

True, my first book, which you say you read cover to cover, didn't keep you out of prison. I feel damn bad about that. And let's be clear, I got love for you. I want to see you happy. I want to see you succeed, and I believe in my heart that you still can. But again, I'm also not into the blame game. Yes, I wrote a book—a user's manual for growing into manhood—but the key is: *You gotta use it!* Your letters hint at how little responsibility you want to take for your current situation. That makes me sad. It leads me to think you didn't pay much attention to my message. You see, it doesn't do you any good to read a book if you don't actually learn from it. So why don't we dead this whole issue and say *both* of us failed. Cool?

You wanted to know if I remembered those letters you wrote me almost seven years ago. You're kidding, right? Brotha, I remember the way each letter would start out with the same kind of doubt you're expressing now. Your bitterness spilled out like warm blood when you told me about your mom dying and your father absent. Your disappointment about living with your aunt, who you were sure was just doing it out of some sort of obligation. Your feeling of being in free fall, with no parachute to save you.

So now the question is, why did I bother to answer you back? You were basically just writing to tell me how I failed you and how little you needed bullshit advice. But I figured the fact you wrote me in the first place meant you actually needed something. Maybe, somebody in your corner? Remember what you said to me a long time ago? You were going to be as successful as my paternal grandfather, Harry, had been. Then, all of a sudden, you disappeared on me. Not a word. . . . Nothing for six years. I thought it was because you were too busy working out that plan. I figured you were making moves. And what's wild is that it seems you *were,* just not the right ones. And whose fault is that? Yours? Mine? Your drunk dad? The fucked-up school system? That girl who broke your heart? God's? Whose?

Now six years later. I get another letter, from a correctional facility. I've got to admit, as I sliced the letter open, seeing that new return address sliced right through me. As I already told you, I was at a loss.

You know what I did after I shoved that letter in a drawer? I shoved *you* in a drawer. Yep. I completely shut you out of my mind. You know what I did next? I did what I like to do when I'm trying to clear my head. I went to look at cars. I'm a car fanatic, got it honest, too—my dad loved cars. He even quit his job to sell cars at a dealership when I was in middle school. Anyway, I headed to the Pomona Swap Meet. A place with a low-rent name, but badass aftermarket cars.

Have you ever wanted a new car? I mean had your eye on a specific model that got your blood boiling and motivated you to fantasize about having the means to get that whip? Well, I know some people who have all the money in the world and prefer to buy a used car and add aftermarket parts as opposed to buying a car new off the lot. Have you ever seen the cars that come off of that show *Pimp My Ride*? These people ride in with clunkers and they ride out with Class. A fresh candy-coated paint, ice-cream leather, a set of rims (dubs and up), a custom wireless hotspot in your dashboard, a Fosgate amp, these things can alter the entire perspective of the driver and the outside world. I like to think of myself as an original composition of aftermarket parts that create a custom person, my best me showcasing my own unique style. *My* coat of paint may be learning another language, or my rims may be my ability to write, but all of my custom parts have to be found, acquired, learned, and earned like looking for the right set of speakers at a swap meet. But none of my aftermarket skills equipped me on how to answer your letter.

So what, right? I don't even really know you, right? At least that's what I tried to convince myself. So I started looking for another way to escape dealing with you. I had some friends heading down to Daytona Beach, Florida. They asked me to roll, so I went.

PIT STOPS

After I connected with my friends in Daytona, I was surprised when they said we were heading to the Daytona International Speedway. Never been there before, didn't know they let Brothas in. Ha. In the parking lot on the way in we saw a sweet 1969 Camaro Z28. Out of curiosity I asked my boy how much one of those would run on the open market. My jaw dropped when he told me he had just seen one sell at the Barrett-Jackson auto auction for fifty thousand dollars! A quick Google search found the original sticker was less than three thousand bucks. Talk about return on investment. Ever seen any race-car driving? I like fast cars myself, and I like to watch the pros race. It may sound stupid, but for some reason endurance racing is my favorite. Little did I know, the best endurance racing in the country is in Daytona, Florida. In the course of a twenty-four-hour race, every car covers more than twenty-five hundred miles. Around and around they roar on a 3.56-mile closed-course track within the Daytona Beach speedway arena—right through the entire day and night. My buddies and I saw about eight hours of it because I wanted to see if Porsche, which has the most overall victories of any manufacturer, could add to its lead.

Doing anything with cars is one of my escape hatches when there's too much of the world coming at me, and I suppose part of what I wanted to escape was feeling shitty about a letter from someone I've never even met. But guess what? All that race did was bring me right back to thinking about you. You quoted back to me that I'd said you and your generation were "the newest perfect models." Just as each year's car model gets better than the previous—more powerful, easier to handle, more endurance—you, my brother, the newest generation, are the most brilliant, the most perfect model of the human species. You *know more* than any generation before you did, right? You're the *2014 Porsche GT of the human species*. You are the human equivalent of Internet-enabled entertainment systems, adaptive and responsive suspensions, and dual-gear, seven-speed tiptronic transmissions. You are turbocharged, even if you don't believe it.

So the sight of those Porsches, Aston Martins, and Ferraris roaring around that track like lions reminded me of *you*. Suddenly I realized that your incarceration hadn't changed anything. I *still* believed you were the newest perfect model. Nothing—not even prison—can take that away from you. I know your options have changed, but you're still that same person with the *same potential*. And I still love you and still believe in you.

Since we're on the subject of endurance racing, let me hit you with something else: At Daytona, as those incredibly well-tuned machines roar around the track and day changes to night and back to day again, *every single car* needs to stop, to get out of the race for a time. They call 'em pit stops. It happens over and over during those twenty-four hours. Even the greatest of the race cars can't make it without those stops.

During a pit stop, each car needs five to twenty mechanics to put it back in shape. After a pit stop, the car is renewed; it's faster and performs better. The new tires and mechanical adjustments are made *in the middle of the race.* And often those adjustments are more important than the shape the car was in initially. The same holds true for you. I don't give a damn about all the mistakes from your past. I only care about you . . . your future . . . and how you can move forward.

What's more, no single driver can make the entire twenty-four-hour race on his or her own. Each car has several different drivers. At some of these pit stops, the new driver is waiting to change places with the old driver. It only takes a split second. One jumps out, and the other jumps in.

I see the span of a person's life in kind of same way. Short, flashy bursts of performance usually don't count for much. It's all about managing to make it over the long haul. Brother, you are exactly like those Porsches and Aston Martins and Ferraris, but you are worth more. They're true performers, but like any machine, they need their pauses. As you go through prison time, the same holds true for you. You're not out of the race yet by any means. You're just off to the side to refuel and make a few tune-ups and adjustments.

Remember, even if a dude can't afford the best car off the lot, as he gets more ends he can add to it in the aftermarket. He can improve it slowly, one new piece at a time. He may say he's trying to "trick it out," but if you really break down what he's replacing the original parts that are either worn out or not the best design and replacing them with these aftermarket improvements. And sometimes after enough improvements are added you can't even recognize the car anymore. I want you to think about your life the same way. What aftermarket parts do we need to add to your education, spirit, finances, family, faith, discipline, courage to change you for the better? So many that others might not even recognize you when we're done. That's right—we gonna upgrade you through the aftermarket and like that Camaro your value will skyrocket!

I'm telling you right now, if you're willing to trust me again—I promise—we can do it. Do I have all the answers? Hell no. But if we work together and access our resources, I know we can help each other. Oh yes, this isn't a one-way thing. I will rely on you to look out for me, too, because there are a lot of areas in my life where I need to be a better man, and by no means have I figured it all out yet.

Are you ready to ride with me? Let's go on this journey *together*. Shit, what have you got to lose? Don't let fears and doubts stop you. Fear is just an acronym for "False Experiences Appearing Real." Let's do this: Hit me back when you can, and let me know if you're in or not. Time's wasting. And BTW, I don't be sittin' in hammocks!

Take care,

Hill

P.S. You know how there are little fortunes in cookies you get at a Chinese restaurant? When I was a kid I used to tape the good ones up on my walls. But then I decided, why not make my *own* fortune!? Since then, I've been writing and taping up motivational words and sayings on my mirror, cupboards, walls, and even on the dashboard of my car. I usually write them on an index card of some sort. I do it to elevate my frame of mind and spirit. I do it because words are powerful, and if I put enough positive ones in me, I get refueled, like a car at the pit stop. Even the Bible tells us, "The tongue has the power of life and death, and those who love it will eat its fruit" (Proverbs 18:21). Writing down positive words is something I want you to get in the habit of doing. Come on, at least try it. I put one of mine in this letter so you can see what I mean.

REFUEL

LETTER 2

The Nature of Freedom

The preparation and experience most necessary for understanding and valuing a great gift is experiencing its opposite.

—Anonymous

Freedom is nothing but a chance to be better.

—Albert Camus

Dear Brotha,

    I'm gonna keep it 100 with you, fam—I'm pissed off. And you might be reading this saying, "Awww, Hill Harper is pissed. I'm real sorry; some actor in his fancy apartment is pissed—*fuck* him!" Whether you're thinking that or not, I want you to know it's true. I'm fed up because we've been exchanging letters for a while now, and I get a letter from you telling me *again* how you don't see or believe that you can break the cycle you're in. And you finish it in your own classy way:

but its not as easy as you try to
make it. you dont fuckin get it how
it is to be where i am. To be who
i am. whats the use of thinking
positive? Huh?
WHAT THE FUCK IS THE USE?
WHERE THE FUCK HAS IT GOTTEN ME?

FUCK THIS.

You know what? Fuck it then. I quit. I guess I can write to you till my hand is sore, but if you don't want to help yourself, then ain't shit-else I can do. If *you* want to see change in your life, then *you* need to be prepared to change. It's that simple. And, to be fair, I know that *we all* go through periods of doubts where we question ourselves. We let the *fear* (False Evidence Appearing Real) rule our egos and the voice of doubt and anxiety drive out all the other sounds. Most fears we carry are faker than a cheap weave. You *have* to use techniques to quiet the voices of fear and doubt in your head before they make you think that you *can't* do something. That you can't break the recidivism, the revolving door that keeps so many Brothas locked up for their entire lives.

Our deepest fear is not that we are inadequate. Our deepest fear is that we are powerful beyond measure. It is our light, not our darkness, that most frightens us. We ask ourselves, Who am I to be brilliant, gorgeous, talented, fabulous? Actually, who are you *not* to be? You are a child of God. Your playing small does not serve the world. There's nothing enlightened about shrinking so that other people won't feel insecure around you. We are all meant to shine, as children do. We were born to make manifest the glory of God that is within us. It's not just in some of us; it's in everyone. And as we let our own light shine, we unconsciously give other people permission to do the same. As we are liberated from our own fear, our presence automatically liberates others.

—Marianne Williamson

Last night, for some reason, though I was home in L.A., I couldn't sleep. I'd finally answered your first letter, but you hadn't answered me back. I began to believe you really had written just to tell me I had failed you.

I kept thinking about your situation and the ways it mirrored the hundreds of thousands of other newest perfect models of your generation who are stuck behind bars in a six-by-nine. I began thinking about your feeling that everybody, including me, has let you down. I found myself trying to imagine what it might be like to be locked up. I began imagining what it's like to be known as a number, not a name; what it's like to be told what to do every minute of the day, what it's like to wake up in the middle of the night, roll onto your back, and stare at bars. What it's like to be told when to shave, sleep, and shit.

The other day I had asked a smart Brother I knew who had done an eight-year bid what was the worst thing about prison. And he said: "For me, prison was terrible because I was idle. For eight years, I had to wait for my life to start again. The day they sentenced me I felt like a ghost, not real. As if I didn't exist anymore. . . . You are expected to be willing to fight in prison, but it's not about winning or losing. It's more about standing up for yourself. Opportunity is low in prison, violence is high, there are mental patients everywhere, gangs, racism, but worse than that, it is just being frozen in time."

I couldn't sleep, so finally I turned on the lamp and reached for the book that was lying half-open on the side table. I hadn't touched it for a long time and I'd forgotten what it was. Turned out it was the life story of a guy who's suffered some pretty rough pit stops on his race through life, some of them just as rough as yours. When he was just a little younger than you, he nearly lost all hope, all belief. He even spent some time behind bars.

I'm talking about Sidney Poitier, the Oscar-winning actor. I should be finished with his book, *The Measure of a Man: A Spiritual Autobiography,* in a few days, and if you want it and they allow it, I'll send it to you.

I myself consider Sidney Poitier a first-class mentor. He's the coolest cat for any generation—smart, classy, successful. He represents strength through intelligence. The thought of what he's achieved, compared to the way he started out, keeps me afloat during difficult situations, especially when I begin to question myself. We all, no matter who we are—no matter where or from what circumstances we come—find ourselves in need of inspirational guidance. I have tried to build my own "personal board of directors" made up of people I know and others, like Mr. Poitier, that I read about.

Sidney Poitier was the very first Black man to win an Academy Award, back in 1964. Almost fifty years later, in 2009, President Barack Obama pinned the Presidential Medal of Freedom—our country's highest civilian honor—on him.

Sounds like somebody born under a lucky star, right? But Sidney is no stranger to fear and doubt. By the time he was sixteen, he was often homeless in New York, sleeping on roofs and doing freelance gigs as a dishwasher whenever he could grab one. Winter came, and he found himself facing it without a hat, a scarf, boots, or even a coat. So he joined the army, just to get out of the cold and have three squares a day. Army discipline only ended up igniting his rage and leading to him throwing a chair at an officer. He admits it was a foolish decision, a stupid way to try to get out of the army. That's when they locked him up while they determined whether he was a nutcase or just a bad guy. If the verdict had been "bad guy," he could have been court-martialed and sent up for twenty-five years.

Sidney calls this period of his life the lowest one of all. But he also calls this same time his "indispensable years." According to him, "the young man must go 'down' in order to find the right path for going 'up.' Call it the 'time of ashes.' In some African tribes the young boys must cover their faces with ashes before their initiation into manhood. In certain Nordic cultures the young boys used to sit down in the ashes by the fire in the center of the lodge house until they were ready to take on their adult role."[1]

Sidney Poitier's time of ashes taught him to fight for his life. It gave him an opportunity to balance the good and the evil impulses whirling through his mind. He put all of these energies where they fit—into the natural order of things, where they'd work to his advantage. So when a situation demanded aggressive energy, he had it on tap, but when it required calmness, compassion, or reflection, he had a supply of that, too.

I'm hoping that your time inside will turn out to be the same kind of "time of ashes" for you, as you move toward a greater balance of light and shadow. By telling you about Sidney Poitier, I'm trying to tell you that "shit happens" to everybody. We've all gone through some hardships in life. We all have a story to tell. Sometimes nobody could have made it happen any differently. Sometimes we play a big role in what happens without even being aware of it. Sometimes we know we've made a bad decision, but we follow through with it anyway. Sidney did all those things, but once he'd learned to temper his impulses, he discovered gold among the ashes. Maybe you can, too.

It may not make sense to you now, but I'm asking you to surrender to your own time of ashes. Most people don't associate manhood and power with the maturity it takes to surrender. But sometimes surrendering can be the most powerful, courageous action you can take. Because when it comes to making big changes, we have to surrender the old, the trite, and the tired to create space for what can be new.

MENTAL FREEDOM

> Conformity is the jailer of freedom and the enemy of growth.
>
> —John F. Kennedy

It all boils down to mental freedom. Yes, I know you're incarcerated; your body is locked up. But does that mean your mind can't be free? Nelson Mandela inspired and influenced the world from a two-by-two prison cell. We may not have total control over what happens to our physical selves in this life. But no one and nothing can control our minds; no one can stem their freedom unless we let them do it. So the next time you feel the prison walls closing in on you or can't take another moment of a bitch-made corrections officer, just remind yourself what Mahatma Gandhi said about his jailers: "You can chain me, you can torture me, you can even destroy this body, but you will never imprison my mind."

"You can chain me, you can torture me, you can even destroy this body, but you will never imprison my mind."

Brotha, can you actually push yourself to get to a place where your body is in prison but your mind is free? I think you can. No, that's bullshit—I *know* you can. Try repeating to yourself out loud, three times in a row, *My body is in prison, but my mind is free. . . . My body is in prison, but my mind is free. . . . My body is in prison, but my mind is free. . . .*

Peace,

Hill

P.S. That picture you sent was funny.

MENTAL
FREEDOM

LETTER 3

Losing Is Learning

There is no better [thing] than adversity. Every defeat, every heartbreak, every loss, contains its own seed, its own lesson on how to improve your performance the next time.

—Malcolm X

Hey, Brotha,

Your letter couldn't have come at a better time and your opening definitely made me laugh!

From what you said in the rest of your letter, where you're at now is like being in limbo. Stuck in a general population jail that has every variety of incarcerated person, from murderers and drug kingpins to petty thieves to guys picked up for smoking a joint.

I know there's hardly any training or recreational programs exist in these temporary joints. I hope your sentencing and assignment to a prison comes up soon, so you have more certainty about where you're headed. The funny thing about certainty is that even if the answer isn't always what we want it to be, at least it allows us to make a plan. Waiting around in limbo must be hell. It's a kind of "bullpen therapy," a system designed to either wear you down so you cop out and take a plea bargain, or numb you to everything going on around you. But we're not going to let that happen, are we?

Hill,

You talked a lot about honesty so i
just wanted you to know that you
trying to explain race cars to me
made think you were the whitest
black guy i ever talk to in my life.

Compared to what's happening to you, this won't sound like shit, but I just walked in the door after a bumper-to-bumper rush-hour commute from a location in L.A. where we shoot most of *CSI: NY*. Don't ask why we shoot a New York show in L.A. . . . because the reason is, like most things, money. Bottom line, it's less expensive to shoot our show in Los Angeles. The producers and the network want to make the show for the lowest cost possible.

THE COST-BENEFIT ANALYSIS OF ACQUIRING MONEY

I have a saying: You can't be free if the cost of being you is too high. I'll explain what I mean by that in a second, but first, let's talk money, a subject that's always on a lot of people's minds. The interesting thing about money is that it influences the choices and decisions we make in so many areas of our lives in profound ways. For example, if you were to ask the vast

You can't be free if the cost of being you is too high.

majority of people who are in prison why they took the actions that led them to be there, most would say, "M-O-N-E-Y."

It's true, the vast majority of crimes committed are crimes related to getting money. Drug dealers sell drugs—for what? M-O-N-E-Y. Burglaries and robberies and auto theft are committed for what? M-O-N-E-Y. Most fights, arguments, and even divorces happen over what? M-O-N-E-Y.

It's often said—and I'm sure you've heard this before—that money is the root of all evil. But I think of it very differently. I think it is our perception of and *relationship* to money that's the root of most poor choices.

Most of us have been taught the wrong things about money. We've been taught that money is a *result,* so therefore we should chase it. I mean, you can't even listen to a song these days—"getting paper," "racks on racks," "get money," "got a condo on my wrist"—we hear it all the time. Money is something to chase, to pursue—a result. But what money truly is—and the wealthiest among us know this—is a *tool,* not a result. Just like a hammer, money is a resource tool that allows us to build the life we want to live. And if we think about money that way, we can use the tool of money to build the most efficient and effective life for ourselves. A hammer is a great tool when it's used for the purpose for which it was designed. So if you're pounding a nail, a hammer is perfect. But if you're cleaning some hardwood floors, a hammer will do more damage than good.

So we have to be smart about using the tool specific to our needs, instead of thinking, "I'm just going to grab this because it's what I need." Now, I'm sure you're sitting there saying, "That's great, Hill, it's easy for someone like you who has all the money in the world to tell somebody else money isn't a result, it's a tool. . . . Only people with money say this, 'cause broke folks ain't feeling this." But I'm not telling you money isn't important. I'm saying that's it's an incredibly important *resource tool.* And like any other resource—whether it's time, knowledge, or experience—effectively using money will make the difference between failure and success. I'm not trying to say money isn't important—it's vital—but what's more important is how we pursue it and use it. We can't just get it by any means necessary. The whole idea of "getting real money" is relative; it's not absolute. You probably didn't hear about this, but Drake recently tweeted, "The first million is the hardest." In response, Texas billionaire T. Boone Pickens retweeted that and responded, "The first billion is a helluva lot harder." Yeah, he did kind of shit on Drake, but that's the point. In T. Boone's circle, Drake's money is "short." In Drake's circle, his money is "long." Yet to people who are homeless on the street, even one thousand dollars could make an immediate impact on the quality of their lives. "Short money," "long money," "big money"—all of these are relative.

Rather than focusing on money as a result, our challenge is how we can back into the plan for our life, what resources in education and training we need to execute that plan, and how much acquiring those resources would cost in terms of money. Once we determine all that—find out how much money we need in terms of food, shelter, clothing, and the other basics of life—we need to do a cost-benefit analysis of how much time and what type of activity will be required to acquire that necessary amount. You may be thinking, "What the hell is a cost-benefit analysis?"

So I'm about to blow your mind right now. Remember in one of your earlier letters you told me that you didn't want to keep working your "stupid minimum-wage job" and that's why you even got to the point of considering dealing on the corner like your Brother Vernon did? Not taking into account the question of whether dealing poison in our community is the right thing to do or not, let's do a complete, straight cost-benefit analysis of that "stupid minimum-wage job" you hate versus the possibilities of dealing drugs on the corner. I think you told me Vernon spent up to eight hours a day either on the block or in front of a certain bodega, and you said he was dealing for eight months before he got arrested for the first time. That's 1,947 hours of dealing. Then you said he also usually got picked to spend a day, sometimes two, in county before he was out . . . and over the past few years Vernon has been out of county several times with stints of a few weeks, and now he's gonna be upstate for fifteen to thirty. That's 131,472 hours for the first fifteen years locked up. Adding those hours he spent waiting to deal on the street brings us a grand total of 133,419 hours dedicated to a life as a dealer. Now, what's the total amount of his so-called earnings during the time he was dealing? For example, let's make it a big number—$200,000. If we divide the amount he earned by the time he spent "earning" it, it comes out to $1.50. So for all the hours he spent on the block and in and out of the system, based on my calculations, he was earning somewhere around $1.50 an hour. If you were at that so-called dead-end minimum-wage job for the same number of hours, you'd make almost five times that amount at $7.25 an hour. Steven D. Levitt and Sudhir Venkatesh actually gained access to three years of records kept by a Chicago gang lieutenant and in *Freakonomics*, Levitt and Stephen J. Dubner wrote:

So J. T.[the lieutenant] paid his employees $9,500, a *combined* monthly salary that was only $1,000 more than his own official salary. J. T.'s hourly wage was $66. His three officers, meanwhile, each took home $700 a month, which works out to about $7 an hour. And the foot soldiers earned just $3.30 an hour, less than the minimum wage. So the answer to the original question—if drug dealers make so much money, why are they still living with their mothers?—is that, except for the top cats, they *don't* make much money.

SINGLED OUT

In your letters, you keep insisting to me that there isn't anybody with worse luck than you. You feel like you've been singled out for suffering. You speak as if you're unique, a rare, tragic case. You say you didn't do what they're accusing you of. You were just there when they found the drugs in the car. You can't stop feeling tortured by the injustice of all of it. You even take that point of view to the max by writing:

> it sucks to be in a loosing situation where everything is going wrong. i havent heard my son rjs voice in months and they fuckin make us share underwear fuckin underwear. its like they think were animals. i try to keep my head up but sometimes it just feels like God has turned away from me.

• • •

Only God could tell me if that's really the case, but I can't really buy the "singled out" idea. Sadly, your situation is far from unique. In fact, it's all too common. I looked up a few figures about our prison system and discovered that it has swollen to such gigantic proportions, it's larger than the entire university system in this country. Pretty ironic, isn't it, seeing that it costs $10,000 *more* to send somebody to prison than it does to send them to an Ivy League college? We've outstripped every country in the world in terms of the number of people we incarcerate. At the same time, the quality of our public education lags behind that of other countries more every year. We're the world champs when it comes to locking people up, yet when it comes to giving people the skills, knowledge, and hope to pursue other alternatives, we seem to suck more each year. Over two million three hundred thousand American citizens call a state or federal prison their home.

Lots of people are making money out of that situation, Brotha, believe you me. You gotta read up on this stuff, bruh, I'm telling you, it'll blow your mind. You see, in the past, state and federal governments ran all prisons. Now the building and management of quite a few have been turned over to private companies—for profit.

Locking people up and keeping them there as long and as often as possible has become an industry. Like any corporation, the companies that build and manage prisons only stand to gain by building more lockup facilities. As of December 2010, in this country, almost 130,000 incarcerated people out of a total 2.2 million are being housed in these private for-profit mills. They work for less than one-fifth of the legal minimum wage and also have to deal with foul food, cramped conditions, and medieval medical care. Our prison system has become a runaway

Our prison system has become a runaway perpetual-motion machine that nobody seems to be able to stop.

perpetual-motion machine that nobody seems to be able to stop. It doesn't seem to matter how many respected thinkers point out its flaws. Investigative journalist Eric Schlosser and political scholar Angela Davis call the whole exploitive system the "prison industrial complex." Davis, in fact, put it very bluntly:

> Jails and prisons are designed to break human beings, to convert the population into specimens in a zoo—obedient to our keepers, but dangerous to each other.[1]

So, Brotha, the real truth is much sadder than what you've been claiming. Instead of being unique, your situation is—in a tragic way—"*normal.*" Normal, at least, for the majority of Americans who are poor or belong to an ethnic minority, or don't have a green card.

I know you've heard it, but maybe can't see yourself as being a part of it. Our prison population doesn't equally represent all American communities. African-Americans are at the top of the list, with a crazy imprisonment rate of more than one out of every twenty-five of us. That's six times higher than the imprisonment rate for white, non-Hispanic Americans. At this point, this country has locked up a larger percentage of its Black population than South Africa did during the worst years of apartheid. In Washington, DC, three out of every four young Black men at some point in their lives end up behind prison bars or in the penal system. As Michelle Alexander, author of a powerful book on our prison system called *The New Jim Crow,* has pointed out, when you're locked up, you're automatically—and sometimes permanently—locked out of American society. Alexander says that our prison system has put in place legal structures that in many ways create a subclass, a class of incarcerated or formerly incarcerated individuals, just like legal Jim Crow segregation in the South before and during the civil rights movement.

> **My heart has already been broken in more than two million two hundred pieces—one for every single person incarcerated in this country.**

Maybe you understand where I'm coming from now. In all honesty, what has happened to you does break my heart, but my heart has already been broken in more than two million two hundred pieces—one for every single person incarcerated in this country.

PRISON SUCCESS STORIES

Now, I'll bet you're asking yourself why I'm being so damn negative in this letter. I just want to make it clear to you that you aren't being singled out. And in certain ways, looking at the makeup of prisons from the economic and race aspect, you might be thinking that there is no way to win. But the system doesn't have to beat you. The truth is, plenty of people have conquered this beast we call the system. There are folks everyone has heard of, like 50 Cent, Michael Vick, and Robert Downey Jr. And there are many other success stories who are not so-called celebrities. Take Tracey Syphax, who did his time for drug trafficking—today he's an entrepreneur, CEO of Capitol City Contracting Inc. and Phax Group LLC.

Syphax took risks as a young drug trafficker but realized that the same attraction to risk was what made entrepreneurs succeed. "I spent my entire young adult life taking risk every day standing on that corner," he said. "In 1995, I took a risk and started my company Capitol City Contracting with my brother-in-law, also an ex-offender, as my first employee." Jay-Z said, "I sold kilos of coke. I'm guessing I can sell CDs." The list goes on and on. Kathy Boudin, PhD, was convicted in 1984 of felony murder for participating in an armed robbery motivated by extremist left-wing politics, during which three people were killed. She was finally released in 2003 and received a doctor of education degree from Columbia University's Teachers College. Today she's a professor at Columbia University School of Social Work. And what about Jim Harris, who was an IV drug user who ended up doing time in the Texas Department of Corrections for possession of cocaine? With the aid of a charismatic volunteer chaplain, he managed to turn his life around and is now a drug-free owner of a computer business.

Finally, let's not leave out Wilbert Rideau, who's now known in the world of journalism throughout the world. He was a death-row inmate in Louisiana who not only became an award-winning journalist while he was still locked up, but who also received one of journalism's most prestigious awards, the George Polk Award. Like you, Rideau claimed he was innocent and unjustly convicted. But he also did something about it. He developed the skills of a journalist while he was on death row, spread the word about his innocence to the outside world, and finally got his sentence overturned. When he got out, he started a program called the Innocence Project to help others who'd been falsely accused.

In your letter you talk about your "bad luck." You chalk up your arrest to "being in the wrong place at the wrong time." Maybe so. But these prison success stories I'm telling you about didn't really have anything to do with luck. "Being in the right place at the right time" did not turn around these people's lives. None of their good fortune *happened* to them. No magic dust was sprinkled on them, they didn't win the lotto, and no one gave them the hookup. They made it happen. They accomplished such stunning life changes and subsequent victories because they never gave up on the idea that they had a right to be unreasonably happy. They knew and believed that they had that right and the ability to create their own lives.

These future giants of music, sports, business, journalism, and education understood that no matter where you end up, it doesn't have to be the absolute determinant of your ultimate fulfillment. Somehow they learned that hope and belief are all you need to move toward any goal. Hope is a uniquely human quality that is the powerful necessary precursor to belief. Why? Because even for the most hardened and cynical, hope gives us the right attitude to be able to believe again. And belief is something that we all carry with us. Sometimes it feels scary to believe in ourselves because none of us want to be hurt by taking a chance, and those old habitual voices of doubt start to creep in and push us back toward our old way of being and old beliefs. But the more you substitute new beliefs, new thoughts, new ideas, new plans, the easier believing becomes. In many ways, belief is like a muscle. You know when you're lifting weights and you first start training a body part? That muscle is small and weak, and you lift the light weights tentatively. But the more you train it, the stronger it becomes, and the weight you used to struggle with becomes so easy to lift that you use it as your warm-up weight. You can throw it around. The same holds true for belief. It's a muscle that we must build and train. We can build our belief muscles by using affirmations,

Even for the most hardened and cynical, hope gives us the right attitude to be able to believe again.

small words or phrases that reiterate our trust in ourselves. As I mentioned earlier, I stick these words up on mirrors and my dashboard. Try coming up with a few of your own, like:

I can do whatever I set my mind to.

I am able to turn things around.

I can have a new attitude about my future.

In your letter, you went into some detail about the deprivations of jail. It's sad to hear that there isn't even a library in the temporary holding place where you are. But that missing library is part of one of the prison's most powerful tools. Everyone in the prison system is forced into living in "jail time," a time of deprivation, and that includes even the corrections officers. I just called your jail and was informed that I'm not allowed to send you more than one book a month.

There's no reason for it except as a means of deprivation. The poison of deprivation is inside the head of that female guard you told me frisks your aunt and treats her rudely on those few times she comes to visit. It's in the lousy food they give you, which you tell me is close to indigestible. But there's an antidote to all that poison, and it works every time.

BELIEF IS YOUR INEXHAUSTIBLE ALTERNATIVE POWER

Your belief is the thing that can't be poisoned by "jail time." No one—including the guards—can destroy it. Belief in oneself is an inexhaustible source of power that is accessible to all of us, no matter what our circumstances. Psychology teaches us that if you tell a person that they are stupid, they will do worse on a test than if you said nothing. If you tell someone that they are a criminal, they are more likely to commit a crime. But the inverse is true as well. If you tell someone that they are smart, the same person does *better* on the test. So the most important thing is what you actually *believe* yourself to be. Saying you will never amount to anything is the perfect way to guarantee that you will never amount to anything.

> **Your belief is the thing that can't be poisoned by "jail time."**

Your current situation is convincing you what to believe, but it doesn't have to be that way. Are you willing to be courageous and vulnerable enough to believe the truth—that you will do great, positive things in this world? The power of belief is waiting inside you like a hidden treasure. All you need to learn is how to access it. What will you use the power for? Will you use it to envision a new future? Once you surrender to belief, nothing can stop you from building a happy life that is specific to you. You can even build that life within those prison walls. As you do, your belief in it will create a kind of momentum that permeates everything you decide to do, every step you take. I *believe* in you, and that belief gets stronger every day.

> **Once you surrender to belief, nothing can stop you from building a happy life that is specific to you.**

Hit me back, Brotha.

Peace,

Hill

P.S. Oh, I almost forgot. I told my man Lemon Andersen, an amazing spoken-word artist who has written and performed award-winning one-man shows and off-Broadway plays. I consider him a true genius. For a period of his life he was in and out of the pen, and he also did a five-year bid before overcoming that life and carving his own path. I told him about you and asked him if there is anything he wanted to share with you. I slipped what he wrote me into this letter. Enjoy his wisdom and flow.

DOPE BOY FRESH

Dope boy fresh.
Mr. Manager, lookout.
Pusher-man on the street
Momma ain't around, so how else I'm going to eat?
Puts me in his Lexus, plush leather seats, tells me
"Forget food, these crack vials could put Jordans on your feet."

I take a couple bundles on the humble
a few bombs on the arm
figure selling poison to my neighbors won't do me no harm
and that was the beginning, then it was all about winning
and living like what I'm doing ain't nowhere near sinning
this money is making me devilish and all about self
yeah I'm selling to my man's moms
cause if she don't get it from me
she gonna get it from someone else.

And I become heartless and Godless,
regardless of what the old folks in my hood thought
so what, I'm selling what killed my mother?
She was her own grown woman

with her own free will, that's not my fault
and you might not like me
but these Nikes make me feel so loved
wonder what happens when I give this hustle
a little more push and a whole lot more shove
probably make Ph.D. loot without having a degree.

My girl's stressing for my time
but what can she do that this paper can't do for me?
Tell her my mind is on that dollar sign, yo
girl, live your life, don't bother mine, sho'
nuff you want time, whoa
love is love, but holler baby wait on line
go tell your mom that your love losing manners
to this blow mixed with Arm & Hammer
it's the next best living,
and if she don't understand ghetto grammar
tell her the new nine-to-five is
cocaine mixed with baking soda
the new payola,
drawing funds out of packages
the new Crayola.

Her eyes stay bloodshot
from my long nights on the block
praying a lot that I don't get knocked,
or fall blood, braaaaattt, to the gunshot
she can't sleep cause of all the mercies,
she mercies me.
I tell her to,

"Just Chill, I got something special
for our second anniversary."

But it lands on the fifteenth of the month
which means a guaranteed G-stack
so that night I tell her that I gotta make a run,

"Baby Girl, I'll be's back," but she don't believes that
copping to me a . . .

"Please, that, like tonight, like, something ain't right.
Like, my heart don't needs that, like we don't, like,
need money, like, I don't even care.
Like, why don't we just go upstairs?
Like my father has some beers, like,
I will let you run an iron, straighten the curlers out my hair.
Like, if I really mean something to you,
then, like, baby don't go nowhere."

Thinking love or the money?
Money or the love?
Should I go straight with my life,
or should I go straight thug?
Love or the money?
Money or the love?
Should I be living like how I'm living
or should I stop pushing dem drugs?
Answer: money might always get spent,
but love don't always pay the rent.
So I'm bent on making this dollar,
even though it don't make any cents.
"Like he never, like, even listen to me that night he got caught, like, I knew that
*   what we had was history."*
What pisses me, is that I'm in jail, you should hold me down.
"Like I'm only sixteen, like, how long am I supposed to stay around?"
Yeah, but you're supposed to be all the way in it, you know, to win it.

"Like remember one thing, like, I was always in it, but the love, like, that I wanted, like, you was never, like, really with it."

Forget you then. I don't even see you being my spouse.

"Like, I never thought, like, I'd be saying it's over, like, let alone in a courthouse."

So it's over?

"Like, over."

Over, over?

"Like, over, like, over."

Then let me go back to my cell and cry on my own shoulder.

BELIEVE

LETTER FROM A LOCKED-UP BROTHER

Hill,

i went back and reread a few of your letters
and i just dont think you get i mean how could
you? its so easy for you to tell me to focus and
stay positive and tofree my mind when your out
there driving your Bentley to csi and checking
time on your Rolex but that shit dont matter
where i am. why are you really doing all this
goody two shoes shit? You like sittin in hamocks
that much? Does writing me make you feel
less guilty?

—rB

LETTER 4

Whose Life Is It?

The Stigma of the Incarcerated

No man is a prisoner and nothing else.

—Archbishop William Temple

The only thing I want to know is what you are going to do next.

—Robert Griffin III

H ey, man,

How are you? I'm on layover for a flight to Iowa from Atlanta, where I'm shooting a film. I've been campaigning for President Obama in Iowa. It's considered a swing state, which means it could swing either way in the election. And since the Electoral College determines who becomes president, each vote is especially critical in a swing state. I think one of the things that make our country great is that it's a participatory democracy. But that only works if *we the people* participate (or are allowed to).

I think it's truly shameful that in many states, ex-felons are prevented from voting and participating in their fundamental democratic right. Once someone has served time (paid their debt) and is released from incarceration and paroled, he should be able to participate in the democratic process.

While in Iowa, I figured I'd pay a surprise visit to a great-uncle who means a lot to me and just had heart bypass surgery. There were no direct flights to Fort Madison, Iowa, where he lives, so I opted for changing planes in Memphis. Not a great idea, because somehow a forty-five-minute layover has stretched into almost three hours.

I suppose there's a lesson in that. The path from one place to another often isn't always a straight line. We may believe it's going to be simple—from here to there—but we end up with unforeseen detours and unanticipated delays. Even so, we hold up by keeping our destination in mind. And some of those detours even bring us benefits, such as the chance my layover just provided for me to write to you. Sorry to hear about that letter you got from your aunt. But what makes you think she's conning you by saying she's had to change jobs? That her new schedule won't let her come up for visiting hours for several months? I don't know your aunt, of course, but a three-page letter seems like an awful lot of trouble just to put over a lie. Why don't you take her at her word and write her back? Tell her honestly about your disappointment at not being able to see her.

We all want to be innocent until proven guilty. Sometimes we have to learn to give people the benefit of the doubt. And if they don't live up to that "benefit," then so be it.

IT STARTS NOW

In your letter to me, you also told me how depressed you were by what I wrote about the prison industrial complex and our country's exploitive prison system. I get it. Jail is like a friend who always asks you to listen to his music— it's wack, but what's the point of saying it? You go on and on about the same thing. Being there unjustly. Over and over, you keep pointing out that you were "framed." I'm sorry, really I am. However, I can't hold back what I'm thinking any longer. The only answer I have for you about all that is: *Whateva, bruh!*

Because whether you were framed or not, you're still *there*! *It's still your life!* And *you still have choices*!

I don't even need to know any more details about the circumstances of your arrest, and I don't care. The only thing you and I have for certain is right now . . . and we are where we are. If you don't forget about your regretful past, you'll keep on reliving it. It's not like you drown by falling in the water—you drown by staying there. And your ass seems to wanna stay.

All I need to know—all *you* need to know—is how you can make a break with the past and start plans for a new life *today*. The most underrated moment is now. "Someday" isn't even on the calendar.

A couple letters ago, when I tried to explain the importance of surrendering to your experience, you wisecracked back, "What kind of game you telling me to learn, Mr. Hill Harper?" My answer to that is, "No game at all."

In fact, I'm telling you *not* to play the prison game, not to play by its self-defeating rules, not to participate in its atmosphere of fear and negativity, not to participate in its methods of setting one prisoner against another—when you should all be thinking of yourselves as Brothers, people who are in the same boat. The prison industry is profiting from your mistakes and wants you to repeat them. You've talked to me a lot about wanting to design games. Well, those are the only rules of the prison game. They're designed to get you caught up, get you stuck, and make you lose. Be in it but not *of* it—be above it. When Nelson Mandela was in prison for twenty-seven years, he never allowed himself to fall victim to the prison mentality. He rose above it for the entire time. And don't try to tell me it's impossible to be simultaneously "in it" and "above it." You can do it!

> **The most underrated moment is now. "Someday" isn't even on the calendar.**

CHOICES

Did you check out the Sidney Poitier book I sent you? After I mailed it, there was nothing left on my night table to read. So when I first got to Atlanta for the movie I was making, I made a quick run to my favorite bookstore down there, Shrine of the Black Madonna, to get something new to read, and somehow I ended up mentioning to one of the clerks that I'm trading letters with a young Brother who's incarcerated. What do you think she did? She led me straight to this book called *The Other Wes Moore* and said I have to read it.[1]

I took her word for it and bought the book, and I have to say it did blow my mind. Wes Moore, the author, was an ex-military officer about to become a Rhodes Scholar at the time of its writing. Just by chance, he happened to read a bunch of articles in *The Baltimore Sun* about these cats who broke into a jewelry store and ended up killing an off-duty policeman. One of them had a name that caught Wes Moore's attention—his name was Wes Moore, too.

Not only did the two guys have the same name, but they were the same age. Both of them were from Baltimore. Both had spent part of their childhood in the Bronx. Both were from single-parent families. Yet one was about to become a Rhodes Scholar. The other was being sent up to do life for murder. Why?

Out of curiosity, the Wes Moore (WM) who went on to write the book started visiting the incarcerated Wes Moore. How, he wanted to know, had such similar paths suddenly taken such different directions? Once the two got to know each other, they discovered that they had even more in common. Both had hated school. Both had hit the streets at an early age. Both had grown up in neighborhoods where it seemed the only chance for community was in gangs. Both had had early run-ins with the cops.

Gradually, WM learned the facts. They're complicated: The twists and turns of each path narrowly kept one Wes out of trouble and just as narrowly kept the other Wes from avoiding problems. WM thought that being sent away to military school was the thing that saved him. But the incarcerated Wes came close to being saved, too. He came within a hair's breadth of leaving the drug trade because of a training program called Job Corps. By the time that happened, however, he was already in deep shit. While WM was in military school, Wes Moore was fathering children he couldn't take care of. While WM was graduating, Wes Moore was experimenting with drugs. By the time WM was in the army, Wes Moore was making the drug trade his profession. So by the time he had a chance to join the Job Corps, his options had shrunk, because he'd already done time and been labeled a felon. Even so, he still had two choices: Job Corps or his old life on the street. Why, then, did he choose to hit the streets again and walk down that familiar pavement to get back on the road to the Big House? For the Wes Moore who'd write the book, a single event was enough to set him down a different sidewalk and a whole series of chain reactions that paved a road toward success. That doesn't mean when the going got difficult, he couldn't have run away from the discipline of military school as "any homie who'd been on the streets would be expected to do." But instead, he decided to take the ball and run with it—first into education, then into an army career, and finally into a life as a scholar. As far as he knows, he built a successful life on a single chance: military school. But to me the genius of his story is not about military school. It's about his taking dramatic, decisive actions to break away from the hamster wheel that his life and upbringing were trying to keep him on. Believe me when I say, man, if he could do that, you can, too.

Life is woven not just from what happens to you by chance, but also what you weave from those happenings, the pattern you create. And sure, our choice of available options plays a part as well. But those options expand and change each time you make a new choice to set your life on a new path.

At the very same time that one Wes Moore was choosing the steps that led directly to the Big House, the other Wes Moore was choosing steps to turn his life around. Either Wes Moore could have reversed his path at *any* moment in his life's trajectory and gone in the opposite direction. One Wes Moore eventually realized that though you may not be able to change your past, you can change the way your past affects your future. The past is where you learn the lesson; the future is where you apply it. And not coincidentally, he's the one who ended up writing the book. Each time you break away from the direction the "system" is trying to push you in, each new idea you have, each new book you read, each new business you create—all of them give you the power to dictate new choices. Today is the tomorrow you were worried about yesterday.

> **Life is woven not just from what happens to you by chance, but also what you weave from those happenings, the pattern you create.**

THE VOICE OF YOUR AUTHENTIC SELF

So now you know: Change a few things. Let me narrow it down some. They say it takes twenty-one days to change a habit. Over the next twenty-one days, change just one thing. That's my challenge for you. Commit to it. Your future may be completely different than it would have been if you hadn't made this one change and the others that will follow. It's all about cultivating the brilliance you already have inside you. I want to help you create a template or system to do just that. To go from the jail you're in to exactly where you decide you want to be.

Why is having a "system" important? Because when obstacles come up (and they definitely will), we need to have something consistent to rely upon. Something that's unmoving and steady. Because when the waters get rough, we need an anchor. And the systems/techniques we learn will be our anchor.

I know there are big hurdles. I also know that some of them are psychological. Way back when, after you read *Letters to a Young Brother,* you wrote to me and described some voices inside you telling you that you're worthless, that you don't stand a chance, that you're a punk. Back when we both were a little younger, you described so clearly those voices of doubt. They were drowning everything else out, you said. You asked me what to do about them.

I told you that it was possible to *choose* not to hear them. I said that I've had to fight those same voices inside me, too—almost every day. They'll never go away completely, Brotha. Even if the members of our family aren't who implanted them in us, history has been one long, false argument in favor of them—for generations, minorities have been told they are inferior. So, in a way, the voices were imprinted in us at birth. Society creates them. And now the prison industrial system has taken over that function.

Those voices get damn loud at times! Lots of times, I hear them just before I walk onto the soundstage at *CSI: NY* to face the camera. I even heard them last week when I was trying to get the nerve up to call a woman I met at a party the night before. But as I dialed her number, I told myself that the fear and doubt in my head are not my real voices. So the question is, when those voices of doubt come up, who are *you* going to listen to? Are you going to give energy to those negative voices or aggressively seek out the true inner voice that comes from an *alternative power inside you?*

The voice I'm talking about is the *voice of your authentic self.* I believe that we all have an inner voice, though the source of it is up for interpretation. Is it coming from God, from the memory of a wise mentor, from a kind of intuition that we're all born with? Wherever it comes from, it has the ability to argue with us, to plead with us not to do this or to do that. It's really an amazing mechanism, but many of us ignore it too often. Most of the answers we seek are there waiting for us to listen to *us*!

The trick is to get into the habit of using the voice of your authentic self as your navigation system. To let it take you from minute to minute. It knows your predetermined destination and will give you directions along the way. It's your own personal GPS. *This is the voice that will give you directions for navigating out of prison.*

I know that voice is rising to the surface for you, Brotha, partly because of the way we've finally started to communicate. I can tell by the content of your letters that you already know the answers to many of the questions you're asking yourself through me. Let's see if, together, we can encourage it to come completely out of hiding and become your authentic navigation system. Because that's the surest way of finding the path that leads gradually beyond those prison walls.

Take care,

Hill

INTUITION

LETTER 5

Mentors and Options

We must dare to think "unthinkable" thoughts. We must learn to explore all the options and possibilities that confront us in a complex and rapidly changing world.

—J. William Fulbright

It is not so much our friends' help that is important as the confidence of their help.

—Epicurus

Hey, Brotha,

Now I'm back in Atlanta once again, from Iowa. We've still got another week of shooting. This time the layover was smoother.

As usual, seeing my great-uncle in Iowa was like a bath of affirmation, despite the fact that I came there with the intention of cheering *him* up. That's when it occurred to me that a good deal of what I've accomplished happened because there were people in my life with great expectations of me, and more than that, they taught me how to navigate a journey to go wherever I wanted to go.

MENTORS

I can tell you from experience that nobody can make it completely on his or her own. We don't have enough to rely on our own supply. No one whose accomplishments you admire or respect achieved those things without help. So, for you to achieve your goals, you'll also need mentorship. Know what you want, and study people who've done similar things. And your mentor doesn't always have to be someone you meet with in person. You can have a mentorship on paper or online.

It can even be a memory of someone you've heard or read about but never met. For example, Paul Robeson, the great singer, actor, and political activist, is my mentor, and he's not here! True, I can't talk to Paul today because he has passed away, but I can read an autobiography about him. I can see how he made the choices in his life and why he made them. And he's helping me continuously, because a mentor helps you navigate the journey and helps you make your choices. He never makes those choices for you or lives with their consequences. You can create an entire blueprint for the next part of your life with the help of your mentors. If they are there to sit and talk with you and answer questions, all the better. If they are not present, you can study their lives and what choices they made and emulate them.

Wanting to do well in somebody's eyes has helped me accomplish so many things. Think, for example, about fathers. My father wasn't alive in this world and inhabiting his body of flesh when I invested in my hotel. He wasn't there with me when I signed the papers. He wasn't there with me when my TV show made the top ten. He wasn't there with me when my book hit number two on the *New York Times* bestseller list, but he was *here* with me all those times. On Father's Day I always celebrate my father, my father's father, and my father's father's father.

I know you felt that way about your mother, even after she died when you were fifteen. Remember how you told me that when you were pushing for good grades in high school, it was the thought of the look in your mother's eyes if she'd been able to see you ace your report cards that drove you on? Now you're probably experiencing the opposite effect: seeing shame in the eyes of your mother because of where you are.

In my opinion, you should be doing the opposite: still relying on that warm, loving, caring look in her eyes as encouragement. Or maybe that look isn't coming from the memory of your mother. Then imagine the encouraging look in *my* eyes. I want to become your mentor through these letters, if you'll let me— your mentor on paper.

OPTIONS: MORE VALUABLE THAN MONEY

As your mentor, I want to talk about how you can increase your options. It's as simple as this: Knowledge is power. Education *buys* you options. It's the single best way to use/spend your time. It's an investment in yourself. The more education you have, the more options you'll have for the working world when you get out. The more knowledge you have, the more likely you are to make better decisions. Good relationships *buy* you options. Good relationships with people, but also to things. Having skill and confidence about using a computer is having a good relationship to a thing.

Human relationships, on the other hand, allow people with common goals to work together. They make possible a new coworker helping you learn what's required at a job. They make it possible for a cat who was also incarcerated to share info with you about programs for finding jobs or a place to live. They make it possible to draw knowledge and information from a mentor. Those kinds of relationships can also get you the best option of all—somebody you can really trust regardless of what happens to you, somebody who'll be there for you unconditionally. Is there anything else that buys options? Absolutely—*money*. In fact, that's all money really can buy—more options. The option to buy a train ticket and go to another town when you can't find a job in the one you're in. The option to rent an apartment so you can work in a particular city if you do find a job. The option to spend a month unemployed if you lose your job while you look for new work. As we discussed before, money is a resource that buys options like that, as well. But money is *not* what most of us have thought it is—an end in itself. Rather, it's a functional tool that will buy us more and more options, if we use it wisely. Any other use of money—for a car that costs as much as a house, for two chains although you already have a few on, for a pair of fresh kicks that could have bought a week of fresh food—is just symbolic, a desperate bid for social status, an ego meal. Other than options, all that money can buy

> **Other than options, all that money can buy you is a fantasy of status and power.**

you is a fantasy of status and power. Ask any strip-club connoisseur. But that power isn't real. It's just that, a fantasy. Run out of money at a strip club, and watch what happens with that fantasy. Money and things don't possess any power. Only people can possess power. Check out what Deepak Chopra said about *things*:

> There is no such thing as a thing. There are only relationships.[1]

Chopra means that an object can only be defined by describing its relationship to something else. Calling something an object with "status" doesn't mean the object itself contains status; it means the way we speak about the object has *assigned* status to it. The object itself has no, or very little, real value. So spending your money to form a status relationship with a thing, associating that thing with power, will only decrease your options.

Limiting options is the number one method the prison industrial complex uses to keep you down. For example, I found out that any correspondence course you might want to do must be done during off-hours, when you're not performing cheap labor for the prison. Not having the time to get the proper education can ultimately decrease options.

You also wrote me about a related, but more sickening, example: There is a rule in your prison of one book per cell per month; and if a guard finds more, he takes them away as a form of punishment. Such a one-book-a-month rule could only exist to weaken you by limiting your options. However, it's what that guard does with the confiscated book that really pisses me off. He throws it in the trash! One floor down from those cells is the chaplain's office. Wouldn't you imagine the chaplain might find a way to make good use of those books if they were given to him so he could loan them out to other interested prisoners—one at a time, like those misguided rules demand? But a corrections officer who destroys a confiscated book is only interested in punishment, pure and simple. He must have been taught that it's in his interest—and the prison's—to decrease your options. Why would he take the trouble to walk down one flight of stairs and hand that confiscated book to the chaplain?

SERENDIPITY

> I am a great believer in luck, and I find the harder I work, the more I have of it.
>
> —Stephen Leacock

Luckily, the number and kind of options we have aren't static. They change all the time. I know there are hurdles for you in planning ways to get some of your options back, to add to your store of them. On the other hand, you never know what the universe has planned for you. Do you know what *serendipity* means? I love that word. The dictionary defines *serendipity* as "the occurrence and development of events by chance in a happy or beneficial way." Serendipity usually happens because of some coincidence. It's often a fluke that ties two separate things in your life together in a very beneficial way.

So, check this out: I was surfing the Internet, Googling "education in prison" and "degrees in prison," figuring some of that information might be able to help you increase your options. And I decided to take a break for a few minutes and check the mail. What did I find on top of the stack? A letter from a dude named Eric Bailey. He'd read my book *The Wealth Cure* while he was still locked up in Elmira, a prison in upstate New York. And now he's out of prison after eighteen years and trying to get back to normal life in his hometown, Binghamton, New York. He wanted to run some ideas past me about handling funds.

Eric mentioned in his letter that while he was serving time, he managed to get two degrees by correspondence, an associate degree in art therapy and a degree as a paralegal. Since I wanted to find out about that kind of thing for you, I picked up the phone and called the dude. That, my friend, is an example of serendipity. What my girlfriend calls "the Mysteries of the Universe Colliding." That kind of stuff is usually a sign that you're on the right track. I'm trying to answer some questions for you, and part of the answer was sitting right there in my mailbox!

One of the things I asked Eric is how he managed to get the money for those courses. He told me he cobbled it together in a really complex way. There was a well-meaning guidance counselor at that prison who thought he had potential and ended up offering matching funds for his education with her own money if he could provide the other half. So he wrote to everybody he'd ever known in his life and asked them to put whatever they could toward the "Eric Education Fund." No amount was too small. He collected two dollars here, ten there. . . . It took him a year, but, with the guidance counselor's matching half, he eventually had enough tuition for two degrees.

He also told me that in the state prison where he last was, they wouldn't even let him use the prison library to study for his correspondence courses,

> **If someone makes up in his mind to do something, he will do it. It may not be today or tomorrow, but it will happen. You can't hold a determined person back.**

or use any table at all. So he took both courses sitting on the edge of his bunk and balancing his book and pad of paper on his knees. He even devised a lighting system so he could study under his blanket after the lights went out. He traded his cellmate some of the desserts he'd been saving from meals for some batteries, removed a couple LEDs from his own boom box, and rigged up a homemade flashlight. When those batteries ran out, he found a way to tap into the wire inside the wall of the cell and run it to the contacts in his flashlight. I'm not saying I recommend creating options by taking such risks—Eric could have electrocuted himself—but you get my point. He was a determined and creative problem-solver, and he was not going to let any obstacles get in his way. If someone makes up in his mind to do something, he will do it. It may not be today or tomorrow, but it will happen. You can't hold a determined person back.

Bailey tells me you can find out about courses by getting in touch with your state's correctional education administrator. I'll try to pull together a list of those offices in every state and send it to you.[2] Since they've begun putting the overflow from state cases in other states' prisons, we don't know where you'll be when you get transferred, so I want you to have the address for every state. As a matter of fact, the federal government has info about the subject, too. You can collect a lot of facts about getting an education in prison by writing to:

Office of Correctional Education
U.S. Department of Education
400 Maryland Avenue SW
MES 4527
Washington, DC 20202-7242

I don't think you have access to the Internet in there, but if you want to ask somebody on the outside who does, tell them to write to ovae@ed.gov for the same information. Or you can contact Infor-Nation Corp., PO Box 520567, Flushing, NY 11352.

I got a feeling you're about to tell me you don't trust much shit put out by the government. And I can understand where you're coming from. Then you might want to get hold of this book Rivers also told me about: *Prisoners' Guerrilla Handbook to Correspondence Programs in the United States and Canada*, written by Jon Marc Taylor, an incarcerated Brother like you.[3] Taylor seems to know what he's talking about. He managed to get a BS degree, an MA degree, and a doctorate by mail while still incarcerated.

According to that book, there are still ways to get free courses in prison, but it's harder now, since Congress decreased funding for Pell education grants in 2011. I also read that students convicted of a drug infraction while receiving federal student aid could become ineligible for future funds under certain circumstances, but that it's also sometimes possible to reverse that ineligibility. We need to find out more about it. Just say the word and we can start researching all of these details together.

I'm gonna need you to stay patient, too. I know the only program in your jail is a mandatory GED course for those who don't have their high school diplomas, and you already have one. But a lot of the state prisons, where you're headed next, have courses in basic office skills and computer repair, and some pre-apprenticeship training in plumbing and even electrician's work. Maybe you can let me know what's available where you're locked up when the time comes. Oh, and another thing. I hope you don't think I believe that becoming a video game designer one day is completely out of the question. Maybe you won't be transitioning right out of prison into that, but any stable job when you get out can provide the options for more education toward that goal. I couldn't tell you one way or another for sure, because so much of that depends on you. But if it happens, it won't just *happen*—it'll be because you made it happen due to a detailed plan. I believe that plan has to start with some kind of self-knowledge and understanding. To be sure, in your case it's important to have an understanding of the game you've gotten yourself into, what society's role in it was, and what part had to do with your decisions. But I think right at this moment it's more important for you to simply understand you.

I bet you didn't know that one of history's greatest philosophers was in prison and died there: the Greek philosopher Socrates. At his trial, Socrates said, "An unexamined life is not worth living." I want you to truly examine your life. Ask yourself questions, be willing to honestly answer them, and most important, don't judge the answers. What impact and legacy do you want to leave behind? What were you afraid of that led you to take actions that landed you in prison? Incarceration does not have to stop you; we are still learning from and quoting that inmate, Socrates, thousands of years later. You, and no one else, determine your legacy. But what really concerns me the most is the part of your last letter where you wrote:

im tryna make the best out of the worsened situation but sometimes even with you support and tryna keep my head straight its impossible to do any even with your support positive thoughts and really trying to take one day at a time its impossible for this place to not get to you. sometimes it really feels like im just falling from the sky with no control over my life. on the low, its something thought even before prison.

Sincerely

Your lost brotha

YOUR PARACHUTE

I think I understand what you're trying to say and I got a question. Did you pack your parachute? No, I'm not talking about landing on the roof of the jail with a helicopter and picking you up so you can parachute to freedom. My question has to do with some of what you wrote in your last letter. From what I see, sometimes you feel like you're falling out of the sky, like you have no control over your life at all. Nothing to grab on to. On a free-fall spiral with no safety net and no one around to help break your fall. You even said that you've felt that way most of your life, even before you went to prison.

> **All our parachutes are individual. They're made from our own fabrics of experience, our own unique pattern for the life we are leading.**

I know that feeling. Most of us have experienced that in one point of our lives or another. The key, though, is to make sure it doesn't last too long. So long that we feel there is no way to stop falling, that we have no control, ever. That's why I want to tell you that you actually have your own parachute. That's right, it's true. You've had one all along. The problem is, nobody's ever taught you how to recognize it, to use it to slow things down and gain some perspective. All our parachutes are individual. They're made from our own fabrics of experience, our own unique pattern for the life we are leading. Our own ways of breaking falls and holding ourselves up when nothing else seems to work. Our own ways of dealing with our individual missteps and victories.

So my question is: What unique pattern is yours? Have you learned how to pack it in a way that you can find the rip cord and pull it, after which you'll suddenly break into a gentle sail? Or do you need to change the fabrics, pattern, or the way you pack your parachute? You were damn right when you said that a lot of the advice you read in *Letters to a Young Brother* won't work in this new environment you're in. Let's see if we can get you a new parachute that will have you floating down to a different type of territory, with hopefully a little smoother landing. You'll have plenty of time to devise some options on the trip down. Let me know what you think about all that.

Peace,

Hill

P.S. To raise money for charity, me and some other actors are parachuting out of a plane at eighteen thousand feet tomorrow. Let's hope my parachute was packed right, the rip cord works, and the chute opens smoothly! If you get another letter from me you know it was all good. If this is the last letter you got, well. . . . Kiss my moms for me! Haha. Peace.

PROGRESS

LETTER 6

Escape Plan

The past is our definition. We may strive with good reason to escape it, or to escape what is bad in it. But we will escape it only by adding something better to it.

—Wendell Berry, author of *What Are People For?*

To do the same thing over and over again is not only boredom: It is to be controlled by rather than to control what you do.

—Heraclitus

Hey, Brotha,

Let me first say, thank you. The drawing you slipped into your last letter is taped to the mirror of my dressing room at *CSI: NY*. I check it out every single time I'm about to walk onto the set and I get a little chuckle out of it.

You'll never guess what I ended up doing. I guess it's another example of serendipity. I was in New York for a few days to go to some meetings and see my agent, and one evening I ended up at this wrap party for a show on Broadway that was closing. Well, the set designer, whom I know from this little off-Broadway play I was in a long, long time ago, ended up introducing me to two dudes, Nick Higgins and his coworker, who are both librarians at the New York Public Library.

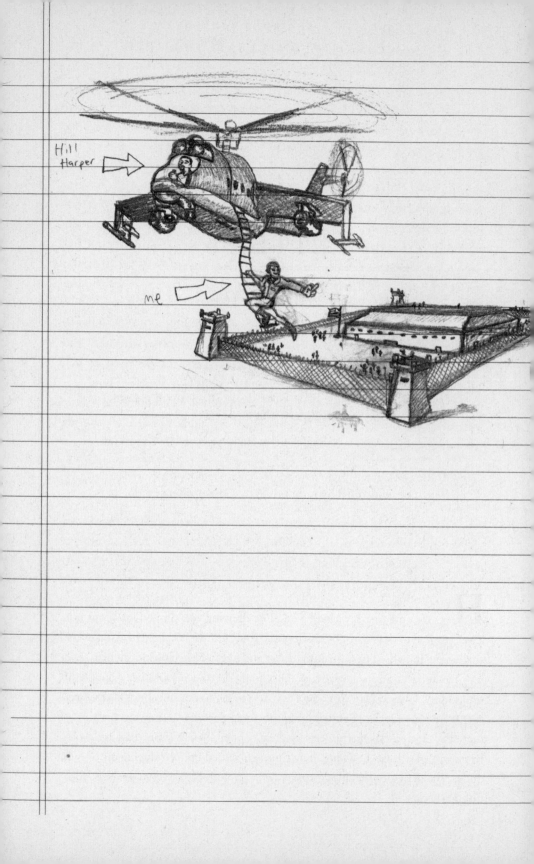

Now, here comes the serendipity: Twice a week they, along with their volunteers, go to Rikers Island to run a small permanent library and wheel around four carts of additional books. They call the operation the New York Public Library's Correctional Services Program. In partnership with the Department of Corrections, they also do a couple of projects based on books. For example, on certain days, incarcerated dads can make a CD of themselves reading a favorite book to their kids. Finally, they also publish an incredible two-books-in-one for the incarcerated: *Connections 2012: A Guide for Formerly Incarcerated People to Information Sources in New York City* and *The Job Search*. Hopefully I can find something similar for the state where the prison you're assigned to will be. I'll send you information about that search after you've settled in.

Anyway, turns out that the next time these two librarians were going over to Rikers was that very next morning! "Why don't you come with us?" said Higgins. "It would be very cool for our fund-raising efforts if we could say Hill Harper was passionately interested in this program."

So, very early the next morning (I think I still may have been a little hungover), there I was in Queens with a giant duffel bag full of books cutting into my shoulder, waiting for the Q101 bus to Rikers with Higgins. When we got there, I had a taste of some of the red tape you've been describing to me in your letters: missing clearance papers that made us wait more than a half hour at the gate, the need for temporary IDs in exchange for our own IDs, having to exchange those temporary IDs for others to change buildings, X-ray machines, pat-downs, and special permission, since I was a last-minute addition. By the end of it, I felt like I myself was being booked. It made me appreciate the loyalty of wives, mothers, and other family members who go through this on a regular basis just to see an incarcerated family member. Maybe it also helps clear up why your aunt can't visit that often. Job or no job, it's an exhausting process.

I was there until late afternoon and must have passed out about twenty-five books. I was so glad to get those tools into the hands of the incarcerated, especially when it had to do with information that could help them form a life plan. But I handed over comic books and thriller novels just as cheerfully. The only thing that really bugged me was when I saw the insecurity or paranoia of a guy being exploited by a scam—when the kinds of books he asked for tended to be about either an unrealistic get-rich-quick scheme, or worse still, one of the many paranoid conspiracy theories. Needless to say, I was a lot happier for a guy when he asked for a book on accounting or even about ways to start your own business. But more on that at another time.

EXONERATION EFFORTS

If you're really serious about devoting all your time to proving your innocence rather than devoting it to acquiring the skills and education to make it when you get out, then it goes like this: There are guidebooks to the process. Apparently, one of the most useful and practical is *Freeing the Innocent: How We Did It—A Handbook for the Wrongly Convicted* by Michael and Becky Pardue. Michael Pardue was imprisoned for twenty-eight years in an Alabama state prison for a murder he didn't commit. Working in tandem with his wife, Becky—Michael inside prison walls and Becky outside—the couple meshed information they found and won his exoneration. If you're really serious about this, your family and friends should read the book, too, and all of you can work together on your goal of being proved innocent.

About one convicted person a week in this country is able to be exonerated, most of them for rape or murder. Quite often it has to do with the thing we deal with the most on *CSI: NY*—DNA—but not always. There are national organizations, like the Innocence Project, devoted solely to correcting the problem of wrongful conviction. And there are a lot of serious studies of this issue. In fact, I've included a list of some of the most interesting books on the subject with this letter.[1] But before you go off on a wild-goose chase, consider how long it took the Pardues to exonerate Michael—twenty-eight years! That's why people who haven't been sentenced to life rarely spend much time on research into this subject.

SOME FIRST STEPS FOR YOUR READING PROGRAM

If you want my opinion, you should use different kinds of books in a certain order to turn your life around, change its course, and ready yourself for things on the outside. However, before we get to that, I've got to tell you about a prison book program I discovered on the Internet. It's called Books Through Bars, and its main purpose is to send free quality reading material to the incarcerated. Check it out. I know you don't have access to the Internet, but I also found out how to contact them by mail or phone:

Books Through Bars
4722 Baltimore Avenue
Philadelphia, PA 19143
www.booksthroughbars.org
(215) 727-8170

You might even want to send them a list of the books you're looking for and see what they come up with. Once you're in a place without a limit on the number of books you can have, I'll hook you up with a few books now and then, too. But don't worry, I won't overwhelm you and make it feel like homework. I want you to enjoy reading and not dread it.

The more you read, the better you get at it, and your comprehension will improve as well. Reading even helps you become a better writer.

Maybe you can organize your reading into these three categories:

1. **Inspiration.** Start by reading stories of redemption, change, or transformation, or any inspirational stories in books, magazines, newspapers, or any other publication you can get your hands on. You'll get inspired by learning how other incarcerated people turned their lives around and what steps they took to escape the prison industrial complex forever.

    Believe me, there is every kind of story. I really like 50 Cent's take on the story of Rubin "Hurricane" Carter—a middleweight boxer who was arrested in 1966 at the height of his career and charged with a triple murder. He was sentenced to three consecutive life terms. According to 50 Cent in the book he wrote with Robert Greene, *The 50th Law,* Carter resisted the demoralizing effects of nineteen years of incarceration by means of risky hard-core strategies, some of which involved a kind of civil disobedience. From the beginning, Carter knew he was probably in for the long haul, so he made up his mind to keep the prison industrial complex from destroying his spirit no matter how dangerous it proved to be. His reason was that he thought if he lost his self-respect in prison, he'd end up back there even if he managed to get released.

Carter figured he could maintain his dignity and self-image as a free man only by refusing to wear a uniform, ID badge, or anything else that made him feel like a number rather than a human being. This, of course, attracted punishment. They put him in solitary confinement, but once there, he refused all television, radio, and girlie magazines—the common accessories most prisoners in the Box beg for to while away their time. Carter told himself that his refusal of these crutches meant there wouldn't be any pleasures the wardens could take away from him. On the other hand, the only thing he could not do without was his mental freedom. To bolster and expand it, he used all his time in solitary to read every book he could get hold of. He eventually tutored other prisoners and wrote an autobiography that attracted people on the outside to his cause. He learned law with the goal of overturning his conviction.

Nineteen years passed, and Carter finally trounced his sentence by legal means and was let out. The next logical step might have been to take a civil action against the state for wrongful incarceration and win a lot of money. Carter reasoned, however, that doing so would mean admitting that he'd been in prison, was damaged by it, and was seeking restitution. He didn't want to think of himself that way. Instead he became an activist for prisoners' rights. In 1999, Denzel Washington portrayed him in the movie *The Hurricane.*

This story also points to the fact that if we could work to overcome racial divisiveness, everyone would benefit. For instance, Bob Dylan (a white singer) wrote the song "Hurricane," and by bridging racial divides, he brought attention to Hurricane's plight.

There are whites and blacks, browns and greens who don't see race first. Bob Dylan is someone who was willing to bridge the racial gap. It's not easy to go against the norm and reach out across race lines. But when you do, it can open up opportunities that you never would have thought possible. Racism is an antiquated way of thinking; we need to be bigger than that limited notion.

Another person who was able to get an abbreviated sentence was Anthony Papa, the author of *15 to Life: How I Painted My Way to Freedom*. Papa is mostly a visual artist, but his book is another unusual, inspiring case of incarceration. He said in a lighthearted way, "[I] painted myself out of a prison cell." Recently, he explained what he meant in an interview:

While I was in prison, I acquired three college degrees and learned how to paint. Seven years later, my self-portrait wound up at the Whitney Museum of American Art, and at that point, I got a lot of exposure to my case. Two years later, in 1997, I was granted clemency by Gov. George Pataki. I basically painted my way out of prison.[2]

Papa spends a lot of his time now fighting the drug laws that led to such a stringent penalty. He feels they're antiquated and unfair.

2. **Learning Your Rights.** Next, learn about the legal aspects of your conviction and the ins and outs of the criminal justice system. I don't mean that you should spend all your reading time trying to prove that you're innocent, since, as I pointed out, that usually takes much, much too long. But you need to understand enough about the law so you'll know exactly what the prison guards and officials can and can't do to you. Being educated about the law and the justice system is a valuable asset. It reminds me of one of my favorite Jay-Z lines from "99 Problems," when he basically rhymes that he didn't pass the bar but he knows enough that he won't let the cops illegally search his shit. If you're denied any rights while locked up, you'll know who to write in order to complain and how to sound intelligent enough about your complaint to get their attention. Play their game until you're in position to develop your own game. You'll also learn about the laws that govern parole, so you can put an immediate stop to any unfair or shady treatment from the parole board.

3. **Learning About Work.** Finally, dig into some training books and textbooks that provide the education and training you'll need to get a stable position in the working world.

Because of your setback, your training and education need to take into account more than one tier of employment. If you tell me that you're reading everything you can find about video game design, I certainly won't say it's a waste. But it's unlikely that you can jump into a job doing exactly that as soon as you get out of prison. Anything worth having is worth sweating for. Your first professional tier probably has to be geared purely toward survival—anything from building-construction helper to plumbing assistant to janitorial work. Once you're solidly set up in work like that, and going back to the street or being sent back to finish your sentence because you're out of work is a dim prospect, you'll use the stability (and hopefully, the saved money) you got from these jobs to "buy options" for furthering your education—maybe by going to community college, technical college, or even night school. If you still want to become a video game designer, you'll be that much closer to it. And just like most things in life, who you know is often as important as what you know. So I want you to begin to think whether you have a relationship with people who can help position you for the type of job you want. If you don't, then we need to begin making a plan about how you can develop new relationships even while you're inside. I'm not trying to tell you not to dream big; I'm just trying to tell you that there are many steps up that ladder toward your biggest dreams. Each step you take is progress, so don't be discouraged. Too many rich minds put affordable dreams on credit. But the harder it gets, the closer you are. Your past cells can't stop your future sales. Legitimate sales. ☺

IMAGINING THE FUTURE

I've spent an awful lot of time trying to get you to stop feeling lousy about the past and focus on your future. Deepak Chopra once asked me, "If you could jump ahead five years from now and meet yourself, who would you meet?"[3] I have similar questions for you. Who do you want to meet—who do you want to be—five years from now? What does this person look like? Sound like? How does he dress? Is he wearing a prison outfit, a three-piece peak-lapel suit, or neither? What is he doing right now?

It doesn't even matter if your sentence turns out to be longer than the five-to-ten-year maximum because of trouble gotten into on the inside. Who are you going to choose to be even if you're still locked up?

I can already imagine this pissing you off. You didn't choose to be in jail, you're probably thinking. So how can you choose where you'll be in the future? But when I say *choose*, I'm not talking about a single decision and its consequences. I'm talking about a series of minuscule steps that lead you in a certain definite direction. At the end of the day, I want you to discover the path that's the best version of who you are and find a way to lead a life that's so happy it's "unreasonable."

So if you're good money, hit me with some answers to those questions.

Soon,

Hill

P.S. Since I've spent so much time in this letter talking about books, I'm including a letter from a friend who spent time behind bars himself and who feels that reading is one of the things that saved him. Dr. Jamal Bryant is the outstanding pastor of the Empowerment Temple AME in Baltimore, Maryland.

Dear Brother,

The only thing the judicial system cannot take away from an incarcerated Brother is his intuition and his imagination. Books give you an opportunity to teleport beyond your circumstances toward what you want or dream. Remember that even though the body is locked up, the mind is still free.

Remember that even though the body is locked up, the mind is still free.

This year is the fiftieth anniversary of Martin Luther King's "Letter from Birmingham Jail," which shows that even while incarcerated, his mind was thinking at a keener, sharper level without the distractions that we have now. Dr. King was able to focus not on the style of life, but the substance and significance of life.

One of my mentors, Dr. Frank Reid, put me on a book regimen of reading a book a week, and every week the subject changed. The first week it was autobiography or biography, because often the news just gives you the snapshot of someone's success but never shows you the struggle of someone's failure. Anyone who has succeeded at something has failed at something first. Michael Jordan was actually cut from his high school basketball team. As he himself put it, "I've missed more than 9,000 shots in my career. I've lost almost 300 games. Twenty-six times I have been trusted to take the game-winning shot and missed. I've failed over and over and over again in my life. And that is why I succeed." Jordan certainly realized the value of persisting when on the face of things, it seemed he had failed.

The second week I read something about our culture or our history. There is a West African word, *sankofa*, that means "to fly forward while looking back." This means in order to push toward your destiny, you have to have a sense of your past. Looking at the full journey of African-American men being in bondage, juxtaposed with being incarcerated by a system that is operating on almost a high-tech level of slavery, would help you to have a greater perspective.

The third week, I read a book on theology. This could have been Islam, Buddhism, Christianity, or any other faith; the tenets remained the same. You have to operate at a level of discipline, studying your theology and looking beyond yourself and seeing how to meet the needs of someone else. Many people who are incarcerated are consumed by some dimension of selfishness, or "What can I get for myself?" But the aim needs to be, "What am I doing for someone else?" Your faith in God propels you to do what? If your goals are what kind of car you'll drive and what kind of clothes you'll wear when you get out, reading will help you develop your personal theology.

The fourth week, I read a novel, so my mind was always moving in a different dimension and I was able to go places that I would never have gone. Ninety-two percent of Black males don't have a passport. Their worldview doesn't go beyond the neighborhood they are in. So reading gives you an opportunity to go places where your imaginary passport has never taken you. The Manhattan Institute tells us that only 48 percent of Black males in this country earn a high school diploma, and of them, one in four will wind up incarcerated. So this is a good opportunity to get your GED and raise your literacy level so you can compete in the mainstream when you're released.

I would recommend the following books to you:

1. The Bible, particularly the Book of Proverbs. This has thirty-one chapters, and you can read one chapter a day. Many of these proverbs were written by King Solomon for his sons to train them on how to rule and be in charge.
2. *With Head and Heart,* the autobiography of Howard Thurman. The title means that if you do not have your head, you'll always lose your heart. It talks about the balance every Black man needs to live with, head and heart.
3. *Brainwashed* by Tom Burrell. This book is about how media has impacted the imagery of Black men and how we should respond to that.
4. *The Coldest Winter Ever* by Sister Souljah. This novel involves a young lady whose father is incarcerated and how that impacts her. It's an amazing book.

In terms of the community's reaction when someone is released from prison, I tell people to treat them like a relative who's been in the hospital for a long time. You will learn to walk again and even how to eat again. If a man is coming out of prison after seven years, the whole world has changed. At the time of this writing, today is the seventh anniversary of Twitter. Think how life has been changed by the impact of Twitter: It affects TV ratings and even presidential elections. The world is different for someone who gets out of prison this afternoon and who has never even heard of Twitter. It's a world that did not exist seven years ago.

So you must be acclimated as a foreigner in home territory and reintegrated into society and technology. As a consequence, there has to be an educational process so that you can be employable even for menial jobs. You can't even work in McDonald's without understanding a computer, so obtaining digital training is key.

The emotional part is very difficult, too, because the loved one has gone through changes in the past seven years. Their son, husband, or brother is a different person from when he went to jail. One of the issues that the Black community is reticent about addressing is that of therapy and counseling. How do you reintegrate, especially with children involved and marriages where someone is coming back home and married to a stranger, or bringing a stranger into her home? You don't know that person anymore. Oftentimes you need another person to help walk you through reconnecting, and a counselor can provide that help.

Mentorship is important, too. Every man who is coming out of prison needs a mentor who is proficient in some area of life. For instance, if a man's son was seven when he went to prison, and now he's fourteen, suddenly the issue is, how do I parent a teenager? Try to connect with another strong Black male who can help you get your equilibrium back.

I hope these suggestions will be helpful to you.

Sincerely,
Dr. Jamal Bryant

DESTINY

IN THE BOX

Hey Hill,

    i got a story to tell you. Here upstate theres nobody we can say is really on our side. i shoulda known better but i went around telling folks movie star Hill Harper decided to lend me a hand and because you was on board i was gonna be good Dumb ass move. This muscles on top of muscles nigga steps to me and starts calling me a liar. one thing leads to another and homie had to catch a fade. whooped his ass with soap in a sock. They threw me in the Box for it. Searched my cell and this asshole cop finds i had more than one book —

The Sydney Poitter book you sent me and that wrongly convicted pardons handbook my aunt sent me. Dickhead threw both of them away. Just so you know solitary aint like the box you might be ~~struck~~ imagine where they toss you buttass naked into a pitch black hole like in oz or something old timer told me thats been gone since the 70s. Your just locked up in a cell by yourself 23 hours a day. A hour a day they let you out of this wire cage for "exeercise" where you can walk in circles and smoke if you want. Even so whenever your ass is locked up almost all day and night you start getting what they call sensory.

deprivation it fucks with your head and comes on mostly at night. Start seeing all kinda shit, even pictures of ~~me~~ you livin your entourage life driving your fuckin Bentley poppinbottles and pullin' bad ones. Prolly chillin w/ Gabrielle Union and shit. And i'm here rolling in the fuckin box. Get the picture "Brother" Hill Harper? By the way you ever fuck Gabrielle? She bad ~~as~~ shit. Anyway point is i'll never be like you i'll never in a million fuckin years and i cant get that outta my mind. So fuck you and all the money on top of monkey niggas like _You._

— Your locked up brotha

—PS send my pic to Gabrielle!

LETTER 7

Having an Impact

When you love people and have the desire to make a profound, positive impact upon the world, then will you have accomplished the meaning to live.

—Sasha Azevedo

The only limit to your impact is your imagination and commitment.

—Tony Robbins

Dear Brotha,

It pains me to think of you locked up in solitary. But maybe it's time to stop comparing your life to other people's, like mine or anybody else's.

The quickest way to waste your life is to compare it. There is a great and unique thing about your life—it's yours. No one else's.

> There is a great and unique thing about your life—it's yours. No one else's.

It's pretty ironic—almost funny—that you were imagining a glamorous life for me while you lay there in solitary. But actually,

I was in jail, too. I'll explain in a minute what I mean. And perhaps, more important than that, maybe you should keep in mind that what counts is having a real friend, not who that friend is or what he happens to do. I'm not trying to play you, just pointing out that my friendship is what counts, not any celebrity you think I have.

YOUR WELL

First of all, I've got to make it clear to you that to the best of my abilities I understand the predicament you face. You've made all the obstacles of your situation as a prisoner more than clear. I know it ain't easy, because none of the options you have now are satisfactory. But no one can *drive* you crazy unless you give up the *keys*.

You're responsible for your reaction to others. Happy people have mastered the art of happiness by controlling the way they respond to what life throws at them. On the one hand, you can be the "nice guy" and play it soft "like a choirboy," as you put it, which means you're bound to get jacked or shanked one day, or even killed in the violence you witness daily. But if you wear your shit on your sleeve and make it plain that you're ready to defend yourself, as you damn well intend to, your ass will end up bleeding at best, or even six feet under. And then, as soon as you do get caught defending your life, there will be no questions asked—no matter who started it, they're gonna send you to the Box like they just did, maybe even slap more time on your sentence if it happens again, which will delay your parole hearing.

But no one can *drive* you crazy unless you give up the *keys*.

I know that you've watched one dude after another play the rehabilitation card and get turned down anyway. You've hit me with one example after another of people who got locked up on charges less serious than yours fifteen years ago but are still in there because they got sucked into joining a race gang and had no choice but to defend the gang's turf—or their own homies would have snuffed them. You explain that you got to be ready to fight if you want to stay alive, but also that things have a way of escalating. Fair enough. But of all the things you've been telling me, I think there's one that's the worst: your telling me you're too old to change, that it's too late for you, and other such bullshit, that you know your game plan was already printed out for you when your mother died and your old man found a new "bitch" (since you used that word, we gotta work on the way you think and talk about women when we get the time later on, my man) and parked you and your brother with your aunt. But those are all crutches. It seems you've held on to so many crutches that you forgot you could walk.

I already told you that I got love for you, but have I said that I do not believe that you're evil or corrupt or hopeless, or whatever else you want to call yourself, no matter what you've done or thought? I believe, in fact, that there's a core of humanity in every single one of us that can't be degraded.

Eckhart Tolle, who wrote *The Power of Now* and has been called "the most spiritual author in the United States" by *The New York Times*, said it like this: "You do not become good by trying to be good, but by finding the goodness that is already within you, and allowing that goodness to emerge."[1] He also said that this inexhaustible supply of goodness "only emerges if something fundamental changes in your state of consciousness."

> **There's a place inside, a source, and if we can find it, we can wash clean all the open wounds that still exist from past experiences.**

My grandfather had an eighty-eight-acre farm in Iowa. They grew corn and lima beans and had cows, pigs, goats, and chickens. I spent most of my summers growing up on that farm. I loved the carefree way it made me feel. Behind the "big barn" (there was a smaller one closer to the road), there was an old well that was connected to this rusty spigot with a big handle on it. There was something about the well water that my gramma just loved. So I'd place a bucket under the spigot and pump that big red handle, and the cleanest water would rush out. It was so cold, clean, and fresh because it was coming from a very deep, unspoiled place.

Inside you there's a deep place that's unspoiled by your life in prison and even by the obstacles before prison. There's a place inside, a source, and if we can find it, we can wash clean all the open wounds that still exist from past experiences. There is a deep well of memories, sadness, passions, and energy inside you. I want you to get to a place where you feel like you can pour goodness and light from it at any time you decide.

GRAVITY

Now, don't get me wrong. Despite all this, throughout your life, there will be forces at work attempting to block you from accessing your well of humanity. But the choices we make are still what determine the effect they have or don't have. In that regard, I like to think these constant forces are like gravity. Gravity is always there, isn't it? It's always attempting to pull us downward. If we jump high, it yanks us back down. Similarly, I've always wanted to be able to dunk a basketball, but the farthest I ever got was grabbing the rim. That dang gravity kept pulling me down before I could manage it.

You can choose to succumb to the unseen forces that are continually trying to bring you down in a way similar to that unseen force of gravity. Or you can come up with ways to beat that downward pull.

I'm going to ask you to do something right now, in whatever type of cell you may be reading this—your own, or solitary, or any kind of metaphoric "box." Whenever you're trapped in your mind or actually imprisoned in reality, I ask you to do something that may seem stupid, crazy, unrealistic, or all three. Close your eyes—do it right now—and imagine in your mind's eye your highest aspirations. Imagine the best version of you. Is it the you playing ball with your son, R. J., when you get out? Is it a version of you shaking hands to complete a transaction for your own first business? Is it a version of you sitting on the couch with your arm around a sweet and sexy lady?

Just imagine that you're living out your highest aspirations. Believe it or not, imagining them is the very first step to reaching them. And I know that when life has hit us with so many disappointments, it's hard to open up and imagine goodness. But do it again now. Just for a few seconds, close your eyes again, and let the vision of goodness, happiness, and love fill your heart and mind.

REBOUNDING

Thinking about our highest aspirations is the best way to rebound from any kind of gravity.

Isn't *rebound* a dope word? It means so many different things . . . like an actual rebound on a basketball court or a rebound in life that consists of coming back up after unfortunate circumstances like time in the Box. A few years ago, you mentioned that you were good at basketball. So let's put that to the test—are you a good *rebounder*?

People think that the tallest person is the one who gets the most rebounds. . . . But that's not any more true about basketball than it is about life. In basketball, the person who gets the most rebounds is the one who controls the *most space* under the basket . . . and in life, same thing. You can increase the amount of space you control in life by increasing your knowledge of it, by learning to know yourself better, and, yes, by adding to your education. The more you know, the more confident you become, the more access you have to rebounds, and the better you handle them. You're ultimately going to get to a place after you rebound where you can go coast to coast and dunk . . . but that's later.

In so many letters we've exchanged, one of the themes that came through is your desire to have some sort of *impact* on the world. You can have an impact, and you will. But first, there's a question you must answer: What space do you want to carve out in your life? On what area of life do you want to focus your time and energy? Where will you be most effective at managing life's rebounds? What training, skills, resources, and other foundational tools will you need to master rebounds and turn them into impact?

> **Having an impact takes a combination of time and hard work, and so many people don't have the patience for, either.**

Having an impact takes a combination of time and hard work, and so many people don't have the patience for, either. Instead, they get seduced by quick hits, quick money, and shortcuts. But let's make one thing clear: There are no shortcuts when it comes to carving out your space. Everything in life boils down to seed, time, and harvest. The seed has to be planted. Then when the seed is watered, over time, the plant has no choice but to grow—when hard work is put in, success has no choice but to occur. Keep in mind that any impact you'll have will be tailor-made just for you. It might be the type of father you will be able to be to your son. It might be the type of business you create. It might be the number of people you'll help—or all or none of the above.

Even if you end up in the Box again, just remember that any desire you have to make an impact must be based on your highest aspirations. And the actions you take and choices you make should all be geared toward building the needed foundation. That foundation must be strong enough to support those big aspirations. As long as that's the case, you have a perfect right to dream big. You have a perfect right to dream about making a *huge* impact. All those amazing things you can and will achieve. Because you're amazing! You'll do so much more than simply *survive*—you'll *thrive*! And I can't tell you how excited I am about your future!

It's already time for me to head out to the airport. I got to fly to Detroit to speak before the Skillman Foundation, a place working to develop good schools and good neighborhoods for children. I'll have to tell you about my time in jail in the next letter.

Treat yourself, don't beat yourself.

Peace,

Hill

THRIVE

LETTER 8

What Is a Slave?

You felt that life was acting upon you instead of feeling like you were in control. You became a worker instead of a thinker. You became a follower instead of a leader—a slave, actually.

—Stedman Graham

Dear Brotha,

Hey, man. You've been on my mind a lot. I've been hoping that you've been taking the time to do the positive visualizations I asked you to practice. I'll be honest, imagining your time in the Box set me off balance for a little while. You told me you'd gone to work to make a chart to tape to your cell wall—a "master list," as you called it, of your assets and liabilities. You seem really hyped about it. What I like best about it is that you're going to use it to figure out a plan. What I call a "blueprint for your life." Although you're going to "dream big," you're not going to pull that dream out of the air. You're going to base it on the things you think you're good at or have the potential to be good at. We all have different degrees of different skills and talents. The goal is to cultivate yours in areas that you enjoy and can and will succeed in.

So, I haven't had a chance to tell you about my "being in jail." A couple weeks ago, I was in my dressing room at *CSI: NY*—we're halfway through shooting the season—and one of the production assistants brought my fan mail into my dressing room. I was going through it, and I got to a thick packet. I looked at where it was from. It was from a jail in upstate New York, so I opened it up. The first thing that came to my mind was you. "Why did they transfer him to a jail up *there*?" I thought to myself. Because it wasn't even a prison, it was jail, like the one where you are now. So I opened the packet, and inside it there was a series of pictures of some young cats in prison uniforms holding copies of *Letters to a Young Brother.*

Also in that packet were these letters from these young dudes, all of whom are between the ages of seventeen and twenty-one. They were part of the mandatory GED program. They'd given these speeches at their graduation from the GED class, using my book as the basis for them.

I was kind of blown away, so I called the warden and said, "Um, thanks very much. What happened exactly?" And he said, "One of the teachers knew about your book and decided to do this program. Eleven of the GED students volunteered to be part of it. We call 'em 'the Program Kids.' I've got a whole lot of knuckleheads."

Now, listen to the words he's using. Right? It really hit me the wrong way. "I got to step into this," I told myself, "if I care at all about those kids who asked for my book." So I told the warden, "Well, okay. Let me send you some more books for all the students in your GED program." Then I hit up Amazon and ordered twenty copies of the book for them. Because I figured they needed more. That's all I did. Then suddenly, I thought of you again, and a light bulb went off in my head. I immediately called the warden back and said, "What if I come down there early next week, so I can meet with some of these young men and rap to them about my program MANifest Your Destiny? And how about if I get everyone in your—" You see, I almost said *school,* though I don't know why I *didn't* think I could say *school,* but I said, "I want to get everybody in your correctional facility a book. How many?" He said, "There's eighty-eight." So I called up Amazon again and ordered sixty-eight more copies of the book.

The following week, I had a few days off so I flew to New York City and took the train far to the north to upstate New York. I walked into this correctional facility to meet these young men and talk to them about my book. But before I did, I thought of you again and I said to myself, "I have to find out what this place is like so I can better imagine how my Brotha is living." So I asked for

"I have to find out what this place is like so I can better imagine how my Brotha is living."

a tour, and one of the deputies—he'd read my book, too, and seen me on TV—said he'd be glad to help.

Turned out that, just like you, some of them had been there for eight or nine months. First the deputy took me to the ground floor. He called it "Entry." That was for people who'd just been brought in and were waiting to be taken before the judge.

No, it wasn't like the movies I'd made playing the role of an inmate or the things I'd read about incarceration. It wasn't even like what I'd imagined when I talked about it with the people I know who have been incarcerated or what I'd pictured when I thought of you. There weren't rows of bars and cells with dudes' arms sticking out from them. This place was very cold and modern, almost like a lab. There were very narrow holding rooms, with thick doors and thick glass windows, and just a bench coming out from the wall. And some of the people inside looked like they'd been there for many hours, even more than a day. Some of the doors had narrow trapdoors cut into them, so that a meal on a tray could be threaded inside the room without unlocking the door or having to get near the person locked inside.

Then the deputy took me to the top floor, the isolation pod—solitary, I guess—for the troublemakers, which must be kind of like the one you were just in. Their cells were even narrower than the holding rooms on the ground floor, and all of the doors had those slots with trapdoors. The entire pod was filled with a disgusting smell. Seems one of the guys had lost it entirely. He was locked in there completely nude, and he was smearing his feces on the thick window of his cell. They weren't going to unlock that cell to clean it up until he gave up and sat down. It had been going on for most of the day. And I thought again of you dealing with an atmosphere like that, and a voice inside me said, "I'm sorry, Brotha, I'm so fucking sorry, man."

So I suppose you were right in a way. You couldn't have explained to me what it was like in a million years. Just like you said. If I want to start at "square one" with you, this is where we start. I must admit that I almost gave in to a sense of defeat, almost got to the point of saying to myself, "What's the use?"

OUR LADY OF LOCKUP

That mood changed, however, after my tour of the prison was over. You see, the deputy dropped me off to a counselor who works in that jail and several others. Her name is Cindy Franz. Her office was like some kind of oasis away from the world I'd just seen. A clean, flowery smell. Books everywhere. Pictures from the last graduation. Some fake flowers in a vase on one of the bookcases.

I began asking her questions about the inmates, and she stopped me right there. She told me that the supervisor of education in that jail prefers to call them "students," not "inmates." I realized I could have called this place a school to her and she would have just nodded. She was that cool. And to prove her point, she began loading me up with all kinds of educational resources. I'm slipping some of them inside this letter and telling you where you can send away for others.[1] Not everything mentioned is available where you are now, but learning about these services will make you ready to reach out for them if they come along when you're sent elsewhere.

There were booklets about getting a "certificate of relief," an official document that can restore some of a prisoner's social rights once he gets on the outside. A pamphlet describing how the local school district is working with the prison to offer courses and training. A handbook of legal terms that anybody incarcerated can use if he decides to put together an appeal. A new work-release program meant to provide jobs for people once they get out, and details about how a local company has decided to take part in it and hire some of them. A prerelease workbook called *Living on the Outside* that covers a variety of situations when you have just gotten out, from getting your ID and other documents, to a list of jobs that might be right for you, to tips about writing résumés and cover letters. Let somebody in your family (your aunt?) know about all these and collect some of this information while you do the same.

Do you know what that workbook said on the cover? It said, "You've been dreaming of the day when you'll walk out of here. *But once on the outside, you'll need a plan to succeed.* This handbook can help you build your future—starting right now."

Once I was loaded up with these resources, I sat down with Cindy to talk for a minute. I figured she could teach me a few things. We discussed some of the reasons for the enormous increase in the incarcerated population. That increase owes a lot to the Rockefeller drug laws, penalties for drug use and sales that were pushed into law by New York governor Nelson Rockefeller in 1973. And the subsequent so-called war on drugs and other woefully misguided statutes, such as *life* sentences derived from a baseball rule! Yeah, "three strikes and you're out" is a cute slogan for politicians getting elected but it hasn't been so cute for nonviolent drug offenders facing life in prison. Across the country people began getting life sentences for what would have been considered a near-misdemeanor just a few years before. But hey, outside of locking people up, baseball is "America's favorite pastime." OK, lemme stop.

VOLUNTEERING FOR SLAVERY

One of the statements that popped out of Cindy's mouth stunned me for a moment. She said, "I tell all my students who become repeaters, 'You're volunteering for slavery.' " When I left the jail and took the train back to the city, what Cindy said began to sink in. My head started spinning. Thinking about the history of slavery in this country. Thinking about you and our letters. As I rode east toward Albany, I tried to put all of it out of my mind, but I couldn't. So that very evening at my place in New York, I found myself putting on an old DVD: *Antwone Fisher.* Ever seen it?

I wasn't aware of it that night, but something in me wanted to review that scene in the movie where the army therapist, played by Denzel Washington, tries to explain to the troubled soldier he is treating why the foster mother and her daughter he was placed with treated him with such vicious brutality. The therapist says that the members of that foster family were victims of *post-traumatic slave syndrome,* a condition passed down from the survival behaviors of American slaves.

> **"I tell all my students who become repeaters, 'You're volunteering for slavery.' "**

The therapist in *Antwone Fisher* was essentially telling his patient that some African-Americans abuse each other just as they were once abused by their white masters. They don't know any other game, and they've "identified with their aggressors." A researcher named Joy DeGruy Leary has studied the syndrome in detail and wrote a book about it called *Post Traumatic Slave Syndrome: America's Legacy of Enduring Injury and Healing,* if you're interested.

Do you know why I'm talking about this? It was Cindy Franz's remarks about "volunteering for slavery" that drew me into the subject. If you compare the option-stealing measures of the prison system to slave-owner strategies, the similarities are almost mind-blowing. Southern slave owners prevented their slaves from learning to read and write when they could. It kept them isolated and dependent. We've already seen how forces in our jails work against reading and educational opportunities for prisoners. Like the slaves of the South, some of whom did learn to read and write despite their masters, you have to be wily and resourceful to get an education in prison. Oases of understanding like Cindy Franz are few and far between in prison. In most cases, the poor choice of training programs, the confiscation of books—it's all there to weaken the resolve and know-how of prisoners. "They're here to be punished, not rewarded" is the common refrain.

There are those who would argue with that, saying a lack of books and courses is merely the result of a lack of funds and a disinterested government, but you and I already know how much of a cash cow the prison industrial complex is for some people. The for-profit prison business is booming. As is the cheap labor production within the prison system.

One other strategy that kept Southern slaves dependent and helpless was violence. Fear of punishment kept them from defying their masters and often worked to set one slave against another. Does that remind you of prison as well? Violence between corrections officers and inmates, between prisoner and fellow prisoner, between gangs, ensures an atmosphere of fear and desperation and keeps the prison body ineffectual.

Well, man, time for me to sign off. My head is weary just thinking about these complex issues. And I'm pissed off I don't have the answers. I hope you don't mind, but I suggested to Cindy that she try to start a correspondence with you, too. It certainly wouldn't hurt to have two mentors on your side, would it?

Much love,

Hill

VOLUNTEER
TO EXCEL

PART 2

A LEAP OF FAITH

LETTER 9

Doing Time

Your time is limited, so don't waste it living someone else's life.

—Steve Jobs

They always say time changes things, but you actually have to change them yourself.

—Andy Warhol, *The Philosophy of Andy Warhol*

Hey, Brotha,

You know what? I'm about to write some things I know you don't want to hear. Maybe I'm mad at myself; maybe I'm frustrated with you. Hold up. There's no "maybe." I'm writing this with some frustration in my heart, but it's real. It's honest. If you want to tear this letter up and use it as toilet paper, go ahead. Best of luck with the edges. You see, Cindy Franz told me how you answered her letter. That answer makes you look *bad*. But because I suggested she write to you and offer to help you, the way you answered makes *me* look bad, too.

"Just send money," you wrote. "I could use some smokes, and more money for the commissary. Oh, yeah, here are the names of a couple CDs I can use. Isn't much I can do but wait while I'm stuck here doing time."

I couldn't believe that, man! Who did you think you were talking to? Especially since she included all those leads for correspondence courses in her letter. To say I'm disappointed in you doesn't even capture how I am feeling. I am so pissed! Not to mention all that "victim" shit you piled on. Making sure she knew you'd had lousy parents, had no money for college, were denied scholarships, saw your older brother sent away to prison for eighteen years, lived with a cold and uncaring aunt, were expected to pay child support for a son after your girl became pregnant, *blah, blah, blah*. C'mon, fam! And the way you presented it: All this stuff "happened" to you. I thought we agreed that nothing merely "happens," that even a life of passivity is a life of choice with its own consequences. Stop letting anger put you in situations you don't deserve. Nobody owes you shit. The sooner you realize this, the sooner you'll start living.

Nothing merely "happens." Even a life of passivity is a life of choice with its own consequences.

LIFE IN THE TREETOPS

I was still thinking of your excuses for trying to con money and merchandise out of Cindy when I dragged myself out of bed this morning at the crack of dawn. It's below freezing in New York already, too cold for fall. Ain't nobody got time for that. But I'm still determined to get in an early-morning run before the responsibilities of the day swallow me up. I wanted to take my mind off the cold and you, so I began thinking about something I went to a while ago.

Last spring, I went to a really cool conference called TED, which stands for "Technology, Entertainment, Design." They invite fifty exceptional people to the conference who are doing something edgy in these fields, and each of them has only eighteen minutes to go onstage and present their ideas with talks, slides, videos, and live demonstrations.

I happened to walk into the place just as a woman named Nalini Nadkarni was up there, talking about her life in the treetops. You heard me right: life in the treetops. In fact, in the world of science, they call her the "queen of canopy research." Nalini has climbed trees on four continents with people from all walks of life—scientists, artists, clergymen, loggers, politicians, Inuits (look it up)—you name it. She wrote a book about those experiences called *Between*

Earth and Sky: Our Intimate Connections to Trees, and that's what she presented: what they call the *canopy,* the world of treetops.[1]

I had no idea I was in store for yet another example of serendipity, because soon it was clear that Nalini was going to talk not just about trees, but about time. And not just about time, but about prisons! And this happened just a week before I got your first letter from jail.

Now . . . you've made it clear that you think of yourself as stuck in jail and that your life's on hold, right? You think of yourself as being in a state of stasis. Because you're locked up, you're as rooted to that jail cell as a tree is rooted to the ground. After all, trees can't go anywhere, even if they want to. But Nalini Nadkarni has another take on trees, and she explained it like this: "Trees epitomize stasis. Trees are rooted in the ground in one place for many human generations, but if we shift our perspective from the trunk to the twigs, trees become very dynamic entities, moving and growing."

Nalini had a totally original way of proving her point. She'd come to the conclusion that by turning trees into artists, she could find out how and how much they moved. Believe it or not, she took a paintbrush and tied the end of it to a twig. She waited for the wind to come up and held a piece of canvas against the brush. As she spoke to us at TED, slides of sketches were projected behind her. Not by her, but by trees! According to her, the way that the tree moved the brush produced art. One of the slides showed a canvas painted by a western red cedar, and the other was a painting by a Douglas fir. They were as different from each other as a Picasso is from a Bearden.

Trees seemingly rooted in the ground can still truly move and create.

And now, what about you, Brotha? How many miles do you think the movements of your hands, your fingers, have covered in the seven months you've been locked up? How many miles have the repeated contractions of your heart covered in a year? You could actually figure this out if you knew how much movement each contraction of the human heart normally represents and you then multiplied that by your average pulse per minute, and then multiplied that sum by the number of minutes in an entire year.

How many miles does the blood flowing throughout your body—the cycles of your circulatory system—cover in a year? What distance do the electrical signals passing through your nerves to your brain cover in a second, a minute, a day, a year?

The biggest question of all is: *What percentage of all that movement have you wasted—flushed down the toilet—with that letter to Cindy Franz?* Are you actively creating a life of movement? Or one that is much smaller than the one you were meant to live?

You see, it's not just that people are *never* in the wrong place at the wrong time—like you claim you were when you got arrested. It's that everyone and everything is in a *different* place at every second, and so are you, at every second of your life.

You can move. But your movement must be guided. Undirected movement isn't progress, it's just movement. And you can't always be *about to* do something . . . *about to* hardly ever does a thing. Your potential must lead to action and action to progress. Do you get what I'm saying? I know that Nalini Nadkarni, the queen of the canopy, does:

> I began to think about ways that we might consider this lesson of trees, to consider other entities that are also static and stuck, but which cry for change and dynamicism, and one of those entities is our prisons. Prisons, of course, are where people who break our laws are stuck, confined behind bars. And our prison system itself is stuck. . . . I decided to ask whether the lesson I had learned from trees as artists could be applied to a static institution such as our prisons, and I think the answer is yes.

In 2007 she started a partnership with the Washington State Department of Corrections. She began bringing science to four of their prisons. Biologists and conservationists came to talk, and their ideas developed into conservation projects right inside those prisons, as more and more and more of the men locked inside began coming to science lectures instead of lying on their bunks thinking about Lauren London and jerking off, or watching TV, or lifting weights.

It's that everyone and everything is in a different place at every second, and so are you, at every second of your life.

Then those same incarcerated men began growing prairie plants that were endangered so they could be shipped out and replanted in Washington State. And then they began to raise endangered frogs to be released into the Washington wetlands. And finally, they started to bring pictures of these growing, living things into the exercise yards and the isolation pods used by the most violent prisoners, the ones who are locked up twenty-three hours a day and aren't allowed to take part in the conservation projects and are only allowed to exercise in the yards for an hour a day.

Why put photos of those plants and animals in a place like that? I think those photos stuck up on the walls of the isolation pod or pasted to the walls of their exercise yard were an attempt to send the message that no one is completely locked up, on hold, shut down, stuck, "doing time"—whatever you want to call it. Because everything that is alive is in constant movement.

You're alive, moving and changing, no matter where you are or what happens to you. From your letters to me I've gotten a sense that you're living in the fantasy world of life after prison and kind of sleepwalking through the time you're doing. That's a very passive way to live, man, and your passivity affects all of us! Ever heard of a Greek guy named Heraclitus, the philosopher? More than two thousand years ago, he pointed something out: "Even sleepers are workers and collaborators on what goes on in the universe."

Most of what Heraclitus said only survived in fragments, but we do know enough about him to understand that his thinking was structured around one fundamental truth: the fact that everything *flows,* or as he was said to have put it: "Change alone is unchanging. . . . You cannot step twice into the same stream."

While you may believe that precious time is being robbed from you while you're locked up, it is possible to transform all those idle hours in gen pop or even in the Box into *all the time in the world* to gain the power of knowledge. Right now, you actually have more time to get an education than most people on the outside. Plenty of time to start putting together a list of colleges, religious ministries, charities, and other services offering courses by mail or free books. I know I may sound like an asshole right now, but quit lying there on your bunk with "time on your hands" when you could think of it as *time in your hands,* waiting for you to mold it. How you use your time now will affect not only you in profound ways, but many who are involved with you, including your son and your aunt and me.

Okay, Brotha. Make sure you hit me back. Let's pick up the pieces and try to go back to where we left off. Speak soon.

Peace,

Hill

P.S. I was speaking to my boy Jeff Johnson about this concept of time, and he told me he wanted to share something with you, so I've enclosed his letter. Jeff is a television journalist, activist, and motivational speaker on topics such as violence and voting rights. He was known as "Cousin Jeff" on BET's *Rap City*. Check out how gangsta he thinks time is.

Dear Brother,

I remember *you*, Brother. I think of *you*. When I am working and traveling I often have *you* on my mind and I wonder . . . what are you doing with your time? Webster's Dictionary defines *time* as "the indefinite continued progress of existence and events in the past, present, and future regarded as a whole." When I read that, it doesn't really hit me. Time, in the Jeff Johnson dictionary, is the most precious natural resource that each human uses to create his or her unique life story. But when you look at your life, how have you utilized or wasted this most precious of resources?

Time is the most gangsta resource because no human can control it in its purest form. It is the only thing you cannot make more of. You cannot get time back, and no matter how much power you have, you can't change the universal laws of time. What you have (or don't have) in life is a direct reflection of what you do with the time you have been given. But it is also gangsta because it is the one true equalizer.

Rich people don't get more time than poor. Suburbanites don't receive more of it than those in the hood, and white people don't have more hours in the day than people of color. Every person on Earth, you included, gets 86,400 seconds a day. Answer this: Have you wasted more of those seconds than you have used to create a life that you can be proud of? So now the better question is, *what are you going to do with your time now?*

No one realizes the power of someone telling you what you can do with your time more than Brothers and Sisters who are locked up. Brother, when you decide to use your time to create a reality that is in opposition to why you were put on this earth, the universe (God) will begin to fight back and put you in a space that forces you to see your life for what it is. You were created for greatness—*not* for prison. Your sentence, your bid, your release date, your probation are all reflections of someone telling you *where* you must spend your time, but no one can tell you *what* you can do with your time. My hope is that you realize the difference.

> **You were created for greatness— *not* for prison.**

You remember how much you and others would complain about the time spent on activities and responsibilities that made you and them uncomfortable? "Damn, I gotta go to work," "I don't feel like going to school," and even "I don't have time to spend with those kids." Brother, do you recognize that old saying that you reap what you sow? That is not always about karma, good and bad energy coming back to you, but it's about your getting back what you invest.

And if we keep it 100, so many of us have invested in more negative activities than we have positive. And just so you're clear, I'm not just talking about Brothers locked up. But think about how much time you invested in the hustle. Learning how to get into it, how to perfect it, master it, and even teach the game to others. Well, your jail time is normally a reflection of that foul-ass investment. Those investments catch up to all of us in different ways, but the point is to remember how gangsta time is. It will pay you back, whether you want to collect or not.

But what would happen if we all, you especially, decided to flip how we use our time? The things we dream about, the people we allow around us, the books we read, topics we study, prayers we lift up, service we give, and love we offer. What would our lives look like with positive investment of our most precious resources in those areas? See, it's not about being soft, letting anyone get over on you, or being less than a man. But a real man is first and foremost responsible to what he has been blessed with. Those gifts you were given to lead other men, to inspire them and push them to go places they otherwise would not go, were not given to you to lead them to jail and death, but rather to power and legacy.

I believe in you. I believe that the world is waiting on you to shift how you use your time. The world needs your energy and investment. The community needs your legitimate business, your time on the block empowering others, and your positive example. Your child needs that time that only Daddy can give. What will you do with your time, Brother?

Some people have more time left behind bars than others. Some of us are out and act like we are not free, wasting time like we can get it back. Some people in prison have invested *so* much time in dirt that they will never see the outside again. *So what?* Invest time on the inside the right way, and your time on the outside will shift. I believe that God gives you life to remind you that you still have time to make *today* right, no matter where you are. So, my Brother . . . what will you do with your time? Time spent learning, loving, and living your best will define your life's legacy. Live well, my Brother; the world needs your greatness.

Yours,
Jeff Johnson

PRODUCTIVELY
USE MY TIME

LETTER 10

A Leap of Faith

Faith is taking the first step, even when you don't see the whole staircase.

—Martin Luther King Jr.

Dear Brotha,

Wow, that was an awesome letter you just sent me, man. I consider it a first in real communication. Does it embarrass you to hear that? I'm not just talking about the apology you asked me to convey to Cindy. It's the fact that, in my opinion, this was the first time you revealed some true feelings. The first time you allowed yourself to be vulnerable enough to reveal some deep truths to me. No false bravado. No unnecessary middle finger in the air. None of that resentment or cynicism about your situation you were hitting me with before, none of that shit about being an innocent victim.

No. You talked about your fears about your sentencing, which is coming up in a couple weeks, and how you really felt about the situation with your son, R. J., your sense of helplessness about not being able to do anything for him. Real-talk. No sulky rhetoric or blame this time. Just your anxiety and fear about your son, your son's future, and your own. It was moving, in a good way. I'm so proud of you, man. Made me feel closer to you. Pause . . . not like that, pimpin'. Slow up. Ha ha.

You also talked about something else that was buggin' you out, and that was the "leap of faith" you say I'm asking you to make. *A leap of faith*—those are *your* words, not mine. I hadn't thought of it that way, and I think it was brilliant that you did. You said I was asking you to give up all the prison codes that locked-up people use to get by—the deceit and the scrambles to rule the roost, the factions-against-factions and race gangs, the drugs that dull pain and boredom. I was asking you to take "a leap of faith" into a whole new game plan I was promising would assure your future, and that was scaring the hell out of you. Well, you need to get the hell out so you can get the hell out.

FEAR AND TREMBLING

What you wrote actually got me thinking about a philosopher I spent an entire term reading when I was at Harvard, as a way of dealing with my own problems. I was full of anxiety about a lot of stuff, some of which seems kind of silly now. You see, I'd just made the decision to pull out of a legal career and go into theater—acting—and was scared shitless about not making it. What the hell does *scared shitless* even mean? Anyway, I was scared about the "lawyer money" I was walking away from and whether or not I'd be able to pay back my student loans. From where you sit you probably think, "Those are some wack-ass fears, Hill." But the thing about fears is we all got them, no matter who we are, rich or poor, Black or white. Fears don't discriminate or play favorites.

I kept picturing the expression on my father's face when I told him I wanted to be an actor, the disappointment, almost a look of being betrayed. In my mind he was saying, "What!? You have a degree from Harvard Law School. . . . What the f— are you thinking? . . . You're gonna throw all that away!?" And then, if I failed as an actor, it would be even worse. I'd have let my entire family down.

So you see, I felt guilty about the consequences of my decision. I was full of anxiety, fear. As my anxiety increased, a so-called friend recommended that I get on the latest tranqs and antidepressants. I've always been afraid of that stuff, thinking that I can fix things on my own. I don't remember how I ended up with a copy of *Fear and Trembling* by the Danish philosopher Søren Kierkegaard.[1] I think I might have bought it a year before for a course on ethics that I ended up not taking. On one of my worst evenings, alone in my dorm room, I picked up the book and started thumbing through it, in an attempt to get my mind off my fears. To my surprise, I found myself reading a nearly exact description of the feelings I was having.

Kierkegaard talks about "fear and trembling" as a type of dread—a strange kind of anxiety directed at no particular object. It happens, he says, when we become aware of our own freedom, our ability to choose our own fate, and also come to the conclusion that the right decision may not even be based on logic or reason but just on intuition. Our fear is not only of what the unknown has in store for us but also comes from the temptation to backslide from our state of mental freedom into something that requires less responsibility, something that society can logically prove to be the best choice, the most moral position. But according to Kierkegaard, there is a higher mentality than socially sanctioned morality that goes beyond logical thinking. It's called *faith*.

In my opinion, I've been asking you to take a leap of faith, to go against almost every code you learned on the street or in prison, to go on this journey with me even if you don't completely see where it's heading. Life is designed to depend upon a higher power. Sure, I've spent a lot of time writing about the logical reasons for my point of view. I've said that when you're incarcerated you're an unwitting upholder of the prison industrial complex and its profit machine. I've told you that Cindy Franz called being locked up volunteering for slavery. I gave you lots of examples of convicts who turned incarceration into a positive experience and emerged as educated, accomplished people after using their time in prison effectively. But I've also talked to you about *your authentic navigation system* and claimed that there is a voice in you that will define your rightful place in the universe if you can only get into the habit of listening to it. The despair and anxiety you're experiencing now might be the terror anybody would feel when they first dare to listen to their authentic voice and—without understanding why—follow it down a new path.

Kierkegaard pointed out that a leap of faith is often an ordeal. He said that it's always accompanied by dread and the possibility of regressing into an easier state of nonfreedom by simply doing what society, family, and community say is right. He means that it's always *easier* to get pulled back into our old habits. That's why most people go back to prison after that exit. I want you to be the person who begins to change that statistic.

As I lay on my dorm bed way back when, reading those pages, I suddenly realized how relevant all Kierkegaard's philosophical issues were to my situation. Wasn't I flying in the face of convention by defying everything that my family and community had expected of me and rejecting a so-called prestigious legal career in favor of acting (a job you don't even need a high school diploma to do)? Realizing that faith alone in my choice would give me the best chance at succeeding gave me permission to stop trying to think of an argument that would convince my family—and especially my father—that my decision was a rational one. *Understanding the reason for my anxiety, my dread—which was based on my inability to support my choice with logic—suddenly put me at peace.* I gave up any attempts to explain my choice to others and began relying 100 percent on my intuition that studying theater was the right and only thing to do.

I think the fear and trembling you've been experiencing comes from a similar conflict. Everything about your environment is telling you that the only way to "make it" is by following the prison code of power-mongering, from which all the repressive elements of the prison industrial system draw their strength. You're on the brink of turning your back on such a mentality in order to have a very different future. It makes sense that part of what you're feeling is dread and anxiety. All I can do to help is tell you that your intuition about changing your life makes intuitive sense to me, and I want to be there to support your faith in it all the way down the line. Listen, Brother, the greatest goals are never realistic. They come with fear, doubt, and insecurity. But every successful person I know pushed through these moments. They didn't allow clarity to cloud their vision. They didn't rely on reality to get by. Every successful person I know foolishly believed they could accomplish their crazy goals, and they did. And so have I. And so will you. Believe without a doubt, and watch what happens.

You know, I'm willing to bet that if you told that dude J. T. you'd given up any attempt to manipulate Cindy or me for short-term material benefits in favor of more lasting rewards, he'd label you a sucker and try to challenge your "manhood." He'd probably come up with a logical-sounding argument that I couldn't answer completely. He might even accuse you of giving in to "the system" or "listening to some Harvard actor nigga who knows nothing about this life."

But in my opinion, J. T.'s the one who has given in to "the system" straight up. He sees his code as the rebel's, but cons, intimidation, gangs, and all that shit aren't really rebellious. They're obeying the oppressive rules of the prison environment. In the end, they're the tools that the prison industrial system relies upon. As long as you talk and act that way, you remain a pawn in their game. You have no power, being moved here and there. Setting one convict against another in a bid for power is only increasing the power of "the institution," so that those prison-profit machines get more cheap labor in order to get richer. From the American Revolution to the rebellion of the Warsaw Jewish ghetto against the Nazis to Black civil rights, no attempt to shift the balance of power has ever occurred without solidarity. But prison teaches each man to set himself against every other and sets groups against groups, so no big shift in the balance of power can ever occur.

So yeah, I'm asking you to take a leap of faith into a planned-out, gradually built new life. But it's a leap into the unknown based on the belief that the universe has much better in store for you. And that better life won't come knocking on your cell door; instead, it's up to you to claim it. Remember, it's a process. Chasing the success before chasing the goal is like a drunken one-night stand. You may get it, but it'll only last five minutes and won't even be remembered.

So don't grow weary, and don't worry. The fact that I see you poised for that leap of faith—which has to be the reason for all the "fear and trembling" you wrote about in your last letter—fills me with joy, because it's gonna be the best gamble you ever took.

Gotta go. I'll be in touch.

Much love,

Hill

FAITH

LETTER 11

Her Point of View

I often hear prisoners' wives comparing themselves to military spouses. Early on, I too offered this analogy to help explain away the blank stares. In the context of: "My husband is incarcerated, but it's no different than his being in the military." Sure, there are similar tenets; partners are away from each other for extended periods; families must figure out how to raise kids, maintain a home, and create intimacy despite distance. Both relationships face difficulty with reintegration. That's where the similarities end. For obvious reasons, prisoners' wives do not receive the same respect as military wives and with another public distinction: military wives *stand* by their partners, prisoners' wives *wait*.

—Reesy Floyd-Thompson, wife of a man serving time who maintains a support website for other women in the same position, PWGP.org

Hey, man,

This might be a short one—though I've said that before and just kept writing. I've got to run out in a minute. I just came back from a quick boxing session at the gym. For me it's a kind of private time, in between airplanes and sound stages and speech platforms. I sparred with one of the interns from my

TV show. He used to box Golden Gloves, amateur. How'd I do? Let's just say he ran circles around me—I'm starting to feel my age! I'm still in the Big Apple wrapping up those exterior shots. I never get tired of the kaleidoscope of humanity that the streets of NYC represent. That's what I love most about New York City; every walk of life is represented and if you're open to it, you will connect with different people of all points of view.

My boy Ryan Holly did eight years a little while back. He told me he felt the same about the city and possibilities for his life. He said, "Coming to New York City for the first time, I experienced things I thought were silly. I saw a play (*The Heights*), and I have never been so inspired by something I didn't understand before I saw it. That play and standing next to humongous buildings made me think, 'Damn, if they can build all this. . . . I should be able to pull a decent chunk of success myself.' . . . And I took off."

Your apology about the way you answered Cindy means a lot to me, fam. I spoke to her, and she told me she totally understands the way you reacted to her at first. It didn't surprise her or turn her off like I thought it would. She's no stranger to the despair that being locked up can cause and the cynical reactions it can trigger if somebody reaches out to you. She's still willing to help if you'll let her, my man.

More important than that, thanks for keeping it 100 with me after I came at you. The next time things get too heavy, get at me, instead of reverting back to that everybody's-out-to-get-something-so-why-shouldn't-I gangsta. If you'd clued me in to the fact that you'd just gotten that letter from Yvette—your son's mom—the very same day you got Cindy's letter, I would have understood a little better why you answered her the way you did. In fact, I put my phone number at the end of this letter. I think it's about time we talked on the phone about the situation between you and Yvette, right?

I'm glad you included Yvette's letter with the one you sent me. It let me see for myself how something like that would put anybody back as much as it did you. I had no idea the mother of your child—your ex—was so deep into cocaine and that you've known her to experiment with "Molly" and that "Spider Blue" or that child protection is trying to take your kid, R. J., away from her and put him in a group home. Yet again, we're seeing somebody who doesn't want to take any responsibility for the consequences of her actions, blaming her descent into drugs on your being locked up. I don't buy that because it doesn't compute.

Sure, your being incarcerated had a strong effect on all your family members, but that doesn't mean you are completely responsible for Yvette's drug use. Unless there's something you're not telling me. There is no doubt that problems are constant. They are inevitable. I understand the want, need, desire to start handling your life in a way that sets you up to be able to face problems and start living accordingly. You have to understand that you are a leader. And people are going to follow you. The question is, are you going to take responsibility for that leadership? You are somewhat to blame for the totality of what Yvette is going through. You are Yvette and R. J.'s role model and you failed to live up to your position. Taking responsibility for the mistakes you've made is the first step toward true manhood.

> **You have to understand that you are a leader. And people are going to follow you.**

It's easy to see that Yvette's problems aren't totally unrelated to your incarceration. As I read that resentful letter she sent you and felt all the rage exploding in it, it almost burned the tips of my fingers. For the first time, I started to think more deeply about what it might be like to have a family member or loved one locked up. I even went on the Internet to see what I could find out about the experience. Although it doesn't excuse her drug abuse and parental neglect, spouses and family members of the incarcerated don't have it easy. I feel for family members and spouses like Yvette, for all they have to go through. If your mom, dad, brother, sister, cousin, son, daughter, niece, nephew, husband, or wife is locked up—damn, it ain't easy.

HELP ON THE OUTSIDE

Do you know there's an entire online community of people dealing with the loss of a family member to prison? There's talk about the situation from every angle—from the practical to the psychological, to the unwitting role played by families of the incarcerated in upholding the functioning of the prison. One website went so far as to compare the grief and confusion of losing a loved one to prison to a death in the family.[1] Even though there's usually a way to keep communicating with somebody who's incarcerated, there's the feeling that he disappeared into some other world—another reality—and the fear that he'll be a different person when he gets out.

The situation of the single mom isn't at all rare these days. Do you know that about two-thirds of the families in poor neighborhoods are being run by, in most cases, hardworking single moms? Sadly, much of it is the result of a father being locked up. A whopping 8.7 million children have parents under some kind of correctional supervision, men and women who are either locked up or on parole. And, of course, a habit of getting locked up has a strong tendency to be passed down to the next generation. Of all the people incarcerated today in this country, 78 percent of them grew up in a fatherless household. Now they're bringing it down the line to their children. It's up to you to break that cycle with R. J.

Some wives and parents posting on these websites touched on the irrational guilt they're tortured by, the nagging feeling that they could have—should have—done something to keep their mate from getting arrested, despite the fact that, in the majority of cases, there would have been little they could do. The worst of all is that it's not just the convict who's stigmatized by being incarcerated; so are all the members of his family. I read stories about families suddenly abandoned by their community, children shunned in school, even in *church*, and being rejected by formerly close relatives.

Some of the stuff I found was geared toward helping wives, mothers, or siblings on the outside to remedy practical problems caused by the loss of the family's wage earner, ranging from tips about tightening the family budget to suggestions for moonlighting jobs that would bring in more income. Your ex, Yvette, must be going through some of that. I know you'd already moved out when you got arrested, but you were paying her child support, and that's obviously on hold now.

What I hadn't really thought about was the kind of depression that sneaks up on some people when their husband or brother or father begins serving a term in jail. Many times it pains loved ones and family even more than inmates. A friend, Jose Vasquez, recounted a story to me: "I was just with a woman whose two sons, brother, and nephew just got locked up. During a conversation with me, she broke down in tears at the thought of these men she loves being locked up. People have a scary image of prison and because of that they suffer so much more." I learned about that in detail in a terrific collection of essays by people dealing with the loss of a family member to prison: *Counting the Years: Real-Life Stories About Waiting for Loved Ones to Return Home from Prison.* One of the editors of that collection, Sheila Rule, traded a thirty-year career as a globetrotting *New York Times* journalist for the opportunity to devote all her energies to cofounding the organization that published that book. It's called the Think Outside the Cell Foundation, and its goal is to end the stigma of incarceration and the effect of it on those who care about somebody who is serving time.

Sheila Rule obviously knows what she's talking about. Through a prison ministry, she met and eventually married Joseph Robinson, a man already incarcerated at Sullivan Correctional Facility. The website they produce together, ThinkOutsidetheCell.org, tries to cover all areas of the incarceration phenomenon for every member of the family; it offers everything from a fledgling scholarship program for the children of families dealing with incarceration to the Prison to Prosperity Fair and workshops intended to equip people just released with social, psychological, and financial tools to help them get back on their feet. And if you want me to, I'll let your ex Yvette know about the book and website as well. Sometimes we all need to hear something more than once to get the message. If she is open to it, I'm going to turn her on to the book and the website when I speak to her.

GOING DEEPER

That book and website aren't the deepest sources of information about the phenomenon, though. *Doing Time on the Outside*, by Donald Braman, a professor of law at the George Washington University, tries to unearth some of the more profound issues.[2] Not only does Braman tell the stories of actual families smashed to pieces by the incarceration of a male parent, suddenly shifting the role of caretaker and breadwinner to grandparents, aunts, or mothers; he also shows how much more damaging than other types of single-parent households this kind can be.

It really made me wonder why our state governments stand by as prisons milk mostly poor people for money by charging triple the long-distance rate for a phone call with family and friends. But it isn't just the added burden of those astronomically high phone bills from the collect or prepaid calls from prison, or the transportation costs, lost work time, and humiliation of inconvenient visits to facilities. It's also the fact that all of it is happening at a time when child welfare programs are being mercilessly slashed. The largest group of people living below the poverty line in this country is its *children*. That's a damn shame! The situation has torn apart some of the poorer African-American, Latino, and white neighborhoods, damaging the life of every family member.

Braman also makes a controversial hypothesis about incarceration that might bother you. He says it serves as a kind of alibi for men to give up their parental responsibility, inadvertently punishing innocent family members with the consequences of crimes they had nothing to do with. Wow. What do you think? Fam, I know it's more complicated than that. But maybe it's one jumping-off point for thinking about things.

Let me go back to what I said earlier. Obviously, I don't know Yvette, and I'm just feeling my way along. But I do know that nobody has a right to hold somebody else responsible for their drug use, and that, obviously, includes her. Still, it's also fairly obvious that once you were locked up, she had to deal not just with her changed financial situation but also with a kid feeling the pain of an absent father. It wasn't just *your* options that were narrowed by incarceration. Hers and R. J.'s were, too. So out of the few choices available to her—for example, trying to make it with a minimum-wage job and doing what she could to fill the parental void left by you with other relatives—she chose to cop out completely and get high, and her situation progressively got worse. Yvette certainly made bad decisions, because worse still, now your kid has two strikes against him. Now can you see how their lives were immediately changed by your incarceration?

I'm not claiming there's much you can do about it. I'm just saying that some kind of positive communication among all three of you could only help. If you can get to the point of seeing your incarceration as something that happened to *all three of you*, knowing you understand this might help Yvette feel less alone, and that might help her to pull it together. Even if that doesn't happen, you'll know you did the right thing. And if neither you nor I can help Yvette, there are definitely things we can do for R. J.

I found another organization that's a treasure trove of resources for the families of the incarcerated, with an emphasis on the kids. It's called the Family and Corrections Network (FCN),[3] and their website has answers to almost every question you might have about this situation: It has a directory of national and local programs for kids with a parent in jail, news about services and projects designed to help children, and a fact sheet listing all the research being done on the problem. And that's only the tip of the iceberg. Just by glancing at the website, I found the "Children of Prisoners Library," tips for volunteers on mentoring children of the incarcerated.

Since you can't get online, I'm going to keep feeding you the information I find on it. What would make it easier is if you send me a list of questions about the subject. I'll try to find answers to them on the website and include them in every letter. It'll be a good exercise for both of us, as we put our heads together to find out more about the issue. Let's make delving into it a joint project, okay? I might even be able to get Yvette interested in all of it. The first thing for you to do is to put in effort to find peaceful ground and exchange helpful information with Yvette. All right? Cool?

At any rate, I'll call Yvette, I promise. And I'll try to get permission from her to deal with child protection about the issue. Do you think your aunt would take in your little man, at least until you got out? That's a much better option than a group home, in my opinion. Either that or your ex has got to go into recovery right away and start attending some NA meetings, so she can get back to being a mother. Those are the only two options.

Whatever happens, R. J. is somebody who is obviously going to play a big role in any of your future plans. Group home or no group home, I'm gonna work at finding a way for you to communicate with him—for example, being able to send him a card for his birthday that you told me was coming up. Too bad the New York Public Library program I told you about isn't available where you are. I'm talking about the one where they record fathers reading storybooks to their kids and then deliver the recording on CD to the kids. Maybe we can jury-rig a homemade version of that process ourselves. I know it's possible to record a phone conversation because journalists use that method all the time when they interview me. So maybe . . . just maybe, I can rig something up on my own phone—for special occasions—and at least record you wishing R. J. a happy birthday or speaking a greeting for the holidays. And then I'd mail that recording to him wherever he is. The sound of a loved one's voice has a lot of power, Brotha. It's healing, and it creates intimacy. I know Yvette won't accept your collect calls, but maybe I can get a recording to R. J., anyway.

I'll hit you up with more on this subject soon, all right? Hang in there. Speak soon.

Peace,

Hill

FIRST . . .
FAMILY

LETTER 12

Hill's Assignment

We're the richest nation on Earth, with the highest number of imprisoned people in the world. Our drug addictions and child poverty are among the highest in the industrialized world. So don't ever confuse wealth or fame with character.

—Marian Wright Edelman

My Man,

I got your "assignment." And let me tell you, there is no assignment I will be happier to complete. I'm so glad you finally hit me up with a list of questions I'm supposed to research on the Family and Corrections Network since you can't get online. What really impressed me is how on-the-mark they are. Now that you've decided to get proactive about making your time behind bars count, I'm finding out how savvy you are about getting to the real core of a problem. So here are the answers to the questions you sent me about R. J.

I spent a long time going from one link to another on the Family and Corrections Network website. It's a pretty massive collection of information. Some of the links I found sent me to articles by caseworkers, recollections of people who'd had a parent incarcerated as they were growing up, statistics about the phenomenon, etc. In trying to answer your specific questions, here's what I gleaned from them:

1. **Should my kid, R. J., be told the truth about my incarceration and why I'm inside or given some half-truth that would be easier for a child to swallow?**

   Ideas about the children of incarcerated people have changed a lot in the last few years. In the past, some child protection agencies seemed to discourage bonds between children and parents who were going to be locked up for a long time. Nowadays, most professionals believe the opposite: Family members and caseworkers should try to *strengthen* the bonds between kids and their incarcerated parents. Part of doing that is to be absolutely honest about where an incarcerated person is, why he's there, when he's likely to come home, and whether it's possible to visit him. So yes, R. J.'s mom, Yvette; or your aunt; or any adult he trusts and sees fairly regularly should explain all of it, taking care to give answers in a way that a kid his age can understand.

   That, however, is just one side of the equation. Children of incarcerated parents don't only need to be clued in about their parents' situation. They also have to be encouraged to talk about their feelings regarding it. Even a kid your son's age might be feeling embarrassed or ashamed about having a parent in prison. Maybe he's sensing the stigma attached to such a situation from the way he's being treated in school (he's in third grade, right?) or on the playground—not only by other children, but by the parents of these children or by teachers. As you know, it can be a fucked-up world out there. Believe it or not, a lot of adults who should know better lack any sensitivity about the ways a child can feel when his father is incarcerated. In fact, research about such kids' feelings is still scant. Social science researchers and social workers are only just now starting to study it methodologically. Nevertheless, several things about it have already been proven.

   Most children are *deeply* affected by the loss of a parent to prison. Grief, guilt, anger, and a sense of abandonment are all common emotional consequences of it. These can lead to poor performance in school; having a "thin skin" that can't withstand much stress, whatever its source might be; or even a higher probability of being attracted to drugs. One paper I read on the subject even compared the behavior of some children with incarcerated parents to the symptoms shown by those suffering from post-traumatic stress disorder, or PTSD, an ongoing condition of severe anxiety and panic attacks that usually comes after exposure to a violent and frightening event, such as a military battle.[1] Man, this is the condition Brothers suffer from after doing tours in Iraq. Can you believe a kid with an incarcerated parent can go through the same thing?

Also—although I know it'll be hard to get your mind around this one—it's a fact that many kids feel that their parent's arrest and incarceration is somehow their fault. These children need to understand that it isn't and that the parent in prison doesn't, of course, blame them—that he still loves them a great deal even though he can't be there. In other words, it could help R. J. to know you love him and that none of this is his fault.

Studies have found that the best treatment for all these symptoms is encouraging children to discuss their feelings, to talk about them often and at length. All their questions should be answered as honestly as possible by an understanding and caring adult, and one of those understanding and caring adults certainly could be *you*. Once you and I find a way for you to communicate with R. J., and if we can arrange for his visiting you, you should already have worked out a way to talk about your incarceration with him. I know it will be hard because you're still working out your own feelings about it, but there is a way to rap honestly and simply to R. J. about such stuff.

2.   **Would it really be good for R. J. to see me locked up?**

Definitely. Even though I do notice how negatively you put the question: Would it "really" be good for him to see you "locked up"?

Let me put it this way: It would be good for him to *see* you—period. Wherever you are, in or out of jail. It will strengthen your parent/child bond, which R. J. needs to mature successfully. Being able to touch each other strengthens that bond, too, and that, of course, can only happen if he comes to you. His being able to see you regularly, to look forward to it, would be best of all.

According to the article I read, regular visitations "normalize" a parent/child relationship. R. J. will learn to accept the fact of where you are and associate that place with the excitement and pleasure of seeing you, not with negative feelings of your being "locked up." Regular visits can also establish your rights as a parent and ensure your ongoing connection to your family, so that when you get out, you can go right back to being an everyday father. In fact, what you say and do right now regarding your son can be critical when it comes time for a parole hearing. And if there has to be a custody fight with either Yvette or children's services after you get out, it could strengthen your position. Successful visitations with your child can be used as evidence of your sense of responsibility for him.

I'm glad you gave me this assignment, because I learned a fact I had never considered about child visitation. It's not only R. J. who would benefit from regular visits to you. According to studies, bonding with their children has been proven to lower the rate of recidivism for people who are incarcerated. That's a dope idea, isn't it? R. J. can help keep you from going back to prison.

3. **If R. J. ever does come for a visit, how can I make him feel comfortable?**

Another great question from you. It hadn't even occurred to me that a man who's been separated from his child for more than a year might feel at a loss as to how to relate to him when he finally does see him. Especially a kid R. J.'s age who was not much more than just a toddler the last time you saw him and who may not even recognize you now.

I checked out the same pamphlet I used to research these other questions.[2] What's funny is that it contains a list of activities for children up to three years old, then it suddenly jumps to those who are seven to ten years old. Your kid's almost eight so I picked the activities from the older age group. You'd better prepare first and find out if your facility has any resources for child visitation, such as crayons, children's books, puzzles, and stuff like that. But here's what you can do:

- Draw pictures for R. J. to color in.
- Make up short stories using his name and yours as the main characters.

- Have him practice his numbers and the alphabet.
- Make up word puzzles.
- Play cards, dominoes, or Legos; read books; use material available at the prison.

4. **Even though my kid is still stuck in a bad neighborhood with shitty schools, is there anything I can do to make him grow up better than I did?**

To research this question, I figured I'd get close to a source for that kind of information. Instead of spending hours surfing the Internet, I looked up a lady I dated for a few months right after I graduated from college. Now she's the principal of a pretty tough inner-city Chicago school, so I figured she'd have some interesting answers. But I hadn't thought her answer would be this unexpected.

She told me about a new theory of education that claims it's not always high grades or the "wealth" of a school that makes a student succeed later in life. Thinking that there's an indelible equals sign between high grades on tests (and high IQs) and later success is called "the cognitive hypothesis." But some new research is suggesting that *character*, not test scores, is a lot more valuable than the grades someone gets. Not only that, but character can be taught, regardless of the IQ level. But how?

She told me I could read about the research that explains how in a new book, which I bought the day after I talked to her. It's called *How Children Succeed*, by Paul Tough. Tough's theory suggests that character is built upon the rhythms of *failing* and then *persevering*. The essential quality that allows a kid to persevere is his ability to put off instant gratification. As evidence of this, Tough describes Walter Mischel's "marshmallow experiment" of the late sixties, which discovered that those kids who could resist eating a single marshmallow immediately in return for the promise of two marshmallows later did better in school and in the adult world because they could build toward long-term goals. This also speaks to the value of exhibiting discipline and self-control, the same thing you and I have been talking about.

Based on these *noncognitive* theories of learning and coping, a group of schools is focusing not so much on preparing students for high grades but on finding ways to develop character. One of those schools, called Infinity, in West Harlem, is a middle school that teaches mostly low-income kids. Another, called Riverdale, is one of the most exclusive private schools in New York. Both schools give report cards that don't evaluate kids' progress at the three R's. Instead, their report cards evaluate *character strengths*. Kids get marks in seven of these traits: grit, self-control, zest, optimism, social intelligence, gratitude, and curiosity.

At these schools, kids learn persistence, self-confidence, and resilience. Failing and then being encouraged to pick yourself up and go to the next challenge with the lessons learned from that failure are the life experiences that promise high achievement. Consequently, kids from *both* schools and backgrounds who are taught to face challenges optimistically, learn from failure, put off instant gratification for a better long-term reward, and keep alive their curiosity are on a true success track. And those habits aren't useful just for kids. You and I need to be mindful of adopting these, as well.

So, it isn't necessarily money or privileges that will give R. J. certain success. High character, work ethic, perseverance, and innovation/problem-solving skills are all much more determinative. Bill Gates, the founder of Microsoft and the second-wealthiest man in the world, dropped out of college. Granted, he got into Harvard, but he decided not to stay. I truly believe in the transformative power of education, but it's not about *where* you get educated, it's about *what* is put in your head. So if R. J. can be made to see that failure is merely a challenge (or even better, an opportunity) rather than a condemnation, that optimism can take him where he wants to go, and that long-term goals are more valuable than quick pleasures, he'll have a great chance for success.

The good news is that *you* can help instill in R. J. many of those lessons *right from where you are in jail*. You can take an interest in his

> **Tough describes Walter Mischel's "marshmallow experiment" of the late sixties, which discovered that those kids who could resist eating a single marshmallow immediately in return for the promise of two marshmallows later did better in school and in the adult world because they could build toward long-term goals.**

school projects in person or by letter, you can challenge him to explain what he has learned from his failures, you can give him long-term professional goals and the optimism to believe in them, and you can encourage him to feel grateful for those things he does have in his life, including your love for him and your interest in him. And, another way he will learn the strength of character to fail, persevere, and

> **Bottom line: Kids emulate their parents for better or worse, and from now on your life is for the better!**

succeed is by watching how you navigate your life. Bottom line: Kids emulate their parents for better or worse, and from now on your life is for the better!

Okay, teach, I think I've completed my assignment. I don't know how helpful this is for you, but I gave it my best shot. And I want to tell you that I really appreciate how our relationship has evolved. To be honest, it's gone from my wanting to help you because I felt sorry for you to my completely respecting you as a man. I consider this a real friendship that is a two-way street.

Peace,

Hill

```
HIGH
CHARACTER
```

LETTER 13

Smart Enough

I know that I am intelligent, because I know that I know nothing.

—Socrates

Are you using your brain today or is it using you?

—Dr. Rudy Tanzi

Hey, man,

I'm at the New York Aquarium in Coney Island, about to discover my next dead body. Ha. I mean my character on *CSI: NY,* Dr. Sheldon Hawkes, is. Per the script, somebody dumped the body in the shark tank, and it's up to Hawkes to figure out whether the COD (cause of death) is shark bites or some other method of murder that came before. I'm just glad those clouds of blood in the tank are really Food Red 17 dye and that the shark's a mechanical one, thank you very much. While they get all the mechanics going, and before they dunk me in that tank, I thought I'd drop you a line.

Dr. Sheldon Hawkes is an imaginary guy, but after playing the same character for several seasons in a row, I began to really identify with him. In 2011, during the eighth season of *CSI,* I did an interview about the quick mind he's been endowed with by our scriptwriters and about the fact that other characters rely on his intelligence. I said I was glad I could counter the usual stereotypes about African-American males by portraying a Black man with intelligence and savvy.

I guess you can tell already that I'm leading up to that long phone conversation we had last night. Kept me up to eleven P.M., and I had to pop out of bed at four this morning to get to Coney Island to shoot this scene. Thanks a lot, Brotha! (You do know I'm joking, don't you? Being able to talk with you on the phone is more than worth a sleepless night or two.)

Anyway, I suppose it was that last letter where I talked about new research in learning and failure that started you thinking about intelligence and the fact that you'd always thought you *weren't* smart enough to succeed. I happen to disagree with that evaluation because I think it's just a case of those negative voices some of us have had fed into us since birth. Remember, I mentioned those voices quite a few letters ago. But at that moment I couldn't think how to answer when you said something like, "Yeah, Hill, you tell me all the shit I can do and all the things I can accomplish and that my destiny is in my control . . . yeah, yeah. . . . But, Hill, I just don't trust my brain or my instincts, I don't trust my thoughts." Essentially, you said that you've already learned a lot of fucked-up things in jail just to get through the experience and that it has impacted your ability to think about things in a clear and smart way.

Wow, that threw me! First of all, it's so astute of you to realize the mental dangers of a bad environment in the first place—and the fact that such an environment can mess with our ability to reason. We heard all about that during the Korean War, when they talked about brainwashing, and here you are saying almost the same about prison. You never cease to amaze me, man!

But after we hung up, I began thinking that if prison can rework your brain like you say it does—actually screw with your intelligence, intuition, and reasoning skills—then why can't the opposite be true? The question is, how can you create the brain you want?

I kept thinking about how to answer the question: How can you become the master of your own brain? Then I remembered a lecture I saw a year ago by this Harvard neuroscientist, Dr. Rudy Tanzi, and what he said about some of us letting one brain area dominate our lives. I guess it's the primitive, survivalist parts of the brain that take the foreground in prison. But does it really have to be that way? The thing to remember—and I think you and I already came to

You *always* have a choice. Always.

this conclusion—is that you *always* have a choice. Always.

As I dragged myself out of bed the next morning at four, I suddenly remembered that Tanzi had sent me his new book, *Super Brain: Unleashing the Explosive Power of Your Mind to Maximize Health, Happiness, and Spiritual Well-Being*, a work he cowrote with one of my friends and mentors, somebody I've already mentioned to you—Deepak Chopra.[1] I'd stuck it on the shelf and then forgotten about it as one responsibility overlapped another and the days followed days. But this time, I took down the book and slipped it into my messenger bag before jumping in the car the studio had sent to take me out to Coney Island. During that entire drive, I sat in the back with my mini book light, devouring the book, and it was fascinating.

Tanzi has been called the "rock star of science" because of his many accomplishments. He recorded the organ tracks for Aerosmith's album *Music from Another Dimension!* and adapted *Super Brain* into a PBS special. Both works hit the charts and were bestsellers. Tanzi views the human brain as a musical instrument that you can learn how to play, eliminating destructive emotions (the bad notes) that are holding you back, opening thinking up to new experiences, and increasing your concentration.

Both Tanzi and Chopra call the brain that most of us use to navigate daily life our "baseline brain," and they believe you can learn to move way beyond it toward states of mental freedom and euphoria that might even reduce the mental effects of aging. Their book is full of research proving that the brain can heal and reshape itself. In fact, its cells are changing and growing just like the rest of the cells in our bodies.

Chopra and Tanzi are convinced that anybody can maximize the power of his brain by reshaping it and transform himself from someone with a mere baseline brain to someone with a "super brain." The "baseline brain" is one that we use passively, surrendering to the feelings and thoughts it creates without trying to control them. People with "super brains" are *active* observers of their own feelings and thoughts. They are controlling their brains, not the other way around. Since everything the brain experiences is either positive or negative, anyone can shape his brain into a super brain by maximizing positive mental experiences. You achieve this by what the authors call "outerwork" and "innerwork."

Outerwork has to do with the kinds of outer experiences you subject your brain to: diet, exercise, stress management, sleep, and intellectual stimulation. *Innerwork* consists of a balance of all the kinds of thinking that the brain is good at, thereby developing a brain that is flexible and creative and adaptable to different experiences. All of this may sound a little crazy to you, but it's all in line with what we've been talking about in our previous letters: figuring out ways to break old destructive habits; taking full control and creatively designing a new plan for our lives; being healthy and disciplined.

And check this out: As I was paging through *Super Brain,* I was drawn to some quizzes in it that are supposed to show whether you're relying simply on your baseline brain or also using it on a higher level. The Creativity Quiz is a true-or-false checklist with choices such as, "I don't ask myself to behave very differently today than I did yesterday;" "I am a creature of habit;" "I like familiarity. It's the most comfortable way to live." All those things are characteristics of a baseline brain. In contrast, the creative super brain would choose the following from the lists in the quiz: "I look upon every day as a new world;" "I pay attention not to fall into bad habits, and if one sets in, I can break it fairly easily."

In an interview, Chopra and Tanzi pointed out that we will die with essentially the same heart and liver and lungs we were born with, whereas our brains are changing throughout our lifetime. All you have to do is invent new things for it to do, and it will gradually reshape itself to apply itself to those challenges. It's just like doing curls or dumbbell bench presses. Over time, if they're exercised, our muscles (like our brain) will adapt, grow, and change. But we have to work them and challenge them.

The two authors subscribe to a slogan they call "ten thousand hours." What they mean by "ten thousand hours" is that applying yourself to any skill for that length of time will allow you to master it: painting, music, writing, mathematics—it doesn't matter what the skill is, who you are, or where you came from. They even go so far as to claim that "the same sense of balance that allowed you to toddle, walk, run, and ride a bicycle, given ten thousand hours (or less), can allow you to cross a tightrope strung between two skyscrapers."

I'll admit to you that I've been worried about aging, wondering how much it will slow me down and whether my memory will be affected. But there was something I read in *Super Brain* that eased my anxiety about that:

One of the unique things about the human brain is that it can do only what it thinks it can do. The minute you say, "My memory isn't what it used to be" or "I can't remember a thing today," you are actually training your brain to live up to your diminished expectations. Low expectations mean low results. The first rule of super brain is that your brain is always eavesdropping on your thoughts. As it listens, it learns. If you teach it about limitation, your brain will become limited. But what if you do the opposite? What if you teach your brain to be unlimited?[2]

Chopra and Tanzi want to overturn some basic assumptions we have about the brain: that its aging is inevitable and irreversible, and that its functions are limited by our particular genetics. They admit that the brain does lose millions of cells a day that can't be replaced, but the brain also contains stem cells that can bloom into new brain cells at any time of life. In their opinion, remaining young, intelligent, and open to experience is merely a matter of emphasizing our higher brain functions. Quite often, all of us are overcome by primitive reactions of fear, anger, or aggression, based on our lower brains, which developed thousands of generations ago, when such negative responses were needed for survival. They call our lower brain a "reptilian brain." Yeah, you got it, just like a reptile, a snake or a lizard. That's the level of brain function that most of us walking around the world are using. But now that we know that the brain isn't fixed, mechanical, or slowly wearing out as we age, there may very well be ways of overriding these reactions with more evolved mental processes that are needed to get ahead in today's modern world.

There are no real limits to the ways the human brain can be shaped by our wills.

So that's my answer to you about your fears that you're not "smart enough." If that's really the case, it's because you're *choosing* not to be smart enough, and such a choice doesn't make much sense, does it? I'm not claiming that you can become a super brain overnight. Or that you can break every habit easily. But you can and will break them to open up to this new life that you are already beginning to create for yourself. There are no real limits to the ways the human brain can be shaped by our wills. For you, me, everyone, it's a process that happens over time, maybe even long periods of time. And just by looking at the way that children learn—by failing and persisting, as I mentioned to you in my last letter—we know that the super brain is not something you can sit back and watch happen. The question of whether or not you've got the will, the discipline, and the grit to start making your own super brain is something that's entirely up to you.

Damn. It's fascinating, isn't it? Let's both of us create super brains!

Also, I thought you might want to play a little "mind game" with me that I thought of. I figured we could cook up a situation that you might design into some graphics someday. It's a little complicated, so pay attention. The name of the game is Getting Out. It works like this: The player is caught within the architecture of a prison, with different areas just like a real prison—cells, canteen, yard, exercise room, warden's and counselors' offices, classroom/library, showers, and toilets. For each location he ends up in, his goal is to make the decisions that get him out as soon as possible.

We can switch roles as the player and the controller of the game system, but why don't we start with me as the player and you as the system? You pick an area of the prison and list one event that could happen there. In reaction to that event, give me the choice of making three different decisions. Each of the three decisions will take me to a different location in the prison. In two cases, that location will be a disadvantage and slow my progress out of prison. In one case, the decision will take me to an advantageous location and speed up my progress out of prison. Gradually, the wrong decisions will make my sentence longer. The right decisions will shorten the "game" and reduce my sentence.

After a couple cycles of events and decisions, we'll switch and play the game with me as the system and you as the player for a couple of rounds.

Here's an example of one round:

Let's say you were to pick a counselor's office as a location. The event you have happening there for me, the player, is:

Event: **I dislike this counselor on sight, and she/he seems to feel the same way. I would really like to talk to the other counselor instead.**

Do I:

Decision 1:   Refuse to talk at all to the counselor until the session is over? (If I pick this decision, I get sent to the warden's office and written up as uncooperative.)

Decision 2:   Tell him/her right out what I think of him/her?
             (If I pick this decision, I'm accused of hostil-
             ity and lose my yard privileges for one week. I
             get sent back to my cell.)

Decision 3:   Politely ask if I could speak to the other counselor instead?
             (Right move! If I pick this decision, I get sent
             to the counselor I want.)

Once I'm in my new location, you can give me a new obstacle and a choice of three new decisions. Then we can switch roles and play a couple rounds with you as the player.

Oops, time to get dunked in that shark tank now. Hit me back on all this, all right!?

Much love,

Hill

P.S. I liked the idea of the transformative power of the brain. It made me reach out to Dr. Tanzi, Harvard professor and neuroscientist and coauthor with Deepak Chopra of the book *Super Brain*. And I told this "super brain" about you, and he asked me if he could write you a letter. Here it is.

Dear Brother,

After the PBS special on *Super Brain* aired, I received three letters from prisoners. All were in for life for homicides, and each person said that no matter how much he tried to overcome his past and the crime he committed and move on, there was a deep-seated guilt that wouldn't go away. Even if they were feeling good one day, they'd wake up the next day feeling like criminals again. *Super Brain* helped them realize that the negative impression was being produced by their brains. It was very comforting to know that the real person—the soul, the mind— is the *user* of the brain and can say, "You know what, brain? Your job is to make me feel bad about this to make sure I won't do it again. That's fine; you're doing your job, but you're starting to get on my nerves now. I want to move on. And let's get this straight: I use you; you don't use me. You're *my* brain! When I have these feelings, I will know that it's not me; it's just my brain doing its job, but I'm the one in control."

It was very empowering for these men to think that way and by-pass some of the negative images of themselves, which create negative feedback loops and limited belief systems and challenge their spiritual recovery. They loved the concept that you are not your brain; you are the user of your brain. "My brain made me do what I did, but I'm not going to let it do it to me again." Those actions were probably caused by a genetic predisposition and a negative feedback loop based on fear, anger, and rage that came out of the reptilian brain, with no control from the rational frontal cortex.

Seeing yourself as more than your brain—whether it's "My brain made me do it" or "My brain is making me feel bad about it now"— shows that this is not who you are. The real you is a person who's aware and mindful of the feelings and thoughts that your brain brings to you, and you can rise above them. You can learn from them, but most importantly, you can detach from them and still move on in terms of spiritual recovery and a positive identity.

Are we really just the sum of our past actions, and the feelings and thoughts that are driven by them? The neural networks in your brain emerge in a recursive way. (A recursive system is a self-organizing system.) Every time you learn something new or think about something new, you are producing new synapses and new connections in your brain. You are physically modifying your neural circuitry. But here's the crux: Every new layer of neural circuitry—every new set of synapses that you make as you learn things and also recollect, meditate, and contemplate—all of this creates new neural circuitry. Every layer that is produced by the prior layer must in turn monitor and regulate the previous layer. There are always built-in feedback loops. So everything new that you learn and do, as it is represented in your neural circuitry, will regulate the original neural circuitry that gave rise to it.

So, remember that all learning is by association. What does that mean for you? It means that as you sit in your cell and contemplate what you did, who you are, and what you wish to be, why you feel bad and how to feel good, you are making new neural circuitry. The good news is, that new neural circuitry must regulate the original neural circuitry, including the historical circuitry that led to your actions, for which you are now serving a sentence. Through contemplation, mindfulness, and meditation, as well as recapitulation or repetition, you can dynamically change your neural circuitry at every level: its neurochemistry, the connections between the neurons, the synapses and their strength, even genetically, simply through contemplation. Therefore, physical change in the brain is possible purely by contemplation.

So what do you want to create as you contemplate what's going on in your life? Because what you create is going to control what you've already done. And that means there is room for correction and improvement at the physical level. However, if you're letting your brain just do what it wants and you're simply being reactive—if you're thinking out of limiting belief systems, guilt, and negativity—that's fine for a while. It's fine to have a certain level of guilt initially, knowing you did something wrong and that you have learned your lesson. But then you have to move on, detach, and reshape. "I know I did wrong, but now I'm going to build my new neural circuits in a positive way."

And that's not just mental; it's physical, too. With repetition, the brain will yield and change. Every single day, with self-awareness of who you are, you are actually changing your neurochemistry and changing your brain physically. And that is a gift. You can do it proactively, saying, "I'm in charge here; I'm the user of my brain; I'm its inventor, its leader, its creator; I'm its shaper." Or you can let your brain do whatever it wants and fall into negative feedback loops, depression, agitation, fear, anger, and resentment. You have to realize that it's your choice, and you have to step up and say, "I'm taking over." When my brain makes me feel angry, I'm not going to be numb to it, but I'm going to say, "I know I'm angry right now. I'm going to observe when I'm angry; I'm going to observe when I'm upset or down about what I've done. I'm going to learn from it, but then, I'm going to detach and move on."

Neuroscience says that when you do this, you re-create your brain and your neural circuitry. This is the way to apply the "super brain" concept to mental and spiritual recovery when you are an incarcerated person.

Yours,
Dr. Rudolph E. Tanzi

```
I HAVE A
SUPER BRAIN
```

LETTER 14

You Can't Keep a Good Mind Down

The philosopher Lao Tzu once said, "When you let go of what you are, you become what you might be." I now know that it wasn't until I let go of who I thought I was that I was able to create a completely new life. It wasn't until I let go of the life I thought I should have that I was able to embrace the life that was waiting for me. I now know that my real strength never came from my body, and although my physical capabilities have changed dramatically, who I am is unchanged. The pilot light inside of me was still a light, just as it is in each and every one of us.

—Janine Shepherd, former Olympic skier who was paralyzed in a road accident and later got a license as a commercial pilot[1]

Dear Brotha,

So it's really gonna happen? And you got no earlier warning from your public defender that you'll go before the judge ten days from now for sentencing? He told you to plead guilty in exchange for a reduced sentence, and in ten days you'll find out how "reduced" it will be. Now you want to know if I think you made the right decision.

Well, according to the information you sent me, I don't see how you had much of a choice other than to take the plea. If I understood what you were saying in your letter, that so-called friend of your brother whose drugs you were caught holding when your car was stopped isn't willing to put his ass on the line to take the heat off you. And you have absolutely no additional evidence that would turn things around. The lawyer was right, I guess. If you had gone to trial, you stood the chance of a much stiffer sentence, and I know the court-assigned lawyers you have to defend you aren't exactly attentive. Those are the facts, man. So, given what's already happened, the question is, how can we get the best results in all ways moving forward?

There is one thing I can do, and I'd be glad to. I can show up in court when you're sentenced and testify to your character, recommending leniency. It wouldn't be a strain for me at all. We've been writing each other for over eight months and rapping on the phone for the last two, so I'm comfortable telling the judge that I have an informed take on your character and that your potential to be a great asset to society is very high. In our phone conversations over the last two months, I feel like I've gotten to know you on a whole different level. Just say the word, and I'll be there.

By the way, that was an incredible book you asked me to get you before you go to court. I bought it for you but stayed up most of last night reading it. I'm going to send it by overnight mail today. I'm talking about *The Diving Bell and the Butterfly* by that amazing French guy Jean-Dominique Bauby, who actually wrote the book after he became paralyzed.[2] Where the hell did you hear about it? You seem to be getting into a habit: Whenever I come out with an idea you like, you take it and run with it, miles farther than I ever thought possible. So here I am turning you on to Tanzi, telling you it's possible to become the master of your own brain—turn it into a super brain—and use it to determine your own future. The next day, you're reading the paper, probably with those thoughts swimming in your head, and you notice a review of the movie *The Diving Bell and the Butterfly*. What do you know? It's about a guy who achieved a nearly *unlimited* state of mental freedom under the toughest conditions imaginable! I dig the fact that you want to read that book before you go before the judge. I can't think of a better preparation for facing the situation.

I'd never heard of locked-in syndrome until you told me about that book. Apparently, it's pretty rare. Bauby was only forty-three when he had the massive stroke that shoved him into a twenty-day coma. He woke up, and he was completely paralyzed. Couldn't even move a little toe or his finger. Could only blink his left eyelid. Meanwhile, his mind was still totally intact, alert. Where was he? What happened? Imagine the panic when you wake up to that! The fear! It reminded me of what you told me about the way some guys react to the claustrophobia of a cell, especially if they get thrown in it when they're passed-out drunk and don't discover where they are until they come to. But Bauby's cell was much smaller, much more cramped. It was his own body. He compares it to being trapped inside a diving bell, or like a hermit crab dug into a rock.

I won't give too much away until you've read the book. I just want to say that the most amazing part is when he experiences the other side of the locked-in equation: *total mental freedom*. You see, his mind isn't locked in. It's as free as his body is paralyzed, and aware of everything. He can see and hear, and as he's lying there on the hospital bed unable to move or speak, his thoughts suddenly begin defying space and time. Suddenly he's zooming out for Tierra del Fuego or time-traveling to King Midas's mythical court. He's imagining the kind of elaborate meals the French are famous for and actually *tasting* them. That's the "butterfly" in the title: his mind and soaring imagination.

You'd think that would be enough. But it isn't. With the help of a speech therapist who reorders the alphabet in order of the frequency with which each of its letters is used, he learns to write! I mean, the therapist recites the alphabet over and over again. Each time she comes to the letter he wants, he blinks his left eyelid. Slowly but surely, he spells out words, then sentences, and then a whole book. Through his words, he's able to invite readers inside his diving bell and make them experience almost firsthand what locked-in syndrome is like. And

i know you read a lot of books so i gota question for you.

How many of these books do you think i need to read to turn things around? Do i need to read he can also take them on his "butterfly" journeys, amazing voyages that prove there are no limits to the human mind. He can inspire them not to give up hope, no matter how hopeless a situation seems at first.

I'd better shut up. I don't want to tell you about every page of the book. So I'll just tell you that I'm never going to throw away the letter you sent me asking for that book, because of what you said in it in your letter.

NO
LIMITATIONS

LETTER 15

Should I Join a Gang?

Like many others I became a slave to a delusional dream of capitalism's false hope: a slave to dys-education; a slave to nihilism; a slave to drugs; a slave to black-on-black violence; and a slave to self-hate. Paralyzed within a social vacuum, I gravitated toward thughood, not out of aspiration but out of desperation to survive the monstrous inequities that show no mercy to young or old. Aggression, I was to learn, served as a poor man's merit for manhood. To die as a street martyr was seen as a noble thing.

—Stanley Tookie Williams, in *Blue Rage, Black Redemption*[1]

The man who makes everything that leads to happiness depend upon himself and not upon other men, has adopted the very best plans for living.

—Plato

D ear Brotha,
        I finally got your letter. Since I'd left New York, it was forwarded to my office in L.A. My assistant sent it here by overnight mail when she saw you'd written "URGENT" on the envelope. Glad she did.

I'm in Toronto now—two weeks working on a new movie. Even though its plot takes place in New York, they're shooting most of it up here. It's a much cheaper way to make the film, and they can find easy ways to make this city look like parts of Manhattan. That's why you couldn't get ahold of me. And I know you tried six times. Every time I called voice mail for my New York number, I could hear that nasal-voiced robot say, "You-have-a-collect-call-from-a-correctional-facility-will-you-accept-the-charges-say-yes-or-no?" I'm sorry I wasn't there. I knew you'd be flipping out after the sentencing. And I'm sorry my showing up in court as a character witness didn't help all that much. I tried from up here to get info about which joint they sent you to, but everybody I spoke to said, "Sorry, but I'm not allowed to reveal that information." Of course, there's no way to receive a collect call on this foreign cell phone I have here in Toronto, so we stayed out of contact. At least I know where you are now.

I agree. Five to ten years is a *shock*. Neither of us saw a sentence that long coming down the pike. I definitely thought it would be something like three to five. Nor did I have any idea about their legal right to ship you to a maximum-security joint for a few months while they wait for a bed in another facility. I called my lawyer for you, and he said they can get away with it.

I know you must be bumming, but look at it this way if you can: At least you're not on lockdown for eighteen hours a day, like in a lot of maximums. I'm glad you get to go out into the yard for "rec," even if it's only three hours. And I understand: That doesn't make six counts a day standing at attention in front of your cell any less of a drag, does it? I can understand your feeling of having something at your heels all the time, ready to bite. You know a bell's about to ring and you'll have to hightail it yet again to the count and run to stand at attention in front of your cell a minute later, or you'll face disciplinary action. But I really don't see the logic behind doing one of those counts in the middle of the night, a guard coming by and shining a flashlight on everybody's face to verify that he's in his cell. But hopefully, you'll get used to it eventually and it won't wake you up any longer. But since it's all new, it makes sense that you can't sleep or concentrate on anything.

I know you're upset, but would it help you to know that I think you handled your arrival at that facility better than I ever could? I'm so proud of you. Going through the indignity of being marched directly to that inspection center they call the "fish tank" as soon as you get out of that long bus ride, being stripped and disinfected and having every cavity of your body inspected to the catcalls of other prisoners—shit, that must have been one hell of an ordeal.

I had no idea that they take every single one of your possessions away and box them up when you arrive. I thought they'd let you keep your CDs and your

Game Boy. What kind of rule is it that only allows you to hold on to one book out of all the stuff you accumulated? And that is only after legal appeals to expand federal laws that allow for only one religious book. I've even heard some inmates say they think the only reason prisons allow Bibles and Korans is because they make inmates soft.

ADVICE FROM AN OLD-TIMER

I know it's hard to focus on the good stuff right now, but I think you should feel good that they put you in with this Sammy, the old-timer who's now your cellie. From the little I know about all this, some of the advice he gives you seems cool—good survival tips I wouldn't ever have thought of. One thing he did say, though, just doesn't compute for me. Call it intuition, but I just know it's wrong.

No way I can disagree with Sammy when he advises you not to put your full trust in anybody, whether he's a fellow con or a "hack" (that *is* what they call prison guards these days, right?). As much as I believe in the power of community, I'm not so naive that I don't know the rules are different on the inside than they are out here. But I don't think Sammy meant you should isolate yourself *completely*, that you shouldn't form any alliances with some of the better members of the prison population. There must be other guys there temporarily like you, despite the high percentage of violent offenders in those maximum-security joints. I think Sammy only means you should be suspicious about any exaggerated kindnesses or extensions of friendship and ask yourself what the person's motive could be.

I also agree with Sammy about not telling anything to anybody that you don't have to, including why you're doing time. Some of the more corrupt ones could possibly use that information to fuck with your rep, or hit up your family and friends and try to scam money out of them.

When I knew you were getting shipped out of jail to a real state prison, I called Petey, a neighborhood friend from my teenage years who racked up some mistakes shortly after and has done time. (He was involved in some kind of chop-shop operation; I didn't really ask about the details.) He still lives in Iowa. We rarely see each other, but because he used to be my homie, I try to keep in touch. Petey got out of Anamosa State Pen two years ago, and he told me it's also a good idea not to address letters to friends and family (me included) in front of anybody, for the same reason. Keep other cons out of your business.

He also told me you got to keep from giving other cons any "buttons to push." Once you reveal an emotional weakness—a bad temper, fear of violence, an easily bruised ego when it comes to a certain subject—the worst people there could use it against you. I don't mean that you should walk around like a robot, just that, in general, these aren't people you can show any fragility to. But that also means that false fronts—like walking around like some badass hip-hop star—can be risky, too. I think the best idea is to keep any swagger you've learned on the streets to a minimum. And above all, don't take things as personally as you might be apt to take them out here. So often it's just that lousy prison system talking, not the individual. Just keep your balance and stay cool.

Sammy's right-on about warning you against arguing about controversial subjects—like religion or race or politics or sexual orientation. I know it must be like a pressure cooker in there. What seems like an innocent conversation to me out here might suddenly explode into something dangerous for you. We can keep those kinds of discussions between you and me. I'm always interested in your take on such stuff. But in general, just don't be "nosy." And, of course—like Sammy stressed—never, ever snitch on anybody or complain to the hacks about somebody's mistreatment of you—unless you want to be put in protective custody for the whole term of your stay at that joint, which I hope doesn't have to happen to you.

I'm sure you know all this after those nine months you spent in jail before being transferred upstate; just making sure you understand why it's necessary because I really care about you.

I was a little taken aback that Sammy told you never to speak to any guard on your own, even when it's just a "Some weather we're havin', huh, dude?" Apparently, even that could be mistaken for snitching by some paranoid con. It's something I'd never thought of. And I'm grateful to him for telling you not to gamble and to stay out of debt to other prisoners, whether it's for card games, tobacco, books, whatever. Don't use "prison credit," or "juggling," as my friend Fabian Ruiz calls it, to get something in advance. Wait until you can buy it yourself. That's one thing that's the same as it is on the outside. But on the inside, according to my pal Petey, the repercussions of not paying your debts are often a lot worse and can even result in being knocked off.

Petey also told me that while he was locked up, guards would sometimes order him to do something that was just plain a waste of time or illogical. Unfortunately, if you don't want to dirty your behavior record, the only choice is to obey. It sucks, I know. But keep your eye on the prize—your release.

The rest of the stuff Sammy told you is all new to me, too. About not talking about another prisoner unless he's present. And not whining about being locked up in the presence of a lifer. And not asking anybody what he's in for or for how long. But do you mind if I add something? Take care of your teeth; I've heard most prison dentists are horrible. And don't go in for prison tattoos (or shooting dope, obviously) because hepatitis and even AIDS can be transmitted through those needles.

THE BAD NEWS OF GANGS

Like I've said, there's only one piece of Sammy's advice I absolutely *cannot buy*. You don't have to tell me that American prison populations tend to divide themselves into ethnic allegiances. I think such separations are stupid and only make the population weaker and more exploitable by the prison industrial complex. But that's easy to say when you're not behind bars.

Because of the way prison culture has developed, I suppose it could be close to suicidal to make those of your ethnicity feel that you're dissing them in favor of a race or culture you're not considered to be part of. My friend says they call it "crossing gangs," when, say, a white guy makes friendly with a Black gang right after he arrives. You know the impression such crossovers create. Even Hollywood's gotten a lot of mileage out of comedies about suburban white boys trying to live the fantasy of being down by law and getting tricked out in baggies, bandannas, and such, and going around flashing hand signs at their "homies"—until they meet up with the real thing. The opposite formula would seem just as absurd—some Black dude trying to tell the Aryan brothers he basically gets their point. Maybe these are jokes in the movies, but Petey stressed being very mindful of not being insulting to your own ethnicity while behind bars. What's more, having a "family" in the social sense, made up of people who share your outlook and interests or who even might come from your hometown, probably does bring an important sense of security.

Fine! I get that. But showing ethnic allegiance by joining a gang is a whole other bag of bullshit. I don't care whether we're talking about the Bloods, Crips, Latin Kings, Black Guerilla Family, MS-13, Mexican Mafia, or some white-supremacist operation. In some cases, even religions are acting like gangs. And as crazy as it sounds, it's sad to say that non-gang-members are termed "neutrals" and are a gang of sorts. I'm fully aware why all of these and many others came to exist, but all of 'em are dangerous hypermasculine distortions of some of the best elements of brotherhood: courage and loyalty.

Whether locked up or free, inflicting harm on—or wasting—a rival to show the depth of your loyalty to your gang looks like a disgusting and pitiful perversion of friendship to me, a vicious mockery of the ties that bind real brothers. So don't ever let anyone convince you that a gang can serve the purpose of a family—regardless of how much you may have wanted that sense of belonging when you were growing up.

My friend Petey says you see that kind of thing happening again and again in the joint: You get pressured to get jumped into a gang and you give in; then you get a dangerous order from your gang leader that makes no sense to you. Now you have to maim or kill somebody you have nothing against but who's supposedly insulted someone else in your so-called "gang family," often in the most superficial way. This order violates your sense of humanity, but if you're in the gang, you've got to do it without asking questions. That's a situation you *don't* want. Petey even said that he's seen non-gang-members in prison get more respect from gang leaders than the lower-level gang members. It is about the way you carry yourself and about being a man.

Probably the worst result of all this is that you end up with a "shot"—an infraction—on your official file. It'll show up at the parole hearing, and your term might end up closer to ten years than five. So ride with yourself, Brother. Ride with *your* last name. You are a man. You are a leader and you're your own man. Good behavior, following the rules of the institution, is the only thing that will get you out as fast as possible, or ensure a transfer to a low-security prison, or maybe even work release way before you've served the minimum five years.

THE LONG ARM OF PRISON GANGS

I did some research about gangs on the FBI website, using a document they publish yearly called "The National Gang Threat Assessment."[2] According to them, there are about 230,000 gang members in federal and state prisons in this country. These members may be incarcerated, but they've managed to extend the sphere of their activities far outside prison walls. When there's a dispute between members of rival gangs that you're asked to take a position on, don't think you're merely defending control of prison territory. More often than not it has something to do with control of drug markets on the outside.

The families of some of the higher-ups in this group may even be involved on the outside. They visit for the purpose of carrying messages or smuggling contraband—drugs and shit like that—and it's not that uncommon for a hit that occurs on the outside to be the result of an order given to a nonincarcerated friend or relative during one of these prison visits. Sometimes, an influential gang leader doesn't even need to rely on visits. He orders his hits directly using a cell phone smuggled into prison for him by a family member.

Why am I telling you all of this? As an example of how far the tentacles of gang power can reach. You may think you're into a gang for survival purposes while you're locked up but have no intention of living that way after your release. If you join one now, you may *have* to stay in it after you get out, and shortly before you get out, you may find you've been assigned the role of messenger or drug courier for your so-called Brothers. They might refuse to "jump you out" of the gang just because you're going home. Instead, you'll be forced to get more heavily involved with the culture.

I guess I should admit now that it's the one thing that makes me deeply suspicious of your cellie Sammie. On the one hand, he's cautioning you not to put your full trust in anybody. Then he turns around and—after knowing you for how long, four days?—starts trying to convince you to become part of his ethnic gang and to undergo an initiation into it by shanking somebody he feels dissed him at the canteen. Yes, I know you're afraid he'll turn against you if you decline and that could put you in danger since, so far, he represents all the support you have in that joint. But know this, Brother: The danger you're putting yourself in by refusing him is minuscule compared to the mess that can come from gang involvements. Beyond everything you've told me about this place and how it's freaking you out, it's this false offer of protection that's worrying me the most. You've got to find a way to bow out of it gracefully.

A SURVIVAL CHART

In the meantime, mind doing something for me? I'm as interested as you are in understanding how to survive prison while holding on to as much of your personal integrity as possible. So why don't you start a "survival chart" and then send it to me to add to? We can send it back and forth that way.

Take a sheet of paper and divide it down the middle by drawing a line. Label the column on the left "Survival." Label the column on the right "Unnecessary Compromises." In the left column, write down every rule you think you need to observe to keep alive and make your stay in that joint go as smoothly as possible. In the right column, list every rule you're being told to follow that you think is a useless, demeaning compromise, a bunch of bullshit based on featherbrained ideas about hypermasculinity. For example, in the left column, you might list "Keep my mouth shut in most situations," and in the right column, you might list "Talk shit about a guy to try to make another guy protect me against him."

SURVIVAL CHART

SURVIVAL	UNNECESSARY COMPROMISES

eanwhile, I'll keep reading about your world, and I'll take the challenge of adding more items to both columns. When either of us thinks the other person has put an item in the wrong column, he'll draw an arrow pointing it toward the opposite column. As it grows, we'll discuss these items when we can start talking on the phone again.

Listen, I got to run, but I'm going to write again tomorrow night about the same subject we've been discussing.

Until then, take care,

Hill

P.S. Below is a letter from my man Lupe Fiasco, a rapper, record producer, and entrepreneur who has something to say about gangs.

Dear Brother,

Everybody within six feet of me has been to prison, whether it is my assistant or my brother, or my cousin who is just now getting sentenced for drug charges. So I have a fully formed relationship with the Black incarcerated mind and the institutionalized mentality. There's no push to learn who the fuck you are and why the fuck you're doing what you're doing and how you can stop, but you *can* stop yourself from participating in it. That's also when society and community come into play. Because if a Brother comes home from prison and he has no place to sleep, that is a failure of the community, a failure of us.

> If a Brother comes home from prison and he has no place to sleep, that is a failure of the community, a failure of us.

From the beginning of time—from the hammer to the wheel to the iPod—humans have had a drive to get things, to have things we weren't born with. The biggest promoter of things we don't need, or things we want, is not music. It's the philosophy that governs the advertising, marketing, and branding industries, that gets people thinking, "I need this," and "Yeah, I need that." And on the surface we can say that a lot of people are in prison because they wanted things—money, or the things it can buy.

But I feel that the real reason so many Brothers are in prison is a lack of understanding of their history and their place in society as Black men. The Black man started as creator of the world, but now we're on the bottom rung of the ladder, especially in America. We've been barred from being fully immersed in the American culture. What is the cause of that? There has been a complete destruction of any type of educational consistency.

A Brother in Harlem who is running for a city council position recently said, "What Brothers need is less entertainment and more focus on real, solid things. Things that they can actually use." Because now entertainment has become commercial. Hip-hop can be used as inspiration, or it can be used to sell things. On the other hand, pure education is not commercial. The history, philosophy, and teachings of the world are not commercial; they are solid and concentrated. That's why your focus on education has to be 100 percent. You control how much information goes into your mind and how much of the past you allow yourself to be privy to. Even in prison you can get a thorough, consistent education, especially because you don't have the usual distractions.

You have to become as smart as Socrates, Sigmund Freud, Carl Jung, Immanuel Kant. You have to be smarter than the people who put into play these philosophies that run the world. As you can see, they were meant to keep you at the bottom of the ladder. But if you don't understand what those philosophies are, you'll never know how they affect you. You are the end product of it, which is "I'm in prison." And you'll probably come back to prison after you leave it if you don't fully understand how the world works. So educating yourself is the way to stay out of prison, once you are released.

I was writing a lyric yesterday about the fact that Chicago has always been a gang city, since the days of the robber barons. This is no-holds-barred because that's how I talk to niggas; I keep it straight, keep it free:

Why do you think all these gang chiefs are deified?
Maybe you realize that gangs were just the reaction after
　　Martin Luther King died.

I wrote those lyrics because a lot of young people in prison have a gang affiliation—but they don't even know the history of how gangs came to be. Some of these gangs originated as community protection when the KKK and white supremacy groups were burning everything down and targeting Blacks. These bands of Brothers would gang together to patrol and protect their community. And with some groups there was a criminal element, so they would take things too. And after that experience you felt a certain commonality because you didn't have shit. If you had kids and were on public assistance, you couldn't be in the house with your kids because that was part of the terms of public aid. And you had to have a job, which you couldn't get in 1965, because niggas couldn't get jobs 'cause they were real niggas.

But these young gang members today do not even know their gang history. If you're going to be a criminal, at least understand the history of your criminality and the reason why you're a criminal! You were supposed to be protecting the community after Martin Luther King was killed, and people got together to keep others from burning down their stores. Do you understand that, young gang member in prison? That is where your gang came from.

When that Brother comes home from prison and he has no place to go—not even a place on the kitchen floor—then the philosophy of "It takes a village" has become obsolete. It's a catchphrase, but we don't really live it anymore. The sad part is, the phrase comes all the way from Africa across the Middle Passage to today. We still say it, but if that village isn't willing to take on the responsibility, then it doesn't matter what the Brother learned in prison. If he doesn't have a world that accepts him and gives him a cushion against the forces working against him, then he's at a loss. So we need to work as a community to support that Brother when he gets released.

Yours,
Lupe Fiasco, Grammy-winning
hip-hop artist

I AM MY
OWN MAN

LETTER 16

What Makes a Man?

> The ultimate measure of a man is not where he stands in moments of comfort and convenience, but where he stands at times of challenge and controversy.
>
> —Martin Luther King Jr.

> Above all things let us never forget that mankind constitutes one great brotherhood; all born to encounter suffering and sorrow, and therefore bound to sympathize with each other.
>
> —Albert Pike

Hey, man,

You didn't tell me the joint you're in is part of the 20 percent of prisons that are privately run, for-profit places—and that it's owned by one of the biggest of those businesses, the Corrections Corporation of America. Maybe you just didn't know it yet. I found out about it by looking it up online.

I can't say that makes me jump for joy. In general, those private-prison corporations win when *you* lose. "Business" means getting the highest profit from the smallest outlay of cash. Their profit motive incentivizes them to provide the least amount of services to as many inhabitants as possible. So do me a favor and send me information about the place as you discover it. Stuff like how the food is, what kind of a medical clinic it has, showers, recreation facilities, what job they assign you and its hourly rate. Just anything you happen to notice. Know what I mean? I do have some friends in Washington, so who knows. . . . Oh, okay, I better not say another word. I know every letter or package you get is examined.

Maybe what bugs me most of all about prison gangs is their distortion of the meaning of manhood. I haven't mentioned it to you yet, but after doing that research on gangs online, I started thinking about a novel I finally read a few years ago after a couple of friends kept raving about it: *The Name of the Rose* by the Italian writer Umberto Eco.[1] There's a movie based on the book, starring Sean Connery, that just replayed on the TCM channel.

The book is kind of like an unconventional whodunit. In the year 1327, a series of mysterious deaths is taking place in a monastery. A visiting friar (the character played by Connery in the movie) is asked to investigate them, as it's clear that some are obviously the result of murder.

It wasn't so much the unraveling of the murder mystery that fascinated me as much as the key symbol of the novel: the *rose*. The phrase "the name of the rose" refers partly to the beauty and meaning of the past that has long disappeared, leaving behind only its *name*. One interpretation of what the book is saying is that most of us go through life bandying about empty terms that are all but drained of their significance. And it turns out at the end of *The Name of the Rose* that the murderer is trying to keep the other monks from finding out about a book that explains the lost meaning of another word. I'll stop there, to avoid a plot "spoiler," in case you want to read it someday.

You probably want to know how my remembering the plot of that book could have anything to do with what I was saying about gangs in my last letter. Well, check this out. Gang values have perverted the meanings of a lot of words: *loyalty, brotherhood, family*—but also the word *manhood*. They promote swagger, so-called brotherhood, and machismo. I'm sure you know what *machismo* means. The dictionary defines it as "strong or aggressive masculine pride," or hypermasculinity. Masculinity is a vital component to manhood. Hypermasculinity, however, is overcompensation for male insecurity. Most men are insecure. Why do you think we wear our hats so low they cover our eyes and our clothes so big they cover our lives? The unnecessary need to cuss and demonstrate a blatant disrespect for people falls under the category of hypermasculinity. We swear radically to express emotions we're too insecure to express logically, and we disrespect others to gain a sense of dominance and control. Ironically, this act of disrespect categorizes one as being out of control.

The philosopher Eric Hoffer says, "Rudeness is the weak man's imitation of strength." The whole flawed code of machismo is central to the male bonding that holds gangs together. But what if we went back to the origins of machismo just to find out whether the original intent has survived? Machismo finds its source in the attitudes of the Latino male. Scholars of Latin American history have been able to trace the concept back all the way to the late medieval period. Machismo was born from a concept known as *caballerismo,* a Spanish word referring to the late medieval culture of horsemanship. The term is derived from the word *caballero,* Spanish for "gentleman." *Caballerismo* referred to a gentleman of high station who valued honor, dignity, and wisdom above all else.

The kind of machismo promoted by the street or the culture of gangs is actually an expression of being "down"—enslaved—by a greater power.

The original roots of machismo had very little to do with the arrogant bravado of gangstas and hip-hop we see today. Some scholars think that it was the importing of *caballerismo* into South America during the colonial period that tainted it with suggestions of violence, recklessness, and contempt for and control of women. These negative connotations crept in when the original people of South America were being put under the domination of the Spanish. But if machismo functioned according to the true meanings of its roots, it would be symbolic of responsibility, emotional openness, and a respect for family.

Gangs exploit all the *negative* connotations of machismo and masculinity, draining the word *machismo* of all its valuable historical worth. The kind of machismo promoted by the street or the culture of gangs is actually an expression of being "down"—enslaved—by a greater power. It's a reaction to the ghetto oppression of minorities. Just as South American machismo was a combination of the old values of *caballerismo* and anger at the Spanish colonial masters who had brought it to that continent along with their exploitation and oppression, today's machismo is a so-called manliness based on rage at "the Man," centuries of prejudice that have driven entire ethnicities into ghettos and poverty. When a member of a minority—and that includes anyone who's incarcerated—behaves toward a member of his community with negative machismo, he's merely replaying the oppressive behavior that he has suffered all his life.

If you look at urban communities, in many ways, gangs are causing an urban holocaust. Last year twice as many young men were annihilated in the name of gangs and drugs on the streets of Chicago as were killed during the same time in the Iraq War. Kanye West highlighted this sad reality on the *Watch the Throne* album, pointing out that 314 soldiers died in Iraq and 509 young Black men died in Chicago. Where is the true war then? And who is really responsible for Brotha killing Brotha?

Be the man you want your son to be and the gentleman you'd want your daughter to date. My hope for you is that you'll be able to discover the true meaning of manhood, which involves a lot more than testosterone or offing somebody on a switch because the prison drug lord who happens to share your ethnicity has commanded you to. In fact, that's the second thing about gangs that turns my stomach: The violence they promote is just an example of social conformity. The "sheeple" (a little term I like to use that combines *sheep* with *people* to denote mindless followers) who followed the dictates of Adolf Hitler in the name of patriotism and German pride were exhibiting a contemptible form of conformity with disastrously negative consequences. In fact, Hitler reportedly once said, "What luck for rulers, that men do not think."

JUST FOLLOWING ORDERS

What makes people into such dangerously unthinking followers? In 1963, a Yale University psychologist named Stanley Milgram tried to answer that question with an experiment.[2] The purpose of the experiment was to measure how willing a person was to obey an authority figure even if the figure ordered him to perform an act that was against his sense of right and wrong. The results of the experiment were so unexpected and so disturbing that it changed some of our basic assumptions about the human brain.

People who took part in the experiment were divided into teams of three. Two of these three were researchers who were acting. One pretended to be the "experimenter" and spoke with an authoritative voice. The second person was pretending to be the "learner," someone who had volunteered for a little money to take part in a scientific experiment on how people learn best. The only person who *didn't* know what was really going on was a real volunteer who'd responded to an ad offering to be paid for taking part in the experiment, and that person was assigned the role of "teacher."

The teacher and learner were put in separate rooms where they could communicate over speakers but couldn't see each other. Before going into his room, the learner had been instructed to casually mention that he had a heart condition. At the instructions of the experimenter, the teacher began by reading a list of word pairs to the learner. Then the teacher would go through the list again, mentioning only one of the words that formed a word pair. It was supposedly up to the learner to remember what word it had been paired with.

Each time the learner made a mistake, the teacher was told to administer a shock to him. The strength of the shock increased by fifteen volts for each wrong answer. The teacher was the only one of the three who did not know that there was no real shock being administered. The purpose of the real experiment had nothing to do with learning and punishment. It was to see how far the teacher would go in administering the shock just because the experimenter, an authority figure, insisted that he do so.

Meanwhile, as the shocks grew in intensity, the teacher could hear what he thought was the learner screaming with more and more pain. Finally, the sound of the learner banging desperately on the wall could be heard; then, silence, as if the learner had died or passed out from the shocks. Whenever the unsuspecting teacher expressed a desire to stop the shocks and leave, the fake experimenter would forbid it with statements such as, "You have no other choice, you must go on."

In the first set of experiments, 65 percent of the volunteer teachers were willing to go all the way to the supposedly most powerful and painful shock, even after it seemed that the learner may have passed out or even died, merely because the experimenter—an authority figure who they thought was a genuine scientist—was telling them to. In discussing the study, Milgram suggested that these results might help explain what the millions of people who carried out unimaginably inhumane orders from Nazi commanders meant when they said they were "just following orders." What they meant is that what they did conflicted with their moral code, but the power of an authority figure giving them orders was strong enough to suppress that moral code.

It seems to me that a good number of cruel and violent acts performed by gang members in prison and on the street might, at least in part, be the result of their "following orders." The leader of a gang uses a host of strategies to establish himself as an authority figure. Those people who recognize him as such are more apt to follow even the most destructive of his orders unquestioningly.

Meanwhile, you didn't mention anything about gangs when we talked last night. I'm hoping it means you found some way to avoid getting jumped into your cellie's gang without turning him into your enemy. I'll be home early Sunday evening. Can we talk about this and other stuff on the phone? I won't rest easy until I know that you aren't going to find your sense of right and wrong tested the way those in the Milgram experiment were.

Speak soon.

Your friend,

Hill

```
┌─────────────────────────┐
│      I  MAKE  MY         │
│  OWN  DECISIONS          │
└─────────────────────────┘
```

LETTER 17

Lockdown

We can easily forgive a child for being afraid of the dark; the real tragedy of life is when men are afraid of the light.

—Paulo Coelho

Seems like every time you come up something happens to bring you back down.

—Tupac Shakur

Dear Brotha,

Now I know why I hadn't heard from you in two weeks—no letter, no collect call. I've been worried, and it seems I had good reason to be. But you're not going to fall for that superstition of bad things coming in groups of three, are you? Seems to me you've had your share of bad luck for the time being with the two things that have just happened.

I guess you didn't want to go into too much detail so as not to snitch on yourself, but whatever you saw, man, I guess it must have been fucked up. I hate to say it, but I think you did the right thing by keeping your mouth shut tight, even if it led to the entire prison being put on lockdown for two weeks. Snitching would have been way too dangerous. Meanwhile, finding out the very same day that your kid had been sent to the group home must have been the last straw. I'm so sorry about all of it.

You mean to tell me that during that entire two-week period, they shut down the canteen and made all of you do with nasty-ass cold food delivered to the cells three times a day? That situation, combined with the inability to go into the yard, must have been unbearable. Add to that those notes you were getting from the gang leader—balled-up pieces of paper passed from cell to cell threatening that you'd be rubbed out if you snitched—and it's no wonder you barely got any sleep. I'm so glad you were able to keep out of the gang your cellie Sammy kept pressuring you about or *you* might have been the one holding the shiv, and God knows how that person is going to end up.

The only response to falling is to pull yourself out of the mud.

My only advice to you is pretty obvious: For every setback, get back up on your feet again, and keep the larger goals we've been talking about in mind. The only response to falling is to pull yourself out of the mud. Everything that's been happening to you lately is all the more reason to stay focused, to put your hopes in that leap of faith we discussed. As for feeling helpless and anguished, that's no sign of weakness on your part. It's a realistic response to what you're being subjected to. This is an opportunity for you to become more alert, more conscious of how each decision you make can have consequences for years to come. I am so proud that you are not bowing to gang and peer pressure. You are strong. You have a plan. And you are building a new life. Stay the course.

After hearing your voice on the phone last night after two weeks of silence, man, I was relieved. You can't imagine what I was thinking. If you're deemed a high-risk offender then they'll usually place you in the SHU (Secure Housing Unit) in a medium-security until they find you a bed in a max. I tried to get you to focus on the better prison you'll obviously be moved to as soon as they find a bed. And once you're in a medium- or even minimum-security joint, there will hopefully be a lot more resources available to you. But oftentimes, max facilities have more resources available. It's a crapshoot that shouldn't be. But we'll deal with whatever and make it work. I'm not at all surprised that your current state of despair is making it impossible to put your mind on the future. You told me that those two weeks of lockdown went by so slowly, they seemed like "an eternity." To your dismay, you couldn't really see the light at the end of the tunnel. In fact, the way you feel now, you said, your release seems like it's "light-years away, an infinite distance from now."

THE THEORY OF RELATIVITY

Wow. After we hung up, I realized the words you used were actually a reference to the *elasticity of time*. Einstein proved that time was elastic—relative—by studying relationships between space, time, and the effects of gravity. After thousands of calculations and a lot of theorizing, he came to the conclusion that the flow of time at every location in the universe differs and also depends on how fast something is moving.

For example, if you're walking at a rate of two miles an hour through a moving train that is going sixty miles an hour, in your own experience you are still walking only two miles an hour. But to someone who is outside the train standing still and is watching it go by with you walking in it, you are walking at a rate of 62 miles an hour (2 + 60 = 62). Anyway, that's what classic Newtonian physics would say. But the problem is what happens to much, much faster moving objects, especially as they begin to approach the speed of light. Then the perception of movement becomes something a bit slower than a moving train plus a person walking inside it. The two figures add up to a bit less. This gets even more complicated when the moving object is so far above the earth that the pull of gravity is weaker. For example, some satellites are stationed approximately twelve thousand miles above the surface of Earth, where the pull of gravity is weaker, and that difference of gravity also affects the satellite's flow of time.

All of this may sound very theoretical to you, but today, even something as common as a GPS device has to take Einstein's theories into account in order to produce accurate readings. The GPS devices we use in our cars and on phones depend on signals from a couple dozen satellites orbiting about twelve thousand miles above Earth and several thousand miles apart from one another. Our GPS uses the signal from each satellite to determine its distance from each. With these figures, it can calculate its location on Earth to within a few yards.

However, since satellites high above are moving through a gravitational field that is a little weaker than the one we are moving through, and since the satellites are moving faster than us, satellite clocks are ticking at a slightly different rate than ours are. That difference is not much more than a billionth of a second. But not taking it into account can lead to a GPS reading that is off by several miles!

Basically, I've just given you an amateur's explanation of Einstein's theory of relativity. Based on this, scientists have determined that if a person or, say, a rocket ship could travel at the speed of light (186,282 miles per second), no time at all would pass for that person. Taking such an idea into account, what would happen if you could leave and return to Earth on a rocket ship traveling consistently at the speed of light for a duration of ten years' Earth time? When you returned, *no time* would have passed for you, but ten years would have passed on Earth. *You would have traveled into the future!*

That is the main point I'm attempting to make, and I admit that, in the context of your current worries, it may sound a little stupid and irrelevant right now. But if you can somehow move into a "mental dimension" in which you can imagine yourself traveling faster than things are moving in prison, it will seem to you as if only a small amount of time is going by, whereas a large amount of time will go by for the prison, and the time you have left in that prison will have passed before you know it. Your time and "prison time" don't have to be the same thing. It's all relative. Right now, you feel as if you're facing an eternity of incarceration. In another context, it may seem much shorter than that.

Don't get me wrong. I know it's unrealistic to think that a person can bend his sense of time when it suits him, despite the fact that our perception of duration is constantly changing. If you think about it, your awareness of the passage of time varies according to the situation. I'm sure you've had the experience of getting absorbed in something so much, or having such a good time, that when you look up at the clock, you're amazed at how much time has actually passed. It's something that happens to us all the time, but few of us know how to make it happen. I'm not saying I know how to make it happen, either, but I can promise you that the more absorbed you are in something, *the faster time will pass.*

I predict that when this difficult period is over and you have moved to a facility where reading, learning, and recreational activities are available, your involvement in them is going to shorten that "eternity" stretching out before you now. Just keep thinking about that. If you can manage to do it, practice creating and using the positive visualizations of your future life that we talked about earlier. Those visualizations can almost serve as a meditation. Close your eyes right now and imagine yourself in a park playing with your son or shaking hands with someone as you close a successful business deal. Both of those things can manifest in your life when you get out.

    Peace and love,

    Hill

PART 3

QUANTIFY YOUR LIFE

MY NEW JOINT

what up Hill?

i know its been a minute since you hit me but
theres a good reason. i finally got transfred
out of maximum security. im not quite sure
where this place is but even if five hours on
the hardest ball bsutin bus seats ever is worth
it to be in a medium security joint. Pullin in
through the gate i could feel my luck changing
and when i got in they give me a key to
my cell like fancy two star holywood hotel or
something. The key is too keep other ouns
from jackin my shit. cool thing is we can come
and go whenever we want and they even got a
common area with a tv, weight room and even a
fuckin xbox. The only thing off my damn cellie
sandro has another muscles on top of muscles no
neck having nigga. covered with tats and deep
in one if you know what i mean. i just dont
wanna say which but we all good at least right
now. i wanna try to keep it that wa yto and
thats part becuz of you. im really tryna listen
to what you say. And now im somewhere with
way more to lose and im ready i want to

do it the right way and make an impact. Those
are your words ha. No excuses form me i need
your mentorship and man am i lucky to have it.
A while back you wrote to imagine in your minds
eye your highest aspiration imagine the best
version of you. its always stuck with me and
guess what the other piece of paper in here
has a list of my highest aspirations. Lemme
know what you think.

—iB

LETTER 18

Your Highest Aspirations

Your net worth to the world is usually determined by what remains after your bad habits are subtracted from your good ones.

—Benjamin Franklin

Hey, Brotha,

So cool to hear from you finally. I was beginning to think I never would again. I'll be honest and say it gave me a kind of gnawing sense of loss. You may not realize it, but I *like* getting letters from you. I look forward to it.

Let's make a deal. Four years ago, I suddenly stopped hearing from you after a routine of at least a letter or two every couple of weeks. I justified it by telling myself that you were living the ideas we'd batted back and forth, so everything was cool. But no big deal; the important thing is that I've heard from you and that you're okay. Which means you and I can start working on building something new, right? How about we look into fortifying our foundation?

A FOUNDATION FOR ASPIRATIONS

As you were sitting on that hard bus seat on your way west, I was on my way west, too—on a much longer trip. I decided to drive from Chicago, where I was for a conference of MANifest Your Destiny, back to Iowa to visit family. I stayed in

Fort Madison again with my great-uncle, the cool cat I told you about who recovered so fast from his triple bypass. We actually had a blast just driving to some of the places in that little town where I used to hang as a kid. Then when I came back home, I got your letter and your list of "aspirations."

The truth is, the items in the list you sent me in many ways are hoped-for fantasies, not aspirations. Fantasies are aspirations without a plan and without the work. And when that cloud turns into rain, the fantasies will come crashing to the ground with it, because there's nothing real to hold them up. It's like hoping to win the lotto. There's no plan for it; it's just wishing for good luck. All those bright ideas won't work unless you do. It's the simple sucka who seldom succeeds that says the road to success sucks. Who said it would be easy? Success doesn't come before struggle in the dictionary or in life. Pursuing success is like going after a boxing title belt—it's yours for the taking, but you have to get your ass in the ring and fight for it. You'll sustain blows and are likely to get knocked down, but you have to get back up and keep fighting. So let's take luck out of the equation, and there's only one way to do that.

> **A foundation isn't something you have. It's something you *build*.**

A while back, I told you that every plan has to be built on a foundation. Remember what your answer was? "Well, I don't *have* a foundation." But see, a foundation isn't something you have. It's something you *build*. I guess it's my fault, but reading your aspirations made me realize we've started things a little ass-backward, now that you're in a new joint and ready for a new plan.

You need aspirations, but all your aspirations will join the wind unless they're built on some *foundation*. And a foundation comes out of the *resources* needed to make it. To make a foundation for your aspirations, you're going to need a checklist identifying which resources you already have and which resources you don't have but you believe there is some way of getting them.

BIG ASS-ETS ERASE LIE-ABILITY

How do you make that list of resources? Let's call 'em *assets*, like we wrote about when you were first in the jail. And what about the resources, or assets, you *haven't* got, and worse still, what about the stuff that is going to endanger your assets? We'll call them *liabilities*. They have the power to *prevent* your aspirations from happening.

Let's say, for example, that you want to be a video game designer, and you start by taking inventory of the assets related to it that you already have. One: You're a very good artist; you can draw realistic-looking human figures. Cool. That's one asset you have already that you can use to make the foundation for your aspiration. What about a liability? It would be better for you—not me—to think of one of those, but I'll suggest one: You have no formal training (as of yet) in video game design.

Now, let's say that an education is also an asset that you will need but don't have, and it's going to cost you a lot to get that asset. Maybe when you have your degree and work in video game design, you'll have spent, or will owe, over $20,000 in order to get it. So what are you going to put in your list of assets? "Twenty grand"? Is that an asset you have or one that you think there's a good chance you can acquire right away? *Yes?* Are you planning to rob a bank? The answer is no. "Lacking twenty grand" is one of your *liabilities,* because you don't have it, and you're going to need it for your aspirations. And it won't be easy to get. Why not put down a related asset that you have now and that might someday result in getting the asset of twenty grand? How about being able to source books and online information listing college loans, grants, and scholarships? That access to info is an asset of yours that directly speaks to eliminating one of your current liabilities. Does that make sense?

SETTING THE TABLE

Well, we're going to make a table with three columns, in which the columns interact with one another. I want you to be completely honest with me, and most importantly with yourself. Let's get this done now. And no "Hill, I'll do it later. . . ." No, do it right now. Remember, "someday" isn't a day on the calendar. Take a sheet of paper and divide it into three columns:

ASSETS	LIABILITIES	ACTIONS

In the "Assets" column, list all the resources you have *already*. I'm willing to bet there are a lot more than you realize you have: the memory of your mother, who believed in you and who often seems to be there right at your shoulder, is one of your assets because it gives you strength under stress. Then there are your street smarts, your intelligence, your ability to draw, read, and comprehend. . . . See what I mean? You have a list unfolding already.

In the "Liabilities" column, list everything that could stop you from realizing an aspiration. (The liabilities should not be on the same line as the assets.) This is going to be harder, I know. But let's start by listing the only one I've mentioned: "Need money for furthering my education and increasing my options." Finally, there's the "Actions" column. This column is actually determined by the "Liabilities" column. It contains suggested actions for turning a *liability* into an *asset*.

Go down line by line. When a line lists an asset, you don't have to write anything else on that line. It's a resource you have already, so no action is necessary to get it. But when you come to a line with a liability, you need to think of an action that will start you on the path toward changing that liability into an asset. As an obvious example:

LIABILITY	ACTION
No money for school	Research how to get loans and scholarships

This list only works if you're totally honest. In a way, this list is about baring your soul. It's easy to boast about the talents and skills you have. It's hard to be perfectly honest about them without exaggerating. And it's even harder to look squarely at the things you need but lack. And remember that you can be vulnerable because it's for your eyes only. It wouldn't be cool for me to ask you to do something I won't, so to be completely fair to you, I've started my own table of assets, liabilities, and actions. Here it is:

ASSETS	LIABILITIES	ACTIONS
Ivy League education		
	Afraid to express or discuss negative feelings	Try writing about them first and see if it helps
Acting talent (I hope)		
Uncle who believes in me		
	Cheated on my ex-girlfriend; don't want to cheat on my new girlfriend	Don't exchange info with new women; work to keep relationship fresh

Active in mission to help young Brothers and Sisters		
	Have trouble chilling out or relaxing	Try yoga, running, meditation

Okay, your turn. We've been choppin' it up by letter and phone for a hell of a long time. But I bet there'll be some surprises for me when I get a look at your chart.

Oh, my fault. Hold up. Listen. Take your time working on the chart. I won't be around for ten or twelve days. I've been invited to the KAN Film Festival in Wroclaw, Poland, as a judge. I said yes mostly because I'll be making a film in Romania in a few months and I wanted to check out the former communist bloc.

Guess I got to start pulling that trip together in my mind. Traveling is getting easier, and I've got the packing thing down to a science at this point. I've got doubles of everything I have at home that I also need to travel: toothbrush, toothpaste, phone charger, a week's worth of underwear, shirts, pants, sports jacket . . . and they're always waiting in my carry-on bag for the next trip. I never unpack them. All I've ever got to do is grab my cell phone, keys, passport, and coat before I head to the airport. Preparation and planning, man. That's the name of the game.

Warm regards,

Hill

ASPIRATION

LETTER 19

Commit to Endure

To endure is greater than to dare.

— William Makepeace Thackeray

Commitment is a big part of what I am and what I believe. How committed are you to wining? How committed are you to being a good friend? To being trustworthy? To being successful? How committed are you to being a good father, a good teammate, a good role model? There's that moment every morning when you look in the mirror: Are you committed, or are you not?

— LeBron James

Hey, man,

I'm back from that film festival in Poland, jet-lagged as hell. I don't regret going, though. It was my first time in a formerly communist country. Signs of it were everywhere. By trying to industrialize the country too fast, they shat on the ecology of some of their regions. I had dinner twice with the organizers of the festival. The stories of deprivation were mind-boggling.

One of my dinner companions had been there in 1970 when the workers demonstrated in the streets to protest food prices and were shot by the dozen. The other guy who was at dinner talked about the squelching of the rebellious

Solidarity movement by the hard-line communists, pitting neighbor against neighbor, even brother against brother. You had to keep your guard up at all times in front of neighbors, even family, many of whom had no compunction about snitching to the authorities about you for some small infraction. Sounds like some of the false friendships and alliances of the prison house, doesn't it?

There was definitely something heroic about everyone I spoke to, though, and it was obvious that a lot of it developed in a context of endurance. They radiated a capacity for it like I'd never seen before. I thought of some of the stuff you've had to endure this last year in that maximum-security facility, and I admired you for the way you handled it. Meanwhile, I'm really looking forward to the experience of shooting that film in Romania so I can find out more about another country in post-communist Europe.

MORE ASSETS THAN YOU THINK

Got your assets and liabilities chart in the mail. You don't do yourself justice! I was expecting plenty of swagga to show up in it. And mostly external stuff. But you did find the courage to go in, and go in you did. Thank you for trusting me enough to share it, fam.

Because you see, most people (especially in my business—the entertainment business) have the habit of exaggerating their masculinity, calling themselves pussy magnets, bragging about how much ass, how much cash, how many cars they get, and on and on. Those who talk the most usually have the least. Obnoxiously flaunting your riches is the same thing as obnoxiously flaunting your insecurities. We all know that kind of arrogance is a way of covering up fears and low self-esteem. Even they know it! But it's the elephant in the room that nobody wants to point to, since they all consider it a technique of "survival." Loud confidence is quiet insecurity. So I was kind of expecting you to come with some of that in the time-honored tradition of the streets when you talked about your assets. Instead, what do I get? A dude who seems painfully aware of what he considers his failings but has not a clue as to how valuable he really is. As soon as you're born, you have value.

If you don't mind, I'd like to discuss a couple of the items in your "Liabilities" column. Maybe things are a lot more complex than you were thinking. What do we have here?

Excuse me, but I can't buy your calling yourself a "lousy father." Naw, I can't let you get away with that. I was moved by how broke up you were about R. J.'s needing to go to a group home. You truly wanted to be there for him. In your

Liabilities

im a lousy father

dont think about consequinces of

certain actions

my vocabulary is small and i read slow

hot temper

used to think i was a leader but

feel like a follower now

heart, that kid embodies everything you care about, right? That's not being a lousy father; that's a father who cares deeply for his son.

That's why we have to find a way to put some of that love outside your heart and into the real world, and bring it to R. J. As I promised, I'll help you work on that. Since the last time we talked, I've spent several hours on the Family and Corrections Network, that directory of national and local programs for families with a parent in jail. I made a couple calls to some government agencies in your city and found out that I could get R. J. here for a visit if the group home signs off on it. And to be sure, I'm not above using the currency of my "name" to talk them into it. The main thing we'll need is somebody bonded (with no criminal record) who can visit R. J. regularly at the home, because I'll be traveling for much of the next year or so. And if R. J. likes the person, I'm hoping he'll get to the point of feeling comfortable getting on a plane with her or him to come and see you. I'll take care of the fare. There's a young woman, name of Lynn, who used to work for me who's very political. She thinks the prison industrial complex sucks and has really taken to what I told her about you and R. J. She's got a vacation coming up and plans to spend it flying to your city to see R. J., if I can arrange it for her. We'll see what happens from there.

As for being a follower and not a leader, I think I know why you believe that. As you've told me on several occasions, you followed right behind your brother as he sank deeper and deeper into street life. At a certain age, all kids need somebody to follow, and Vernon, your big brother, was the only paternal image available to you, your only mentor. But I've seen you stand up to me and stick to your principles on lots of occasions (even when you're wrong, ha ha!), which is why I think you're a leader in training, my man. Once again, it's just something that needs to be actualized. So do me a favor: In the "Actions" column, on the same line as "I'm a lousy father," write something like "I'm going to try to communicate with my son." You'll write a letter to him when you feel you can handle it. Then, go to "Feel like I'm a follower."

THE ENDURANCE FACTOR

> Endurance is not just the ability to bear a hard thing, but to turn it into glory.
> —Charles Barkley

The fact that you've already weathered two incarceration environments means you've got some skill for it. What's more, making it through a maximum-security facility is proof that you've learned adaptability. So put those two assets on the chart: endurance and adaptability. You got those, Brotha, just like the formerly oppressed people I met in Poland. They are flourishing now, and so will you!

Take care,

Hill

ASSETS AND
LIABILITIES

LETTER 20

Cleaning House

The price of hating other human beings is loving oneself less.

—Eldridge Cleaver

Hey, Brotha,

You were definitely on one tonight. But I totally get it. How long ago was it you wrote your aunt to tell her you're on the verge of turning your life around? That you were working with me on a plan, and that part of the plan is getting educated, which is going to cost some money? Was it about a month ago? She should have at least answered.

Then she shows up unannounced on visitors day, and it's like a great weight has been lifted off your chest. You feel less alone. It makes perfect sense that you'd think she'd come to talk to you about the money you want for books or a couple of the correspondence courses that we talked about. Instead, she walks in there with a hostile attitude, saying she wants to get some things off her chest. She proceeds to lay into you for asking for money for a correspondence course. And just before she leaves, she casually mentions—as if it were an unimportant detail—that she can't let you live with her when you get out.

I hate the way your aunt handled telling you all this. Obviously, it was her way of dealing with the guilt, anger, and embarrassment she felt about letting R. J. end up in a group home. But maybe if your aunt had let you know this stuff earlier, rather than ignoring your letters, you wouldn't have gone off on her like you did, telling her you're convinced that she merely tolerated you when you lived with her and doesn't give a damn what happens to you now. Then ending it by referring to her as a "skanky ho."

Come on, man, really? I know you were pissed, but c'mon, that's one place I can't go with you. At some point in history, some very rage-filled person sat down and made a long list of words meant to demean all women of the human species. And the pejoratives stuck. Who knows why; perhaps it grew out of horrible childhoods, boys resenting their moms and letting that resentment leak onto all women in general. But for others—and I suspect you've been one of them—all that "ho" business is just a casual, thoughtless, and childish way of perversely asserting male dominance to cover insecurity. You know, of course, that the word is short for *whore,* which means "a woman who engages in promiscuous sexual intercourse, usually for money," but I don't believe you think that has anything to do with your aunt. As for *skank,* when it's not meant to refer to a steady-paced reggae dance, it has other meanings, such as "sleazy person," and even insinuates intent to swindle or deceive, but for some reason, I've never heard anyone use it to describe a man, only women. It's not a very interesting word, root-wise, as it only goes back to the sixties. So do me a favor and find a more articulate, more original way to express your anger at your aunt, or anybody else, when you're talking to me. Cool?

IMPERFECT LOVE

Have I ever mentioned to you that my name, *Hill Harper,* is a tribute to both my maternal and paternal ancestors? I think of it as a kind of acknowledgment, as if I were standing in front of them and saying:

> Hey, if it weren't for you guys, I wouldn't be here. . . . Before and after y'all were forced into slavery, you struggled to create a tradition of African-American achievement from generation to generation, straining against the heavy limitations that society imposed on our race and culture. You struggled out of slavery and through Jim Crow to achievement against the odds, at the pinnacle of which I am standing today. I wouldn't be here without you!

Does that mean that the generations that came before me are responsible for my achievements? *Hell no!* Were the Harpers all lucky sons-a-bitches with silver spoons in their mouths from the get-go, whereas most of the Brothas of the same race were born into hardship and poverty? *Bullshit!* Something even worse than poverty, known as slavery, was the case in this country for earlier generations of Harpers.

All I can really thank my ancestors for is putting me on this earth with lungs that could breathe and legs that could walk, and some examples of African-Americans who strove for success and finally got it—examples I could focus on, *if I chose to*! And I am doing that. And I want you to do that, too. I've pointed out to you on many occasions that it's up to us to do what we do with whatever we happen to be given.

Was everything my father or mother did wisely thought out? Ha! *Are you kidding?* Was I ever hurt by a family member, made to feel neglected, under-appreciated? *Who isn't?* Do I also respect my parents, my grandparents, my aunts, and my uncles, and feel gratitude toward them, because they did what they could? You'd better believe it!

HOW WE HEAL

I don't know much about your aunt, but from what you've told me about your pops, Jarvis, I have some inkling of what he must have gone through. You said Jarvis wasn't a bad dad until he got laid off and couldn't find a job. Obviously, after that he no longer felt like the principal protector of the family and started to pair low self-esteem and booze. When drunk, he'd take out his frustration and feelings of ineffectuality on his wife with behavior that got more and more out of control and increasingly violent. That's when your aunt had to step in to help.

Should you ever forgive your pops for that? Grudges are cancer. Hate feeds it. Forgiveness cures it. I'm suggesting you try to comprehend the things that caused your father's destructive behavior. That's a starting platform. Eventually, it might offer you more than one option for evaluating your pops. And it might even begin to heal some of those old wounds from him that you don't wanna even admit you have. Wounds heal, but unresolved issues don't. Scars tell stories of resilience and survival. Don't be scared to get scarred.

What about your aunt? I believe you when you say she did a sorry job of parenting, that she was cold and detached. You've mentioned several examples.

It doesn't erase the fact, however, that she did make the decision to take you in and support you when your father went away, rather than just letting you go to a group home. Why she did this is the most important thing about her to strive to comprehend. You see, this conversation you and I are having isn't about the quality of care she provided, but about the fact that she did provide some kind of care by taking you in. The only other interesting or helpful aspect of the issue is the ways in which you *used* that care, and we know that part of the way you used it was to make a series of decisions that made you end up where you are now. Whether there was lots of care or only a little, the results could have gone either way. The same goes for me: As I said way, way back when we started communicating, what happened to you could have easily happened to me. . . . .

Maybe this is a cruel thing to say, but just taking you in and saving you from the claws of child welfare was *more* than she owed you. Can you really resent her just for not wanting to give more? Resentment about somebody not giving enough always comes from one identical source: a failure to *own* your own life, *claim* it as yours, take responsibility for it, and say to yourself, "Well, I'm the one running the show here, so whatever happens, *I'm* responsible." Believe it or not, a true understanding of that fact can produce an exhilarating sense of freedom.

Do you remember R. J. when he was two? What kind of things did he do? During the period in every child's life they call the "terrible twos"—when an infant first learns that he's actually a separate being, that his consciousness is more than a suction machine attached to his mother's breast or bottle, the moment he learns that *he's* the one in control of his actions—he starts to enjoy all kinds of mischievous acting out. Almost everything he does is to say to himself over and over, "*I'm* the one who threw that spoon from my high chair—all by myself. . . . *I'm* the one who grabbed that piece of candy and stuck it in my mouth without waiting for somebody to feed me."

Did you see R. J. take his first few steps? Did you see a look of pride, mastery, and excitement on his face? I don't think there's a child in the world who's thinking, "Mommy, why aren't you holding me off the ground longer, rather than making me walk on my own now!" No, he couldn't have been more delighted about being a "little man." As a matter of fact, a lot of moms who are overly attached to their kids dread the arrival of the terrible twos, because that's the moment when their child realizes he's not totally dependent on them.

I'm using a metaphor here, of course. But in one fundamental way, you're like that kid embarking on the "terrible twos" as you move into a mode of independence and life planning. In fact, your aunt is entering her "terrible twos" as well, in a way, having put off making her own family in order to take responsibility for you and your brother.

You know, Brotha, you're heading toward thirty, way beyond the age when people are thought to need parenting. You're a grown-ass man! I'm just your friend. Even so, sometimes I get pleasure out of trying to take care of you, out of thinking of you in a paternal way. But does that mean that a few years from now, when you ask me to do you a solid and I just might not be able to do it, you'll go around saying I betrayed you, left you high and dry, that "I ain't shit?" I could never believe that.

Peace,

Hill

ANCESTORS

P.S. Someone I admire, Dr. Benjamin Chavis, wanted to write to you about using your time wisely while you're in prison. Dr. Chavis is cofounder, president, and CEO of the Hip-Hop Summit Action Network and president of the Education Online Services Corporation. Here's his letter:

Dear Brother,

When you are incarcerated, don't just serve time; make time serve you. The time that you now have before you will be a time for reflection and future planning, but you must make sure that you use the time you've been blessed with and the life you've been blessed with. You must see your life as a blessing, not as a curse, and that is what I mean by making time serve you.

The prison cell does not have to be a cell of isolation. It depends on how you see that prison cell, and more importantly, how you see yourself. I was unjustly incarcerated in the 1970s as a member of North Carolina's Wilmington Ten. Throughout my time in prison, I never allowed myself to feel separated or isolated from the civil rights movement or from our people's movement to gain freedom, justice, and equality.

When you are incarcerated, don't just serve time; make time serve you.

Human beings adapt or adjust, but remember, dear Brother, that you are not the prison cell. You are *in* the cell, but you are *not* the cell. The container or boundary that we may face in life—whether we're in prison or what's called the "outside world"—can only confine us if we allow it to. You have to be aware that at the end of the day, it is *you* who decides the quality of your life.

Prayer and meditation are important while you are incarcerated, but study is also important. Study yourself and know yourself, and study your environment and those around you. You should also express yourself. The best expression in life is self-expression, and to that end, you should keep a diary. Believe me, every day of your life during prison confinement, you should express not only how you feel but what you are learning from this experience. Transformation can take place even in a steel box, because transformation takes place first in one's consciousness. If you want to change the world, you first have to think about how you see the world. Changing the world starts first by changing yourself and changing your own consciousness.

Reverend Martin Luther King Jr. taught me so much when I worked for the Southern Christian Leadership Conference. Dr. King told all of us staff people in SCLC never to become bitter, because bitterness only distorts the beholder. You may feel that the world has wronged you, and that may be true. Or you may have wronged yourself. But it is not the wrong that you should focus on. Instead, focus on how to make the situation better and how to make it right for yourself, even while you're incarcerated. Self-improvement starts there.

It's a mistake to say, "Well, I'm gonna get better when I get out." You can get better while you're in.

It's a mistake to say, "Well, I'm gonna get better when I get out." You can get better while you're in. While I was incarcerated in North Carolina, I enrolled myself in Duke University and got a master's of divinity magna cum laude. It was not easy; I don't want anyone to think that it was easy. But I mention it because you have to set high goals in life, even while you're inside a prison cell. And then you must strive. Rather than let your confinement adjust you, you have to adjust the contours of your confinement. You can't move the steel cell bars, but you *can* move how you think through those bars and not allow your consciousness to be confined.

I never felt alone while I was in prison because I stayed in constant touch with my family. You should also stay in touch with your loved ones. Loneliness is a sign that you feel isolated, but I want to encourage you. One lesson I learned while I was in prison was never to let the forces of my confinement break my spirit. Keep your spirit strong. What I mean by "your spirit" is your inner essence—not only what you think about, but your soul, your vibration, how you see the world, and your aspirations.

Yes, you can have aspirations while in prison, but plan how to execute them. Study is very important. Prepare yourself and read everything you can. If they allow you to have a newspaper, don't just read your favorite section; read everything. Words are very important. Reading, writing, studying, and reflection are all part of the universal process of self-development. Self-preparation and self-preservation are important too, because you preserve yourself by preserving others. You help yourself by helping others. You expand your vision by extending the grace that God has given you and the blessings that you see. To sum up, I want to encourage anyone reading this letter to not just serve time but make time serve you.

Yours,
Dr. Benjamin Chavis

LETTER 21

Straying

Drug misuse is not a disease, it is a decision, like the decision to step out in front of a moving car. You would call that not a disease, but an error in judgment.[1]

—Philip K. Dick

My Brotha,

I can't even front on how much your letter put me out. Once again, almost three weeks without a sign that you're alive and breathing, fam. Then I get your letter, and to be perfectly honest, it set me off—from a partly selfish point of view. I kept wondering how much of what happened was my fault. I kept thinking, "What have I done to this dude?" I kept thinking. "Obviously, I'm not helping."

It never would have occurred to me that you'd backslide into smoking weed out of fear of having a deficiency in assets after I wrote you my reactions to your chart. I thought you could handle it. If you reread my last letter carefully, you'll see that I truly believe you have a lot going for you. As I said, your lack of options is *environmental,* which means it's *not* permanent unless you decide it is. I wouldn't have guessed in a million years that worrying about something like that was going to drive you into a bout with contraband.

Now I get the picture, Brotha. Just like your Yvette, you figured staying high is a way of avoiding anger about your aunt, anxiety about the future, and everything else. You felt like I was asking too much of you by wanting you to take an honest assessment of yourself, right? And you were worried about being pressured to jump into a gang again, especially since your cellie Sandro is an OG in one of the Nations, right?

What was it you said? "I'd never get involved with that stuff on the street, Hill, but in here, lots of things are upside down. Having control over some drugs is a chance for a possible power play in the future, when you could end up needing that power most." So you've decided to set yourself up as a drug middleman for quick money, and you're numbing your guilt about what you're doing by staying high.

Even if I was in favor of the dealing—which I certainly am not—I'd tell you what any idiot on the street knows: Never get high on your own supply. A dealer's job is getting others hooked. (Don't think that's a business strategy I admire them for.) But you yourself are not developing *any* kind of business plan here. You're looking for a quick fix, some *quick assets*. I can barely believe some of this, it's so scatterbrained. Let me make sure I got this right. *Becoming an in-house drug dealer is your well-considered plan for the future?*

It pains me terribly to say this, but I don't want to hear from you until you've dropped this weak-ass plan. What sense does it make? I'm not qualified to mentor somebody who's high all the time or involved in any way with illegal substances. So this may be my last letter.

THE HYPE MAN

One more thing before I sign off, Brotha. Are you hip to the term *hype man*? You probably are. It's an old hip-hop term for the man on the mic who backs up the MC. He hypes up the crowd and provides a kind of texture to the main rapper's words. At certain points, the hype man puts his own two cents in, which keeps the rhythm going and adds an occasional new layer. The back-and-forth between the MC and his hype man is really based on the old call-and-response style of music that you can trace through the blues all the way back to Africa.

Hype men have been doing their thing for years, in fact. You know Flavor Flav. He was Public Enemy's hype man early on. Even Jay-Z started off as a hype man for Jaz-O and Big Daddy Kane before he came into his own. Tupac himself started off that way for Digital Underground. Hip-hop experts (including my friend Lupe Fiasco) consider Busta Rhymes's hype man, Spliff Star, to be the greatest hype man ever. Well, I wanna be your Spliff Star, your Flavor Flav. Will you let me be your hype man? You know, have your back? Do you trust me enough to let me be there for you, for this journey we are about to go on *together*?

You may think the hype man is just the "second fiddle," but to most rappers, achieving synergy with the hype man is what makes the act. When a dude's head is in the right place, he understands that success requires an *ally*, a hype man. A good hype man is the most important resource, or asset, a rapper can have.

> **We all have the capacity to live phenomenal, unreasonably happy lives, lives of impact and legacy, but we can't do it alone.**

All hype men and all rappers understand this. They've spoken out and said so. For example, when Eminem's hype man Proof was shot and killed at a Detroit club, Eminem asked Mr. Porter to fill his shoes. Mr. Porter made it clear that the role of hype man is something that comes with a lot of responsibility and he was afraid he couldn't live up to expectations.

Any rap fan can tell you that Porter's commitment to Eminem won out, and even though Porter wondered if he was really capable of bringing it to the table, he just had to. He said:

> Em is like my brother. So it's like, if my big brother was hurt and he couldn't take care of my mother or something like that, I would have to do that, and he would expect that of me. And it was the same thing with Em. I didn't think twice, because I wanna have his back like he always had my back. And I was like, Who else is gonna do it? It didn't make sense any other kind of way. Me and him have been around each other for years, before all of the—where he is right now.[2]

Read that carefully, man, because there it is in Black and white: Every successful plan requires a loyal ally. And I feel that way about you, Brotha. If you'll turn your back on the drug thang, I'm willing to play your hype man for a while, but only if you value me like Eminem values his hype man. I'm gonna try everything in the book to get you back into the game and help you stay in it, if you let me. I'm gonna be in your ear and in your head reminding you of one essential truth: We all have the capacity to live phenomenal, unreasonably happy lives, lives of impact and legacy, but we can't do it alone.

I'll be behind you as you move from being a passive participant in your life to an active one. I'll be there as you go and take control, move forward, make a difference. In letters and when we talk on the phone, I'll show you the way to overcome your micro-quits—those little, barely noticeable strategies of giving up that, strung together, mean failure. I'll share lessons from people who have risen to meet challenges large and small, who have achieved their goals by mustering the courage, the will, and the grit it takes to succeed. I'll give you the tools you need to achieve a brilliant life.

I'll give them to you, but you need to take them and use them. There's no backing down, no telling yourself it's too hard or scary or saying you don't feel like it today and you'll take a break and pick it up later, or deciding you'd rather get high. No! This is *now*. If you don't take control now, you're letting more of your life slip away.

I'll do everything I can to motivate you, my man. I'll be the one who's saying, "You can do it! You can make it happen! You can *win*!" But you have to keep one thing in mind. Whatever I say, whatever encouragement I offer, can't be more than "cheerleading" or hype. Cheerleading and hype are wonderful gifts from a friend because they pump up the energy level. They increase the possibility that you'll have the stamina for your long journey. Having people cheering for you is important, but cheering doesn't break tackles; you have to run the ball. It doesn't give you the playbook, either. You need a playbook. You need a system. That's what a coach is for, and that's what mentors are for: to help you develop your playbook. That's what they are there for—to help you.

So which is it—dealing and sniffing, or working with your hype man? Just say the word, and say it soon.

Peace,

Hill

**START
BREAKING
TACKLES**

P.S. I'm enclosing a letter from someone in the music biz who knows a lot about spiritual surrender. I mentioned you to Russell Simmons the other day, and he wanted to reach out to you.

Dear Brother,

As a person who believes in spiritual practices, first I go to what happens on the inside as a way to evolve into a more healthy physical condition. The environment is always going to affect you, but you choose a lot of the environmental forces. For example, you can be in the ghetto, but you can also be in the church. You can be in the ghetto but also be in meditation. You can surround yourself with elements that can draw you out, but your job is to look inward.

Just like freedom when you're out of prison, freedom while you're in prison comes from personal and spiritual freedom. You can be free while you're in jail, just as you can be locked up while you're on the street. There are people in prison who don't suffer, and there are people on the streets who do. This is a choice that each individual has to make. Of course it's easier to make this choice while you're surrounded by people who are happy and free. But you can see people who *appear* to be more successful or happy out in the world but who are doing things that lead to suffering, and they can suck you in too. You have to make the choice.

> **You can be in the ghetto, but you can also be in the church.**

The nature of spiritual evolution is simple. If you find yourself on a train going the wrong way, you get up, go to the other side of the tracks, and go the other way. This is how an individual has to treat his own life. Despite what the friends and the sheep are doing, find different friends who are going the other way on the tracks. Or if there aren't a lot of people available, find it within your heart, from the inside out, to move in the right direction. The person who is locked up has to look inside in order not to promote a cycle of more suffering.

People say, "That's bullshit. I've heard that before." But I'm not making this up. It's in the Bible, the Koran, the Torah, the yoga sutras, the Bhagavad Gita, the Buddhist scriptures. Every person who sought to relieve the suffering of humankind promoted the same steps, and every one of them was revered because their wisdom changed the lives of so many.

You have to learn that late-night drinking is a headache, but early-morning meditation is a freedom. Until people do enough meditation, they still have doubts that it isn't true or they think there's a shortcut. "If I just cut these corners, then I'll be better off." Anyone who gains faith in the truth lives by it, but you have to gain faith from experience, from actually doing it. Even if you find yourself in prison at age thirty-six or forty, at any minute you can make a change. It's not like "As soon as I get a shot" or "As soon as I get freedom." You have to start to create a different mind-set when you're in prison. In fact, there's no greater place to begin, because that's where you have time alone to learn to look inside.

I just wrote a book on meditation because I've seen its effects on the homeless, on people coming home from war, on people in prisons. I talk about mantra-based meditation, using the mantra *rum*. You sit and be patient, and repeat the word *rum* in your mind. Or you can inhale on *let* and exhale on *go*. At first your mind will go crazy like a monkey in a cage, but if you're patient, the mind will settle. Your mind will try to trick you into moving, but if you set an alarm for twenty minutes, in a few minutes you'll say, "Oh, I'm meditating." And then your mind will settle even more and you will transcend those thoughts even more.

There is no trick to meditation; you just have to have patience. If you make a regular habit of it, you find that what's outside is less important. Every thought doesn't have to affect your nervous system or create emotion or bad energy. When you become the watcher, which is the person who meditates, you see the world in real time and things move more slowly. The fluctuations and the noise that the mind creates—which is the only cause of suffering—dissipates. When the mind is settled, there is nothing but bliss. The things that you think are causing great stress are actually very small.

Meditation is a great gift for people who are incarcerated because you can do it anywhere, and stillness is the thing that promotes the most happiness. So this is my gift to you, Brother—the gift of meditation. Use it and you will become a happier, more peaceful person.

Yours,
Russell Simmons

THE RETURN

Hill,

i know its been a long time since we last talked
but i had to figure this out on my own. Truth be
told i didnt even open your letter for a month
after i got it cause i didnt want to hear your
shit. when i did open it as always you helped me
understand it was really my shit i was dealin with
(dealin with. Get it?) i wound up meetin this old
timer on a 20 year bid who was readin The Man who
outgrew his prison cell: confessions of a Bank Robber
by Joe Loya. The old dude actually gave it to me
after he finished and i couldnt put it down. it was
kind of a dark time for me but im trying and think
im past it so i hope you write your brother back.

—iB

LETTER 22

Forgiving

The reward of the evil is the evil thereof, but whosoever forgives and makes amends, his reward is upon Allah.

—Koran 42:40

The weak can never forgive. Forgiveness is the attribute of the strong.

—Mahatma Gandhi

Hey, Brotha,

It's about midnight in L.A., and it's a little more than forty-eight hours since I got back from New York. But now I'm flying back to New York yet again to film some exteriors for *CSI: NY.* Just settled into my seat on the flight I've become all too familiar with, the red-eye from Los Angeles to New York. It leaves Los Angeles around eleven thirty P.M. and then arrives around seven thirty A.M. the next day in the Big Apple. Guess it's obvious why they call it the "red-eye," because your eyes tend to look bloodshot when you land, since you've slept so little on the plane. I never get any ZZZs, so I decided to write you a letter.

Taking off and climbing to thirty-five thousand feet, seeing the glinting lights on the ground get smaller and smaller, I imagine what you are doing right now. Are you asleep? Or are you under your covers with a rigged LED light reading a new book? So I pull out your latest letter, and damn. Shit, man, I guess when it rains, it pours. That letter you got from your locked-up brother, Vernon, must have come as a surprise. Did you even know Vernon was in a federal pen now?

I totally get how hearing from him made you feel. I know it hurts, but I actually think it's a good sign. I'm gonna remind you of what you said about it in your letter:

miss the shit out of my bro and his letter really bugged me out. He so into prison life now and i dont think he ever gonna change. Fuck the Prison industrial complex. i never told you this but when i was 13 vern got jumped into a gang and everything changed then. nobody would fuck with him and because he was my bro nobody would fuck with me. i thought he had real power i thought he was cool and it kills me to say this but it was just bullshit Hill. it was fuckin bullshit and now it feels like he betrayed

• • •

Wow, man, I'm so proud of you for seeing so clearly. It makes me feel like everything we've been talking about is worth it. I can see why that letter got to you. You still really care about Vernon. And that's *good*. You know? It's too early to talk about now, but once you get your plan together, maybe you can pass on our method to him. If you tell me to, I'll even send him copies of the letters I wrote you. Maybe he'll grab on to them and use them as some kind of life preserver.

I've got a confession to make, though. You may not have even noticed it, but I disappeared a little on you, just like I complained about when you acted that way to me. It doesn't matter that you're used to people playing it that way—coming and going when they damn well feel like it without so much as cluing you in beforehand. But it took me a lot of time to write this letter. Your letter about Vernon came in the mail three weeks before I climbed onto this red-eye to New York. It was obvious you really needed me to answer.

Then why didn't I? Man, I can't believe I'm about to tell you this. This is very private stuff that I usually don't even share with my closest friends. Think of it as a tribute to you. I just have a feeling you can understand.

Truth is, I was trying to deal with my own resentment. Your reaction to Vernon's letter was too close to one of my own issues for me to be able to answer right away. My older brother, Harry, and I barely talk. Since our dad died in 2000, our relationship has become distant. I haven't seen him in at least seven years, and the most we've said over the phone is a "Merry Xmas" and "Happy birthday," which means we talk no more than two, three times a year. No letters, no e-mail, nothing. Most people don't even know I have a brother. And here I am, "Mr. Giving Advice" . . . and I can't even clean up my own shit. I'm ashamed. It makes me feel like a fraud. A hypocrite. Who the fuck am I to give advice when I can't even talk to my own brother?

It's all these years later, and I still haven't let go of the resentment and pride and just forgiven him, and I feel ashamed about that. Here I'm trying to teach you about forgiveness and moving on, and I can't even do it within my own family. I'm sorry to you. Sorry to my brother and his family, and sorry to myself. I need to be better. Maybe I should write my own blood brother a letter, huh?

When you see the other side of an issue and finally get in touch with the other person's point of view—especially when it comes to love and family—it's powerful. I guess guilt was part of it—guilt for never realizing he was suffering when he did things that I thought were wrong.

But it was more than guilt that came flowing in on me when I suddenly understood some of his pain. It was regret, the feeling that something had been wasted that didn't have to be. The last eleven years, wasted. I kept brooding on the fact that if I'd been able to see him and the situation clearly then, he and I might have shared our lives together over the past decade. And then I reached a third stage regarding my brother: I felt *empathy*. Empathy is a deep sense of sympathy for a person, based on sharing their point of view.

EMPATHY MEANS FORGIVING

Your letter made me realize *my brother's* pain, when I was just focused on *mine*. I understand your resentment at Vernon's attitude toward life. But could you be playing the blame game I just described with him? Sure, Vernon was older and automatically served as a role model, but was Vernon himself old enough or mature enough to escape the influence of the street without a father or a mother to rely upon? Understanding that is an example of empathy. It was like one minor who needed protection trying to protect another minor who needed it. However, even as minors, we build our own house. Both of you are paying a price for the way you each built yours.

I just wonder if Vernon's writing to you might be the perfect opportunity to square things with him. More than that, instead of fuming obsessively about what your big brother owes you, maybe it's time to think of other ways to rebuild a family for yourself. For example, what about your own responsibilities for your own son? And yes, *I know* I need to listen to my own advice!

GRATITUDE

> To speak gratitude is courteous and pleasant, to enact gratitude is generous and noble, but to live gratitude is to touch Heaven.
>
> —Johannes A. Gaertner

One of the best ways to nourish a relationship is to express your *gratitude*. Gratitude is an extremely undervalued characteristic—we all need to express it, but few of us do, and fewer still express it well. So why don't we try right now to work that muscle out a bit? It's time to write a letter to someone who's had a positive impact on our lives. Whoever it is, I'm willing to bet that as grateful as we are to them, we've been totally inadequate when it comes to expressing that gratitude. It's time to change all that. I'll write one, too.

Oh . . . shit, I'm really afraid I'm going to lose you after I say this next thing. But just think about it; you don't have to do anything about it until you feel ready. Do you remember one of the things you said when you were talking about your aunt was, "her worry (maybe) about what was going to happen to me in the future"? Yeah, I know you think she was cold and only took you in because she had to. But her worrying about what was going to happen to you in the future doesn't jibe with that exactly, does it? Also, did your aunt really have to take you in? She could have said no and let you go to a group home like the one R. J. is in now.

Are you following me? I don't know your aunt. But something about her—a sense of responsibility for family, or maybe even some real affection for you— made her take you in and also made her worry about your future. I know you have a lot to complain about regarding her. I'm not putting you down for those complaints, and I believe that you're telling the truth about them. But you can have both: complaints about things she did or didn't do and *gratitude* for the things she *did* do.

Maybe taking you in was so much responsibility and created so much extra pressure in her life that she just didn't have the time or energy to reveal the caring that was behind it. I don't know for sure, obviously. All I know is that if you can bring yourself to the point of writing her a letter expressing gratitude, it could change everything. Especially if you could combine it with forgiveness for the mistakes she did make. And when your relationships change for the better, your life always changes for the better. I want you to have as many allies out there as possible when you get released. It would be very cool if you could get on some kind of positive footing with your aunt.

This is an exercise I myself have used on several occasions: sitting down and writing a letter to someone, mentioning the positive aspects of their impact on your life. You need to tell them how and why their giving has benefited you and them.

That's the first part of the letter I hope you'll write to your aunt. The other half of the letter is probably going to be a little harder. It's a letter saying you're sorry.

Saying you're sorry, really sorry, is always hard, especially for people like you and me who sometimes feel that admitting error is a black mark on our self-esteem. We let our false pride and ego get in the way. But it actually takes more strength and courage to be able to swallow pride and say, "I'm sorry." It's one of the best things we can do for our own personal growth and evolution. If we say we're sorry, then we can freely move on, not burdened with guilt, ego, or unfinished business. In doing so, you will feel more authentic and complete. A loop will be closed, a hole filled.

Put yourself in the shoes of your aunt receiving your note of gratitude and apology. How much impact would it have on her? How would she feel to get a note out of the blue saying she was responsible for something good in your life, that you apologize for some of your deeds and forgive her for some of hers? How would you feel if you got a note from a friend who remembered something hurtful he did months or years ago and finally came around to saying he was sorry?

> As long as we cling to the past, God himself cannot prevent this horrible fruit-bearing in us.

No one ever wrote about the subject of forgiveness better than Simone Weil, Brotha. She was a French philosopher who, although of Jewish birth, studied Christian mysticism and social activism, and died of starvation during World War II, perhaps because she refused to eat more than those deprived of food during that time. This is what Simone Weil had to say about letting go of the past and forgiving:

> Having forgiven our debtors is to renounce the past, en bloc. To accept that the future is once again virgin and intact. . . .
>
> In renouncing in one stroke all the fruits of the past without exception, we can ask God that our past sins not bear their miserable fruits of evil and error in our souls. As long as we cling to the past, God himself cannot prevent this horrible fruit-bearing in us. We cannot attach ourselves to the past without attaching ourselves to our crimes, for we are unaware of what is most essentially bad in us.[1]

It just occurred to me how cool it would be if you could reach a state of forgiveness—or call it "compassion"—for Vernon as well, despite that letter you just got that only provides more evidence of what a poor mentor he was for you. After that, who knows? Maybe you'll get to the point of trying to square things with Yvette, and even your father.

Don't get me wrong. I'm not disrespecting your reaction to Vernon's letter. I told you already that I'm impressed with and proud of your new ability to see through all that jail swagga. Nor am I disrespecting your resentment at your father for abandoning you. And I'm not belittling the things you needed that your aunt couldn't give. All of it is valid and understandable. If Vernon went bad and continues to get worse, it might even be the case that he now needs some guidance from you. Maybe that's the reason he wrote. You've grown and matured since we started corresponding, so this could be your chance to become somebody's mentor for the first time in your life. Wouldn't it give you a sense of accomplishment if you could mentor your older brother?

Wow, I've been thinking about or working on this letter to you almost the entire five and a half hours in the air. We'll be touching down in just twenty minutes!

Best,
Hill

FORGIVENESS

LETTER 23

Mental Health

Have you forgotten that, once we were brought here, we were robbed of our name? Robbed of our language. We lost our religion, our culture, our God. And many of us, by the way that we act, we even lost our minds!

—Khalid Abdul Muhammad

My Man,
    It's ten P.M. here in New York. Haven't mailed that letter I wrote on the plane yet. I used the only time I had when I got back from the airport to fall out on top of the bedspread in my New York pad for about three delicious hours and then drag myself to a meeting with the director/producer of *CSI: NY* to discuss the exteriors we'll be doing tomorrow.

It's hot as hell here in the Big Apple, just like it is every summer. But that won't stop 'em from pasting a few fake autumn leaves on some trees in Central Park to shoot scenes that are supposed to be taking place in the fall. The worst part of this is that I gotta be dressed like it's fall for my shots! I'm supposed to be at a crime scene near the lake in Central Park, checking out a stiff they just dragged out of the water.

I really should be getting my winks pronto, since our call on set is for six thirty A.M. tomorrow. But I feel like I owe you a little more communication. I want you to know that I completely understand what you said on the phone tonight, that you don't want to square things with your aunt just yet and that you're not ready to write her a letter. And I get why you don't feel like reaching out to Vernon, either. These things have to happen when you're ready for them to happen. I mean, it took me eleven years to see what happened with my brother from his point of view. But you're a newer, more perfect model than me, so it doesn't have to take you that long. I'm saddened to hear about how down you say you are right now, that you've been feeling more and more lonely and depressed, and that you're still afraid you're not smart enough to turn your life around. You sounded really sad on the phone. In a back-door kind of way, you hinted that you still don't feel worthwhile in any area of your life. It gave me a terribly sorrowful feeling in my chest. But even though we sometimes make mistakes, let each other down, and worse still, let ourselves down, you and I can do more and have more resources at our disposal than at any time in history.

PRISON PSYCHOLOGY

Do you know that you're far from alone in the way you feel? I've been doing some reading about the psychological aspects of being incarcerated. Turns out that there's a much higher rate of depression and other mental problems in prison than there is in the outside world.

I've got to admit I was shocked by the statistics I read. Seems that about 55 percent of incarcerated men in this country have symptoms of either depression or other mental illness, have been diagnosed as having a mental illness, or are in treatment for some form of mental illness. For women in prison, it's even worse; about 73 percent are suffering from mental problems. And it's no surprise that most incarcerated people, male or female, don't get any treatment for their illness while in prison. This, common sense says, would be the perfect time to do so. But what can we expect when people are suddenly uprooted from their families and communities? When they spend the day trying to resist the dehumanizing forces of the prison industrial complex? When "punishment" is deemed more important than reentry?

I know that spouting a bunch of statistics isn't going to make you feel any better, so let's talk about you. You know by now that to see clearly where you are and what direction you're heading, you've got to understand how you got there.

You don't heal a body or fix a car without first figuring out what's wrong inside and what caused it. You can't lead a life of value and impact without a slew of insights about why you failed to do so up to now.

Yes, the environment you're in is responsible for a lot of the confusion, depression, fear, and resentment you say you feel, but we can't make any dramatic changes to that with a snap of our fingers. Developing a political consciousness about your situation could be empowering, but I know you need more right now. Let's use the "triage" system for your problems for a little while. *Triage* is a medical term that comes from a French verb meaning "to separate" or "to sift." It's a way of assigning degrees of urgency to medical emergencies to figure out what order to treat them in. So let's call your bad mood an "urgent situation" and see if we can think of the fastest remedy for it.

In my opinion, one way you can improve how you feel is to talk with someone about it. I'm hoping there are some good counselors in the joint where you are and that they'll offer an ear you can respect in talking about your emotions. But these are things that you and I can discuss, too.

I really do understand how you're feeling; I'm not just paying you lip service. Sometimes it feels like you're standing in front of one of those automatic baseball batting cages. The problems come at you one by one, and at first you tackle them that way, at a steady pace. Even though it's challenging, it's still doable. Then, suddenly, one day, it starts to feel like the pitching machine has gone haywire and the problems are being pelted out too quickly and with too much force. It's like one baseball after another is coming at your head, and they're too fast for you to hit them. They're coming from left, right, and center. You can't keep up, so you throw up your hands—not so much in surrender as in self-protection. You stop moving; you simply stand still. Is that an accurate description?

I've gone through "the blues" myself several times. Most recently it centered around rejection.

Not too long ago I had a screen test for the lead of a pilot for AMC about a politically ambitious Philadelphia DA. My dream has always been to be the lead of my own award-winning show, and this presented the perfect opportunity. With shows like *Mad Men*, *The Walking Dead*, and *The Killing*, AMC has been winning numerous awards, and it has become one of the most respected cable channels. And it was as if the role was written for me, given the fact that I graduated from law school. The character fit like a glove. I have read a lot of TV scripts, but this was—no lie—one of the best I'd ever read. I did all my work, studied real hard, and man, I wanted this job so bad I could taste it.

My agent was excited. I felt so connected to this role that I couldn't imagine anybody else playing it but me. I was so excited about the entire thing. Everything seemed to be going my way, and I thought I had nailed my audition. I gave it everything I had, and I walked away thinking this job was mine for sure. The next few days were full of anxiety. I was walking on air one minute and then freaking out the next. Finally, my agent called to tell me that I didn't get the job.

I have to tell you, I didn't see that coming. I was devastated. Even though I used things like the mental reminders to get out of the funk, I'd find myself right back in it not long after. I was feeling the same way just this week with the ending of the ninth season of *CSI*. And then I got your letter, saying that you're having a hard time, too. Even though it wasn't a "happy" letter, it came to me as a blessing. You'll find out why soon enough. But back to my story about the role.

For weeks, I walked around with what felt like a huge weight on my shoulders. What made it all the more stressful was that I didn't feel that I could talk about what I was going through. I did try a few times. I confided in a couple of my close friends, but they just didn't get it. I don't blame them, though. When I listened to myself talking about my problems, it didn't sound like I felt. They sounded trivial, not worth the energy I was putting into them. I probably had too much pride to acknowledge how down I really was. But all the shit in my life was making me miserable, and I had no clue how to deal with it. Or pull myself out of it. And you know what was even worse? I bet from some of the things you said to me last night, you can relate to this, too: I felt guilty about feeling down. Isn't that crazy? It's a weird, irrational feeling of thinking I let myself down and all others (family, friends), too.

It seems like you've got a voice invading your thoughts, too. Even in the Black church, there is still so much stigma about mental health and depression. "Fellas shouldn't get down . . . that's some pussy shit. . . ." And I understand that you can't reveal too much to your cellmate or dudes on your cell block. But is it wrong for you to be down and feel sad sometimes? No, it isn't. We all get the blues. It doesn't matter how much money you have or don't have, how good your job is, or whether you are currently a free man or incarcerated. You are allowed to be sad sometimes, because sadness is a part of our journey—but only a part of it.

My former classmate President Barack Obama said it best: "It doesn't mean that you can't get down sometimes. Everybody does. But always remember that being defeated is a temporary condition. Giving up is what makes it permanent." So, you and I need to make a pact. Number one, we're not going to allow other people to project negative energy onto us. Number two, we're not going to beat ourselves up if we do get down sometimes.

Okay, enough about what could be wrong. Let's focus now on what you can do to make it right again. When I was going through the blues, one of the things that kept me going was simply moving my body and breaking a sweat. I'd go out and play football, shoot hoops, whatever I could do to get those endorphins traveling through my system. I know you said the only thing you feel like doing is staying in your bed and you've been skipping your daily exercise hour, but, man, you've gotta figure out a way to motivate yourself to do it, even when you don't really think you're up for it. What I realized was that the times when I *least* felt like exercising were the times when I *most* needed to exercise.

> There is nothing "weak" or "soft" about having the courage to ask for help.

When we do feel down, we're not going to wallow in it; we're going to do something about it. We're going to seek out professional help and counseling if it's available to us. There is nothing "weak" or "soft" about having the courage to ask for help. And you know what's a testament to all of this? This letter. Writing to you on this plane has elevated my spirits. I'm no longer anywhere near as down as I was when I began writing, and it just proves to you that giving and receiving mental reminders works. Ya see, man, maybe you're helping me out more than I'm helping you! Thank you.

THE BLUES VS. DEPRESSION: RECOGNIZING THE DIFFERENCE

You're probably wondering what the difference is between the blues and clinical depression. Well, the short answer is that one is a temporary emotional response to a set of situations or circumstances; the other is a more prolonged condition. It's still an emotional response, but it lingers because of the chemical changes that have taken place in our bodies.

In other words, all those challenges that melted into each other to create that huge "everything" you wrote about may have been what brought you down, but what's keeping you down and "checked out of life" may be a chemical imbalance. The mind is part of the physical body. Every hormone or chemical that exists in our bodies affects our moods and our mental state.

Every change that we have in our mood is either caused by or will bring about a shift in our body's chemical levels. When we're mad or frightened, our adrenaline levels increase, making the heart race. When we exercise or play sports, our body releases endorphins, which have been proven to spark a certain type of happy feeling.

I want you to know all of this because you were so damn hard on yourself on the phone last night. Your words were hard for me to hear because I know they're not true. That's bullshit, man! And somewhere deep down, you know that.

There is good in every person, and I have seen the good in you. You care about R. J. and are very concerned for him. You've tried to help some of the new inmates who don't know the unspoken rules of the cell block. And you've been patient in dealing with your cellmate's rants, even when he gets on your nerves. That's what bothers me most: the fact that whatever you're going through is hindering your ability to see yourself as you really are.

Mental health is as important as physical health—maybe even more so, because if you can't function, then how are you supposed to go on with your life? When we're not feeling well, such as when we have a cough or a migraine, we immediately take stock of our condition. We start adding up all our symptoms and trying to match them to an illness. We start monitoring those symptoms to figure out if we're getting better or getting worse. And if we suspect that we're getting worse, we take medicine or see a doctor. When it comes to our mental health, though, we're not conditioned to pay the same attention or to have the same set of responses. We're told by most people to just "deal" or "get with the program," or "take it to Jesus," and I'm sure nobody in your cell block would suggest seeing a mental health professional. So what I'm saying to you is that since you've been feeling bad for several weeks now, maybe it's time for you to make a health service request so you can begin to figure out, with a trained professional, what you're going through.

Whatever you choose to do, and whatever you eventually find out is going on with you, whether it's the blues or clinical depression or something entirely different, I want you to know that you don't have to feel like you're alone or any less of a man. So many folks on the inside and family members on the outside are dealing with the blues or clinical depression. But they get up every day and go through the motions, rather than admitting it.

None of us smile or laugh all the time. And we don't expect to, so we also shouldn't expect to be sad all the time, either. Being sad all the time could mean that you're falling into depression. Life is about moderation, so there is nothing we should be *all* the time. But at the end of the day, one of the best things that I can do to deal with sadness is to give myself a mental reminder. Mental reminders work almost as well as the real thing. That's how powerful our senses are. I'll explain what I mean.

Actors do the mind-body exercise of visualization all the time. It's about evoking what's called sense memory, and what that means is that you use and recall an experience you've had before, through one of your five senses. You think about what something tasted like, looked like, smelled like, felt like, and sounded like. You know how sometimes a song will come on the radio and it'll remind you of a particular time and place, and you start to feel in your body how you felt in that time and place? That's what sense memory is, and it's at our disposal all the time. So when you're feeling down or sad, you can let your senses take you back to times when you felt great and happy. Remind yourself through your senses what you were experiencing at the time. During the twenty-seven years that Nelson Mandela was locked up in prison, he said that he would "mentally stay free" by using this technique of sense memory. You and I really don't have to fall victim to feeling down and sad. We can change that condition.

According to the Mayo Clinic, mild depression often doesn't respond to antidepressants, but severe depression can. Talk therapy can be an immense help as well, although I know it may be tough for you to find a counselor in the prison infirmary. Meditation, mind-body exercises, and pure and simple exercise have also been shown to help with depression, particularly mild depression that comes and goes.

CHANGING THE WAY YOU ACT

When you are depressed, a poor self-image can make a little mistake seem like a huge defeat. Write down your upsetting thoughts and feelings, and the negative events that triggered them, to help you analyze why you are feeling this way. Many experts feel that you can change the way you feel by changing the way

you act. When you're depressed, typically you don't feel like doing anything, but if you can just make yourself get out of the cell and go to the yard for
exercise hour or to the day room, you'll start to feel better. Tell yourself that
what you do *does* count. Make a list of the
things you do each day, and give yourself
credit for them. This is one way to start feeling a little better.

**You can change the way you feel
by changing the way you act.**

When you talked about how you'd
"checked out of life," you said you stayed
holed up in your cell, not really sleeping but
not really doing anything else. You said you even thought about committing sui-
cide a time or two. Now, I'm no doctor, but to me that sounds like a classic case
of clinical depression. Reach out to someone.

I don't want you to isolate yourself so much that you cut yourself off from
people who can help you. If you are having suicidal thoughts, even just toying
with the idea, then you need to go to your health service provider at the prison
infirmary and get some help, no matter what the dudes on the cell block would
say if they found out.

Therapy makes a lot of people uncomfortable, though. There's the whole
issue of stigma. There's also the fear that some people have of talking to a
stranger about their private business. Most of us aren't used to being that vulnerable in front of strangers, but it's no different than taking your clothes off in
front of your physician for the first time. I would think there would be a health
professional, a support group, or at least a chaplain in the prison who could listen to what you're going through. Don't allow judgments to stop you from seeking help if you are seriously depressed and down.

Also, owning responsibility for crimes and developing a sense of remorse for
them have proved to be some of the most therapeutic and character-
building experiences an incarcerated person can have. They also make parole
more likely. You see, once the parole authorities and/or the victims of certain
crimes sense that a prisoner truly understands the consequences of his actions,
they're much more likely to let him out of prison. The Osborne Association
(which has been dedicated to helping incarcerated people through education,
job training, and psychological counseling for eighty years) does not shy away
from the hardest cases inside prison walls.[1] Their Longtermers Responsibility

Project is devoted completely to helping prisoners with long sentences who've committed homicide-related crimes. The treatment method was developed by Kathy Boudin. She was a political activist about forty years ago who was locked up for a crime related to homicide that occurred while she was participating in a bank robbery. Boudin devised the Longtermers Responsibility Project with a professional therapist who specializes in restorative justice.[2]

Members of the Longtermers Responsibility Project keep journals. They also do weekly writing exercises with the whole group. They craft detailed descriptions of their crimes and their role in them, and in vivid detail they try to describe the harm they think was done to victims and their family, friends, and neighborhood. Finally, they write a letter of apology to the family of the victim and devise a plan for making amends and serving their community. They also invite guest visitors who've been victims of a crime to speak to them.

What do they get out of this? Self-insight, a feeling of responsibility for their own actions, remorse, and the clean slate of finally being honest with themselves and others. When they do get released, the Responsibility Project becomes part of their parole plan in the outside world. But whether the Responsibility Project leads to their release or not, it teaches them how to communicate and how to express themselves when it comes to personal relationships. They become more tolerant of other people. They up the odds in their lives for getting along more smoothly with family members, friends, and employers. They begin to feel *connected*.

Do you think there might be a similar organization in the state where you are? I just hope you're on the same page as I am with this, and don't think I'm accusing you of doing anything you did not do. What interests me about the Responsibility Project is that it makes people truly aware of who they are and, maybe for the first time, reveals the links between their actions and their consequences. Hey, here I am ready to sign off and it's already midnight. I should sleep like a corpse until the alarm goes off at five fifteen A.M. I'll try to mail both these letters on the way to Central Park in the morning.

Much love,

Hill

P.S. Just as I was about to send this letter to you I was speaking with my friend Chloe Flower. She is one of the world's best classical crossover pianists. I told her about how much you like music and she wanted to write you a short note.

Dear Brother,

Music can be utilized not only for passive listening but, more importantly, for inspiration and healing. I hadn't really thought of music in this capacity, and I started to realize I had kind of taken it for granted.

Even before Hill told me, I *knew* that you like music because there isn't anyone in this world who doesn't appreciate music in some capacity. You see, music's greatest gift is its lack of prejudice. Music is not the monopoly of the elite or the wealthy, but rather the right of *all* people, rich, poor, Black, white, healthy, sick, free, or incarcerated. And you can use music, a free and easily accessible resource, to improve the quality of your life.

Historically, classical music has been associated with old, white, wealthy Europeans. But you know what? This last year alone, I have done classical collabs with popular musicians like Nas, Céline Dion, Timbaland, Beyoncé, Smokie Norful, and Babyface. And I wasn't there as a traditional pop session musician, playing four chords over and over again. Instead, I fused my classical-music knowledge with their pop records to create a unique and innovative sound.

Music has the ability to provoke profound emotional and mental reactions in humans. That is why I suggest listening to classical music or even your favorite popular music as much as possible, especially when you are feeling anxious, depressed, angry, sad, or negative. Certain musical chords possess the unique ability to instantaneously alter your mood without your even realizing it. It can change your brain chemistry in seconds and produce mood-altering chemicals like endorphins and serotonin, similarly to exercise and sun exposure. Music is the shortest path to the feeling of happiness, compassion, and empathy. Both within the walls of a prison and outside, it can help create a culture of respect and compassion.

And even if you don't have access to technology, you can still enjoy music. You can hear it in your head, sing it in your cell, make your own beats, or just listen to it on any device you can get.

Because I don't know your personal music preference, I chose some classical pieces that I am pretty certain you will enjoy. You will know if your brain likes them when you see the hairs on your arm rising during those "goose bump moments." Although many music therapy playlists are motivated by personal preference, the musical elements of a song are actually more relevant than your musical taste when it comes to affecting your mood and brain chemistry. What I mean by "musical elements" is the rhythm, chord structure, timbre, and dynamics (louds/softs) of a particular song. These elements in music can quickly trigger very specific emotions such as happiness, empathy, and even sadness.

So check out these songs when you can. Music and any art form can be "freeing."

J. S. Bach: *Goldberg Variations,* aria

"Jesu, Joy of Man's Desiring"

Chaconne in D Minor for violin (or piano)

Henry Purcell: "Dido's Lament," from the opera *Dido and Aeneas*

Ludwig van Beethoven: Symphony No. 9 (he was deaf when he wrote this, believe it or not)

Piano Concerto No. 5, first movement

Frédéric Chopin: Piano Concerto No. 2, second movement (love song)

Pyotr Ilyich Tchaikovsky: Piano Concerto No. 1, first movement

Jean Sibelius: Violin Concerto in D Minor, first movement

Giacomo Puccini: "O Mio Babbino Caro," from the opera *Gianni Schicchi*

Johann Pachelbel: "Pachelbel's Canon"

Wolfgang Amadeus Mozart: Piano Sonata K. 448 (this was found to decrease the number of seizures in epilepsy patients)

Johannes Brahms: *Alto Rhapsody*

Sergei Rachmaninoff: Piano Concerto No. 2 (the third movement is incredible)

Start out with these pieces and let me know what you think! And please reach out to me if you want more listening suggestions. I didn't want to overwhelm you with material, but my list of tear-jerking, goose-bump-causing, gut-wrenching, beautiful classical music is endless!

Yours,
Chloe Flower

MY SYMPHONY

LETTER 24

The Seven C's

To act coolly, intelligently, and prudently in perilous circumstances is the test of a man.

Adlai Stevenson

Happiness is not a destination; it is a way of travel.

—Anonymous

H ello, Brotha,
    Well, it's late here in L.A. A few hours earlier, I was tempted to go on
a late-night run and just clear my mind. But I think I'm just going to crash. First,
though, I feel like writing about a few things.

SUCCESS IS A SYSTEM

In your last letter you wrote, "Hill, man, all I seem to ever experience is bad
luck. Dude, I know it's cliché, but I'd rather have no luck than this fucked-up
bad luck."

    Well, I don't believe in bad luck. I believe that if you change the way you see
yourself, you will change the way you see the world—thus affecting your choices,

actions, and outcomes. Thereby shifting from so-called "bad luck" to planned-for positive results. Making that shift is a lot easier if you embrace what I call the Seven C's.

If you can master the Seven C's, you will find a way to live divinely among the mysteries of the universe. Now, that may sound like touchy-feely bullshit to you, but I promise that it works. Take it from me: I probably have the best "luck" in the world, even though I've had cancer, been in car wrecks, been fired from jobs, had my heart broken—but I am blessed! And it's led to success. It's all in my reaction to these events. Make sense? I hope so.

Success isn't a secret—it's a *system*. I'm on the road a lot and have had the privilege of meeting quite a few interesting people from a lot of different backgrounds. The ones who are successful—the people who've made it in business, the arts, sports, education, or public service—all share some common traits. And they are not things they've been born with or been given. In-stead, they are traits they have worked hard to groom and foster in themselves.

> **Success isn't a secret—it's a *system*.**

I've identified seven of these key traits. They are: courage, curiosity, cre-ativity, collaboration, confidence, character, and completion—I call them the Seven C's. I'm even gonna throw in a bonus C at the end of this letter. And just like the Seven Seas that cover Earth, these C's have global significance. They challenge us, they sustain us, and in the end, they help us to bring out the best in ourselves. So, we're going to build those seven muscles and put you on the way to a fuller, more complete life.

Remember my mentioning Anthony Papa a few letters ago? He got out of prison by developing his talent as a painter (creativity). Joe Loya, author of *The Man Who Outgrew His Prison Cell: Confessions of a Bank Robber*, was able to break the grip of prison and recidivism by changing his mentality, having faith in himself, and rediscovering a talent for writing he'd discovered as a kid and forgotten (confidence). Hurricane Carter, by striving to get an education (curi-osity). Wilbert Rideau, by trumpeting his cause and not giving up until he got himself off death row (completion).

The root of the word *courage* is the Latin word *cor*, which means "heart." How can you be courageous and make decisions from your heart? Well, in some ways you have already shown a lot of courage during your stint in prison. You refused to become a member of a gang, which took a lot of cojones, my man. You wrote to R. J asking for forgiveness, which took guts. Not to mention that you've survived behind bars. Now it's going to require true grit to face a whole new world where almost everything will seem unfamiliar to you. But take heart, my friend. Remind yourself that others have come before you and have successfully navigated the waters of the free world after incarceration.

We spoke about **curiosity** in an earlier letter where we talked about reading and continuing to be informed about the world, being curious about the way others navigate their lives, cook, clean, love, play, work. A base level of curiosity is required to be able to ask the right questions—and only if you ask the right questions will you be creative.

Once you are released, you'll have an even greater opportunity to stay informed. Use your local library, check out as many books as you can, read several national newspapers, take advantage of the Internet on the library's computers. Technologically the whole world has opened up since you've been incarcerated, and you have a lot of catching up to do. Try to see it as a fascinating avenue to exploration, and it won't seem so daunting.

Creativity is another major component of success that's required to solve complex problems. For instance, the forces at work against you when you get out will be complex and vast—so it will require creativity to beat them. You'll need to find housing and a job, and overcome the obstacles and roadblocks to those goals.

And once you get established, I'm going to ask you to come up with an idea for your own business. If you're going to go into video game design, think about creative ways to use your skills. Everything from menus to billboards to Internet ads to business logos makes use of graphic and video game design, so the world is at your fingertips. Be as creative as possible in coming up with ideas for your business venture. The sky's the limit.

Collaboration is key, and later I'm going to devote a whole letter to building your own personal board of directors. They will collaborate with you on your path to success, ensuring that you don't have to go it alone.

Confidence is the fifth piece of the pie, and one that you'll gain over time as you accomplish more of your goals. For the time being, getting a place to stay is priority number one, and after that, finding a job that will cover your basic needs. You'll start to feel more and more confident as you find yourself integrating into the outside world, and that self-assurance will feed upon itself and blossom.

Character is one of the most important keystones of success but perhaps the most difficult to define. Martin Luther King Jr. made a famous statement about it: "I have a dream that my four little children will one day live in a nation where they will not be judged by the color of their skin, but by the content of their character."

Make sure that from now on, when you are judged by the "content of your character," it holds up to the high standard set by MLK and our other illustrious ancestors.

The final C is **completion**. Complete that correspondence course and go on to the next. When you tell someone you'll do something, be sure to do it, and *do it right*. When you begin your new job, complete all your assignments in a timely manner. Finish what you start, and enjoy the sense of accomplishment that this gives you.

One more C that I'm going to throw into the mix is **calm**. *Merriam-Webster's Collegiate Dictionary*'s definition of calm is: "a period or condition of freedom from storms, high winds, or rough activity of water." There will always be storms in our lives, but our ability to find "freedom from storms" will dictate whether we consistently experience "good" or "bad" luck. As I said earlier, most people think the storm or obstacle is just that, but instead, it's how we *react* to it that determines our "luck" . . . our "fortune" . . . our future. Staying calm, refusing to take things personally, and not reacting with anger is an attitude that will help you immensely as you adapt to the world beyond prison.

```
THE
SEVEN C'S
```

Hill—

middle of the night writing you from my dark
ass cell but theres something i really gotta tell
you Hill. i dont know why now or where this is
comin from but i just woke up out of nowhere
and just knew i cant keep lying conning you no
maore. its so hard to keep lying to everybody
even urself. i dont really want you to hate me
Hill but if you do its ok cause i gotta do this.
Those drugs i got nabbed for were moine. im
in here cause of my own decisions and it aint
nobody else fault. i took the stupid chance to
deal drugs not Jordache or no one else. im sorry
i lied to you for so long.

—iB

LETTER 25

Flicking the Switch

If you live without awareness it is the same as being dead. You cannot call that kind of existence being alive. Many of us live like dead people because we live without awareness. We carry our dead bodies with us and circulate throughout the world. We are pulled into the past or we are pulled forward into the future or we are caught by our projects or our despair and anger. We are not truly alive; we are not inhabited by awareness of the miracle of being alive. . . . You are what you are looking for. You are already what you want to become.[1]

—Thich Nhat Hanh, *No Death, No Fear*

My Friend and Brotha,

Thank you. Thanks for being honest with me. Thanks for choosing to be vulnerable and honest. I was just about to help you finally launch into your plan when I got your note. I feel like framing it, and I'll treasure it for the rest of my life! I was hoping I could open your eyes a little and get you to take a deeper, more honest look at your life. I underestimated the amount of courage you had.

Sorry I could only talk a minute when you called a half hour ago, but we are shooting in an area with almost zero reception. I could tell right away you were afraid I'd come down on you for what you'd just written me. Cuss you out or something. Even threaten to break it off between you and me. Excuse me for chuckling. No, no, my man. All I feel is pride in your honesty.

By finally facing the true facts of your arrest, you flicked a switch onto a new life. Yes, that quickly and unassumingly you glimpsed a view of a better identity. A different self than the one you'd been living.

When you sat straight up in bed the other night and admitted responsibility, you were having an epiphany. Just as flicking a switch instantly fills a dark room with light, flicking the switch on your state of mind, which once relied on being bitter, inauthentic, defensive, and full of low self-esteem, shifted the focus of your mind from the unresolved hang-ups of the past to a clear view of the future.

EPIPHANY

What is an epiphany? It comes from an ancient Greek word meaning "to reveal." At the birth of Jesus, when the three Wise Men, or Magi, first laid eyes on the infant, the force of what they were gazing upon made them fall to their knees in worship. That moment of seeing Jesus for the first time is called the Epiphany.

Nowadays, *epiphany* stands for any great revelation or sudden understanding, the moment when a switch flicks on in our mind and immediately clears up a source of confusion. Such moments don't come very often in anybody's life, and you've just had one of them, Brotha. You are, however, only at the *gateway* of a new life. It's like starting afresh and being given another chance—almost like being reborn. Beyond that gate revealed by your epiphany stretches a vast, majestic landscape of achievements waiting for you to explore. Now every decision you make starting at this gate that you have reached will be checked against the blueprint you will create for an increasingly successful life. Yes, I know you're in an environment where everything is programmed to keep you from flicking that switch and to keep you enslaved to the prison mentality. You still have to submit to roll call three times a day, no matter what you're in the middle of, just as you had to do when you were at the max-security joint, but at least there's no roll call with a flashlight in the middle of the night. Nevertheless, you've explained how hard it is to concentrate on a book you're trying to read, or even a letter you're writing, because of the potential threats all around you and the necessity to watch your back. I now understand that you can't even lower your guard during our phone calls because sometimes they eavesdrop on those calls as a routine way of collecting information about cons. The lousy food doesn't help much either; it compromises your energy. I can't, of course, do anything about that, much as I wish I could. But there might be some things dragging you down that I can do something about, such as the guilt you told me you feel about not being able to help your mother when she was abused by your pops, the memories of watching in horror when you were a little kid and asking God to keep her from getting killed. All I can do about that is explain that any child would feel the same way, but it was never your fault, and you have to give that hurt inner child in you permission to move on. Tell yourself it's okay. You're an adult now, and the childhood wounds don't serve you any longer.

If I can do anything to help, it's to give you "permission" to let go of the past, to stop finding fault in it and use it instead as an objective basis for understanding yourself. That's easier said than done, I know. But look at the facts: If I didn't see great potential in you, an enormous capacity for sensitivity and understanding, you would not be my friend. And you *are* my friend, Brotha. The other thing that will help you the most is external . . . and that's positioning yourself to get a job upon your release and then continuing to build your foundation in the areas of your interests. I personally think you should be an entrepreneur and start your own business. I don't want you ever to have to be beholden to someone else "giving" you a job. But more on that later. Have a great night!

Warm regards,
Hill

EPIPHANY

LETTER 26

End Points

If you have a long-term goal for yourself, one that you have imagined in detail, then you are better able to make the proper decisions in the present. You know which battles or positions to avoid because they don't advance you towards your goal. With your gaze lifted to the future, you can focus on the dangers looming on the horizon and take proactive measures to avert them. You have a sense of proportion—sometimes the things we fuss over in the present don't matter in the long run. All of this gives you an increased power to reach your objectives.[1]

—50 Cent and Robert Greene, *The 50th Law*

Hey, Brotha,

      I was sitting at home yesterday thinking about the life plan you want to build, which is really both a career and style of life designed to bring contentment. Lots of times, starting in our mind at the end point and thinking backward from it makes it easier to build a plan than starting with square one. The place that you want to get to is "Me, living with R. J.," and a beautiful end point it is. Starting with a goal or end point and reasoning backward to determine the steps necessary to reach it is an example of backward induction.[2] That's the process of reasoning backward in time, starting with the end point and going all the way back to where you are now starting out. Sometimes, backward induction can help determine the very best sequence of decisions. As explained in a Wikipedia article on the subject, backward induction proceeds by first considering the *last time* a decision might be made and determining the most logical choice for such a decision based on the probability of your desired result. The process continues backward in your mind step by step, until you've determined the best decision for every step in the process . . . at every point in time.

Every action we take has a probability of success or failure, based on the particular life situation we are in at the moment we make the decision. The same decision can be a good one at certain periods in your life and a bad one at others.

For example, let's say you got out of prison two months ago and your end point is to form a family with R. J. This end point is all you can think about. You have no savings at all and suddenly have to choose between a steady, low-paying job that would not make enough to support R. J. and a much higher-paying job being offered by a friend of your aunt that would give you enough money to support R. J. but that you aren't sure you have enough training for.

In this situation, I'd strongly counsel you to take the "bad job" until you had savings and more experience and had earned the trust of your community. Now, let's keep the same end point in mind and imagine that you've already been out of prison for several years, have been working at the bad job and saving money, and now want to quit that low-paying job in hopes that a better-paying one will work out for you. I might advise you to take such a risk if you have enough savings to fall back on, especially since you need more money to support R. J. So at some point, you'll need the good job, because the bad job will never make it possible to support R. J. The big question is, when is the *optimum moment* to switch jobs? We'll keep talking about this after your release when the job issue is right in front of you.

Hill

FINISH
TO START

LETTER 27

Warm-ups

If you spend too much time warming up, you'll miss the race. If you don't warm up at all, you may not finish the race.

—Grant Heidrich

Have a plan. Follow the plan, and you'll be surprised how successful you can be. Most people don't have a plan. That's why it's easy to beat most folks.

—Paul "Bear" Bryant, legendary football coach

Dear Brotha,

You wouldn't believe where I am! Remember that gig in Romania shooting a movie I mentioned a while back? It's a modern-day Western that's mostly being shot in the Carpathian Mountains (where Dracula supposedly flourished), to save money, of course. So, howdy, cowboy, from the "Wild West" of the InterContinental hotel in Bucharest, Romania's capital, where they've left me on my own for a few days as they finish the location scouting. That gives me time to devote to your plan. Let's start with some warm-ups.

WARM-UP 1: SETTING A GOAL

I think you know the drill at this point. Your goal has to have some kind of appropriate relationship to where you are right now. For example, why would someone who's designed great furniture for a home-furnishings company be happy mapping out a path that puts him at the head of the accounting department? So, Rule 1 of setting your goal is that it should be *well thought out*. Now, if someone just starting out wants, for example, a career in sports, he'll need to create a plan that's flexible enough to get him into the business without banking on being at the top of it in the beginning, or even on the field. With 450 pro basketball players, 750 Major League Baseball players, and just shy of 1,700 NFL players, the odds of making the pros are slim at best. Most pro players have been training their entire lives—their bodies, minds, and talent—for excellence in these pursuits. Since childhood they've put in hours and hours of training. So it would be foolish of me to say now, "Oh, I want to play pro ball." But perhaps I could work in the executive offices of the team, if that was my passion. I may have to start washing dirty socks in the locker room, but that would be my first step. That brings us to Rule 2 of setting your goal: You need to be *flexible* about the outcome.

Let me be clear here: I am not telling you that you have to bail on your dreams. Just the opposite! Chase that dream hard, and work your ass off to make it happen. If you're an active participant in your own life, you will lead a life free of regret, no matter where the journey brings you. Take me, for example; I played football in high school and was pretty good. However, I'm not over six feet and don't top a hundred eighty-five pounds, so my chances of making the NFL were always pretty slim. But I loved the game, and I played hard, and that effort got me recruited to play at Brown University. If it wasn't for football, a small Ivy League school in Rhode Island probably wouldn't have been on the radar for a kid from Iowa. I

> **If you're an active participant in your own life, you will lead a life free of regret, no matter where the journey brings you.**

went to Brown because of football, but once I landed there, I got to know a whole new world—lots of new worlds—including exposure to the theater, acting, politics, and economics. I followed my passion—football—and even though I didn't get an NFL career, following my passion led me down the right path and exposed me to new doors to walk through. So that's what I meant by Rule 2 and staying flexible. You need to be adaptable, in other words! We need a foundation that's wide enough and thick enough to support not only the end goal, but all of the steps needed to achieve the goal and the possible variations that could come during the journey in pursuit of that goal.

WARM-UP 2: QUANTIFY YOURSELF

Okay, my man. Like a boxer getting ready for the big moment, I want you to watch yourself in the mirror taking a few jabs, imagining your own image as the opponent. You'll use your assets to vanquish "his" liabilities. All I really mean to say is that you're going to take a hard, thorough look at your own assets and liabilities. I know we've done that before. This time, however, let's try to be scientific about it. We talked about assessing how we got to be where we are. That involved taking stock of personality traits. Now it's time to dig a little deeper. The more we know about the details of our lives, the more we can adjust our behavior to get it to where we want to be. It's time to live a quantified life.

I'll explain what I mean. Say my goal is to lose ten pounds, and despite switching to nonfat milk, eating less red meat, and doing thirty minutes of aerobic exercise every day, I still can't get close to my goal. Something else is going on, and I need to dig deep to understand what it is.

Gary Wolf, a contributing editor at *Wired* magazine, has developed a system to help in that effort. He calls it the Quantified Self, and he's among a number of thinkers who advocate tracking everything that matters to us in our lives.

Want to lose weight? Log everything that goes past your lips—everything, every drink of water, every peanut, every can of Coke, every sandwich. At the end of a week of this sort of tracking, you would have a pretty good sense of what is really going on in your style of eating. We think we know what's happening within us day-to-day, but we don't. We have subjective perceptions and biases. And these are especially sharp when it comes to how we view things like eating or exercising. This works extremely well for many. Want to save money? I don't care how much or little money you make; if you write down and track every penny you spend, and budget accordingly, you can and will save money if you choose to. (That is if, of course, you earn more than enough for the bare necessities: food and shelter.) The numbers don't lie. If we're religious about tracking ourselves—whether it's a question of learning to eat better and lose weight, learning to exercise better, saving money, or even learning to get more sleep of a higher quality—by objectively *quantifying* everything, we'll get an unvarnished look at what we're really doing.[1] There are all sorts of tools that can help with this process, from pencil and paper to apps for your cell phone or tablet. (Don't tell anybody, but at this very moment I'm wearing the UP wristband that came out from Jawbone. I got it in one of those "swag" gift bags. Usually the stuff in those gift bags is good, but this is really cool. Not only does it tell me how much and how intensely I moved during the day, it also measures the deepness of my sleep by keeping track of how many times I wake up and how restlessly I move while actually sleeping. I'm hoping to use it to up my burning of calories and to get more rest. Let's keep this between us, though.) As Wolf points out, whether our goal is to get fit through more exercise or start a business, unless we track ourselves with discipline, we can't be sure we're staying on the right path. In fact, the data may show us that despite our best intentions, we're actually being *less effective* than we can be.

For example, I found that for me to have maximum productivity, I had to make a list every night for the next day. So each night before I go to bed, I write out a list, down to the minute, of how much time I am allocating for this (writing) or that (exercising) or the other things (dinner with friends). If I don't do that, my days just go from one to the next, and I am not sure what I've accomplished specifically.

And what about your system of quantification as you execute your own plan over the long run? First of all, you can start doing the exact same thing with your time in prison. I want you to begin to sketch out each day the night before. Allocate time for certain activities: reading, writing, exercise, meditation, sleep, daydreaming, practicing new skills (language, writing, or drawing skills). Quantify the amount of time you'll spend on every activity every day inside. This will prevent your days from just blending together.

I suggest breaking your big flowchart into a bunch of smaller ones with shorter-term goals. For example, your flowchart can still start with "Me, Locked Up," but make the end goal something closer. The next step in your chart, as you have it now, "Release," is too big a jump. How about making the end point of this flowchart "Me with a Skill Useful for the Workplace." However, my main point is *how* you'll use your assets to satisfy the goals of the flowchart. Therefore, you need to get hold of, or draw up, a calendar for the coming months with boxes big enough to make notes for each day of each month. In the box for today, briefly "quantify" your education. It should probably say: "Have GED." That's about it. It's your starting point. Then, for *every single day* that follows, list any activity or effort you'll make to achieve your goal of obtaining a GED or an Associates degree, and so on. Keep in mind that these goals will always make it more likely for you to be granted release by the parole board and to survive in that world without coming back.

So, for example, if you manage to order a book that is relevant to your education, in the box representing the day you ordered the book, write something like: "Ordered a book on beginning video game design." On the days in which you've done nothing to further your education, just write a big zero in the box and underline it. Finally, when you have an entry describing an effort at education for a day, after the descriptive phrase in the calendar box, assign a score from 1 to 10, based on the effort expended to accomplish it. Finally, set yourself an educational-goal score for every month, and set it a little higher for each successive month. At the end of the month, add up all your numbers and see if you met, went beyond, or fell short of your goal. Just one more thing: Your evaluations are not about your opinion of the success of your efforts. They're about the *degree of effort* you put into trying to get the education you need every day.

Just remember, my Brotha. All such information that we collect is in the service of reaching our goal. I've included a small checklist for you that you can use to make sure you've stuck to the task of quantifying yourself. Funny, ain't it? This little list will be a way of quantifying your effort at getting educated.

Love,

Hill

GOALS

CHECKLIST

- ❏ I have set up a system to track my behaviors
- ❏ I have rigorously followed the system for a full week
- ❏ I am having "conversations" with myself and make schedules for each day the night before.
- ❏ I am tracking multiple daily activities that are bringing me closer to my goals.

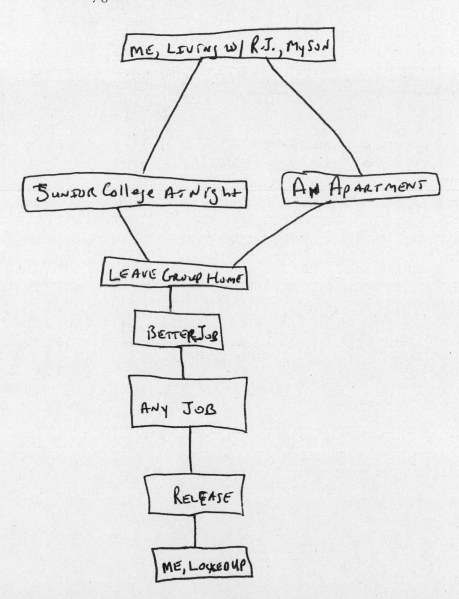

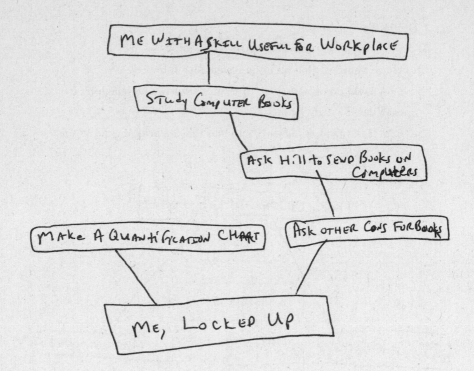

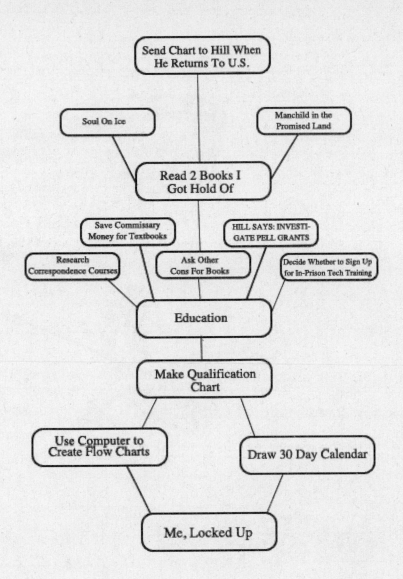

PART 4

BECOMING AN ACTIVE ARCHITECT OF YOUR LIFE

Hill—

i wrote this letter to my son but dont have
the guts to send it. i dont know why im sending
it to you but here it is.

Dear R.J.,

Hey buddy its been a while since weve talked
because of where i am. i know your aunt told
you some stuff but you should really here the
truth from me. im here because i screwed
up. i sold drugs and got caught. Dont make the
mistakes i made dont ever get caught up with
drugs R.J. its not worth it. Look where selling
dope got me. i let down everyone who ever
loved or cared for me and i aint do nothing
with my life. i know you want to see me but
i never wanted for you to see me like this
behind bars like a dog in a cage. i dont even
feel like a man anymore. i should be taking you
to park and teaching you how to hoop. i miss you
so bad and wanna just chill with you. Your aunt
told me that you think its your fault that im

in prison and that breaks my heart its my fault not yours. You didnt do anything wrong and your the newest most perfect model. its hard for me to say this but i need to ask you something do you ever think you can forgive me? For not being there right now for being dummy and sellin drugs taking the easy way out. i know now i wasnt being a real man i was letting you down. if you forgive me since i love you so much thats all i care about. im hoping you say yes. i think about you everyday and wish i could be there with you. Please forgive me for messing up both our lives and if you let me i promise i will make it right.

Love,

Dad

LETTER 28

Developing Your Blueprint

In my country we go to prison first and then become president.

—Nelson Mandela

We are what we repeatedly do. Excellence, then, is not an act, but a habit.

—Aristotle

My Man,

How great it was to hear your voice on the phone last night. I know I sounded a little hoarse from that flu I'm getting over, but hearing how "up" you were was like a tonic for me. But more than that, seeing the letter you wrote to your son blew me away. You are amazing, and I'm so proud of you. I think it's clear that you are more than ready to dive into talking about your blueprint and being an active architect of your own life.

BECOMING AN ARCHITECT

An architect is someone who designs and draws the plans for houses and buildings for a living, right? And a blueprint is what an architect starts with. Just like that guy designing the next twenty-story building, you need a blueprint, too.

A building shown in a blueprint is gradually erected, the structure built. It's the same for your plans for your own life. An architect's goal or dream is to witness a structure that she created in her mind being built in the real world—a structure made of brick and mortar, not just on paper.

ENVIRONMENTAL CONDITIONS

Often even a seasoned architect has to make modifications to a blueprint. Why? To improve it, but oftentimes he has to make modifications because of environmental conditions. You had a plan on paper, but once you went to see the actual land or building site, you realized there was a big rock that couldn't be removed or a beautiful tree that you want to keep. So you decide to modify your blueprint and build around it. You make modifications to your plan based on the environmental conditions that are unique to the property upon which you're going to build. And for the purposes of our discussion, that property is you—your life.

Your "environmental conditions," like boulders blocking the construction of a high-rise, have caused you to make a lot of modifications in the last couple of years. But that's okay; we just incorporate those environmental conditions into our plan.

FOUNDATION

Your foundation is made up of resources such as education and job training. It provides you with support and stability. And as you might think, the size and layers of your foundation are directly proportional to the dimensions of your dream. If you have a thick dream but a thin foundation, the building will collapse because the foundation can't support it.

You've said that your dream—your final goal—is a very big one. You want to be a video game designer. In order to reach that goal, you'll need the money for college. Once you get that, you'll need sophisticated skills in computers, software, and design. So eventually you're going to need some very big foundational elements. The foundation for your goal is education, the money to buy options like education and housing and food while you're being educated, a degree, and proficiency in computers. This is your ultimate foundation.

But there's another foundational element, which is faith. Without faith it is nearly impossible to achieve your goals; you won't get very far. Faith is the mortar that will hold together the bricks of your foundation: education, job training, preparation for your goal of being a video game designer.

FRAMEWORK

Now let's look at our framework, which supports the entire structure. An architect has to decide, given the size and scope of the building, what materials he or she is going to use to create this structure and how thick it will be.

What are the elements of your framework? Your son, your friendship with me, choosing a career you enjoy: All of these elements will rise from your foundation to build a beautiful structure that is airy and open enough to let the light in yet strong enough to withstand disappointments and setbacks.

But remember that your framework has to take environmental conditions into consideration as well. Let me give you a real-life example. I own two apartments, one in Los Angeles and one in New York. They're both roughly the same square footage. Both have roughly the same ceiling height and same number of bedrooms and bathrooms, but they were built by two different architects. The blueprints are relatively similar. The foundations are relatively the same thickness, but the frameworks are completely different. One is made of wood; one is made of brick. Which is which, and why?

The strongest warriors can make modifications to their journey because real strength is flexible and adaptable.

Because of environmental conditions, the New York home is brick, and the one in L.A. is wood. New York winters are much colder than those in L.A. The wind blows, and brick is pretty good at keeping in warmth, right? But in L.A., earthquakes are more likely, so you have to build the framework out of wood because it can bend. It's more flexible than brick.

On the street and in prison, they teach you how to be made of brick, and it's a very rigid structure of "beingness." You've got to "be hard." You gotta be a warrior and move through life with a warrior mentality. But sometimes it's just the *appearance* of being made of brick; sometimes it's just fake swagga and machismo. The strongest warriors can make modifications to their journey because real strength is flexible and adaptable.

Check it out. The best running backs who have the longest careers are not the ones who take the direct hits and just keep going. They're the ones who dodge the hits. *"You ain't gonna hit me. Uh-uh."* Those guys have the longest careers and the most touchdowns because they're malleable and flexible. They aren't "brick-headed."

There's one more detail that's essential to any structure, to any framework or life plan or blueprint, and that is . . .

THE DOOR

A door does what? It lets people in, and it also lets 'em out. A door is essential for the success of any structure, because there are people we need to let in who are essential to achieving and maintaining our goals and dreams. No one can do it by himself. Tiger Woods, the greatest golfer in history, has a coach! Why does he need a coach if he's better than anybody who's ever played? *Because you can't*

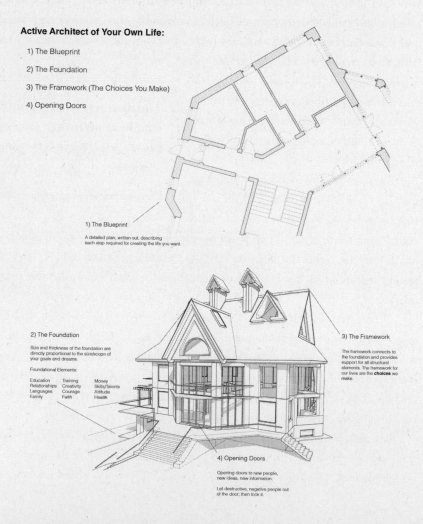

Active Architect of Your Own Life:

1) The Blueprint

2) The Foundation

3) The Framework (The Choices You Make)

4) Opening Doors

1) The Blueprint

A detailed plan, written out, describing each step required for creating the life you want.

2) The Foundation

Size and thickness of the foundation are directly proportional to the size/scope of your goals and dreams.

Foundational Elements:

Education   Training   Money
Relationships   Creativity   Skills/Talents
Languages   Courage   Attitude
Family   Faith   Health

3) The Framework

The framework connects to the foundation and provides support for all structural elements. The framework for our lives are the **choices** we make.

4) Opening Doors

Opening doors to new people, new ideas, new information.

Let destructive, negative people out of the door; then lock it.

do it alone. No matter how good you are. This is where mentors, supporters, family, and other human connections come in.

As for letting people out, there are people whom we have to let out of our lives in order to get where we're going. If we don't, we'll get poisoned, because what they are carrying is "catching"—they're toxic. They will inhibit us from getting to our goals and dreams. They'll lead us right back to the street and then abandon us, letting us go where the day takes us. Those are guys who should be escorted out the door.

These are the key components to being an active architect of your own life, man. Approach them by being proactive, not reactive. That's part of thinking ahead and blueprinting. It's foundation building, having a solid framework. And it's also about bringing the right people into your life and letting out the ones who don't need to be there. On that note, unless you tell me otherwise, I am going to send your letter to R. J.'s aunt to give to him. It's time he heard truth and love from his father. Proud to call you my friend.

Talk soon.

Warmly,

Hill

```
BLUEPRINT
= PLAN
```

LETTER 29

Erasing

The ability to forgive and the ability to love are the weapons God has given us to enable us to live fully, bravely and meaningfully in a less than perfect world.

—Rabbi Harold Kushner

Hey, my friend,
　　You were in the darkest mood on the phone last night. I've never heard you sound so on edge. And you want to know something? I don't blame you a bit, 'cause now that I know why, I feel exactly the same way. Don't think I'm saying I feel hopeless. Fuck no! In fact, when I hear about an injustice, the anger it causes in me acts as fuel and makes me more determined than ever!

Moreover, I have to apologize. At some point, way early in our correspondence, when I was still green about this subject, I mentioned casually that I thought many Pell education grants had been eliminated. That was a prime example of something I've warned you against, opening your mouth or going ahead with a plan without bothering to do the proper research. So before I left for Romania, I said you should look up those grants and apply if they were still around.

Well, *you* were the one who did the correct research, which makes me proud of that mind of yours, man. And as you pointed out, Pell Grants *are* still available—just *not for you*.

Are lawmakers trying to say that they haven't read article after article or book after book by or about incarcerated people—some of whom were locked up for life or were on death row—but who have changed their mentality completely by developing an interest in learning? Or who were even put on death row wrongly? And in every single case, *their* education has benefited *other* people! Some of them I've mentioned already: Martin Luther King Jr. with his "Letter from Birmingham Jail"; or Stanley Tookie Williams, who wrote one of the most impassioned condemnations of gangs shortly before he was executed; and Wilbert Rideau, whose internationally circulated journalism revealed inhumane conditions in prison. Or Malcolm X, and on and on. Isn't that enough proof? As I said, that pre-'94 decree was bad enough, but it pales in comparison to the post-1994 decree, which flatly states that a prisoner cannot get a Pell Grant. This is a case where getting po-

> *Adaptability* and *flexibility* are **two keys to success.**

litically active could make a difference. If we elect different people, we could have different standards. *Everybody* has a right to an education. Everybody!

Okay, so let's modify our plan, because you and me—we decided we're going to be active, creative, flexible architects of our own lives and not let ourselves be defined by the point of view of others. We have the resourcefulness to move on without ever thinking about Pell Grants. And you know why? It's because *adaptability* and *flexibility* are two keys to success. We will take out our pencils and redraw our blueprint right around that lack of Pell Grants, just as if it was a big rock in the way!

TECTONICS

Tectonics is a word used to describe big changes in the layout of Earth's crust, how those crusts shift, and how they change the surface of Earth. And sometimes that means earthquakes. Well, you and I can handle any situation.

Let's be philosophical, man. We know things shift. In fact, things that seem hopeless today get repaired by the universe, even if it takes an earthquake. If you don't believe me, just take a look at one of the most "hopeless" prison-industrial-complex states in the country, Louisiana, which has a higher percentage of people locked up than anywhere else in the *world*. Louisiana is a state that is home to a smaller, even more discouraging world known as Orleans Parish Prison, which is a hell of rats, roaches, suicides, and stabbings.[1]

Now add a single individual to that portrait of discouragement, Leo Hayden, the prison's director of a recent ten-week reentry plan for inmates leaving prison, who brings busy days of coursework in computer training, money management, résumé writing, job interviewing, and anger management to those same cons who used to sleep all day. Hayden knows what he's doing, too. He's a former NFL running back whose interest in drugs sent him up for five years.

These days there has been a giant shift in the prisons of Louisiana. Inmates leaving all Louisiana state prisons get some version of that ten-week program (even though a large population of those incarcerated in Louisiana's local prisons are still sleeping all day). But my point is that, if the tectonic plates beneath the prisons in Louisiana are shifting, and more and more of its wardens and state officials are beginning to admit the value of reentry programs, and if *Louisiana* prisons can begin to change, then just about anything can.

This is a good time to mention that you've got to add a second, parallel branch alongside the one leading to your education as a video game designer. It's time to show it on your blueprint. Running in the same direction as your plans for getting into college is the technical trade you're going to begin to learn.

Didn't you say the new training courses started in a month? So choose your initial, temporary "first" career path now, whether it be plumber's assistant, building maintenance, auto mechanic's assistant, or construction. I've included a copy of the blueprint you sent me with this letter, to show you where to draw in your parallel work survival plan.

And oh, I forgot to mention: It so happened that just when you told me about the Pell disappointment, I was looking into another source for scholarships, and as soon as I have all the info, I'll send it to you. I was saving that one for last. Stay strong, man. Hold tight to the plan. Keep straight and tall, even if the earth trembles beneath you.

Peace and love,

Hill

GRANT YOURSELF

P.S. One last thing, fam. I was on the phone with my buddy Enitan Bereola last night. He's the bestselling author of this contemporary gentleman and etiquette book called *Bereolaesque*. I'd love for you to meet the guy. He has a heart for Brothas and Sistahs. I told him about you and he insisted on sending you something.

Dear Brotha,

It's a crying shame when we live in a world where some men would rather be blackmailed than be a Black male.

By the looks of VH1 you're all dumb. You're full of cum and only interested in drinking Coke and rum with girls barely twenty-one. And though your woman is the one, you can't seem to stick with just one—"some" is more of an adequate sum. And it definitely ain't no fun if the homies can't have none. Your only talent is picking up a football to run or picking up a gun to stun someone, then proceeding to mug someone 'cause that's what a thug would've done. They say women outnumber you in college seats, and you're so used to hearing the word *no* that *yes* sort of sounds like defeat. They'll keep feeding you this BS as long as you're willing to eat because that's what they want you to believe.

My soul bleeds when they say you just move keys and smoke weed because in reality you sow seeds. They say our women just sew weaves slowly while we sell trees, ducking and dodging the police in our big-rimmed, dark-tinted SUVs. They think you're dumb thieves so they put you on blast, *The First 48*—A&E—for all to see and agree. They think you're illegitimate . . . illiterate, can't read—wear watches for shine but can't tell time. That's what they want you to believe.

It was said that if you want to see a Black man on TV, you'd have to turn to *America's Most Wanted*. No, no—all you have to do is turn to CNN and look into the Oval Office. Though you're too frequently overlooked, overbooked, and counted out, I see you and I appreciate you.

I appreciate you for thousands of years of excellence, from pyramids to presidents.

From effort to excellence, if you don't hear it from anyone else—Brotha, I appreciate you. Like all men, you were created in the image of God, so appreciate yourself, and learn to appreciate your neighbor. If you don't give your Brother some time, the system will.

Your family,
Enitan Bereola II

LETTER 30

True Access to Education

He who opens a school door, closes a prison.

—Victor Hugo

The roots of education are bitter, but the fruit is sweet.

—Aristotle

Hey, Brotha,

What'd I tell you? What seemed hopeless a couple days ago certainly has picked up today. I can't promise anything yet; I can only tell you that I'm on a mission—to throw as many possibilities in your lap as I can. But it's up to you to investigate them and see if they pan out.

I got frustrated surfing the web and looking for education opportunities for incarcerated people. Don't get me wrong, I found a lot of them. One of them, which was started at Bard College in New York State, is called Bard Prison Initiative (BPI).[1] BPI creates the opportunity for incarcerated men and women to earn a Bard College degree while serving their sentences. It's the largest program of its kind in the United States and enrolls 250 men and women in prison, with choices of over 50 courses each semester. By 2011, Bard had already granted 157 degrees to BPI participants and enrolled a total of nearly 500 students. The degrees they award are full-fledged, with courses taught by the professors who teach on campus.

In fact, the Bard program has been so successful that it led to the organization of an academic group called the Consortium for the Liberal Arts in Prison, designed to support other innovative college-in-prison programs throughout the country.[2] Now Wesleyan University in Connecticut and Grinnell College in Iowa have similar programs, and they're trying to develop the same thing in ten more states within the next five years.

I looked into those developments and discovered the Alabama Prison Arts + Education Project; a literature-study program in Dorchester, Massachusetts; the Prison Outreach Program at Georgetown; the Lipscomb Initiative for Education at the Tennessee Prison for Women; Marymount Manhattan's Bedford Hills College Program at Bedford Hills Correctional Facility; Ohio University's Correctional Education program;[3] and about five other programs in other states—even the Hudson Link for Higher Education in Prison program at Sing Sing. But I couldn't find a damn thing in your state!

So I went on this website PrisonLinks.com but got frustrated because the links I happened to choose took me to pages that didn't exist anymore. Then I clicked on "Inmate Educational Programs," which took me to what seemed like a grab bag of good information and people trying to sell things. But that's where I also found the Prison University Project, a college made up of a few portable trailers and a laundry facility inside San Quentin State Prison, where about four hundred incarcerated students take twenty different classes as the teacher competes with the noise of dryers and washing machines. And I was thinking, of course, "Damn it, why didn't he end up in Cali to do his bid?"

THE PRISON COLLEGE FUND

Then suddenly—bingo!—my eyes lighted on another link, for the Prison Scholar Fund (facebook.com/PrisonScholarFund). It was their statement of their mission that got me excited: "The Prison Scholar Fund invests in incarcerated students, empowering them to realize their post-secondary educational aspirations, and advocates for correctional reform, bolstering grassroots pressure to amend the Violent Crime Control and Law Enforcement Act of 1994."

There we go. There's always an answer if we stay open and patient and keep searching. It was the list of values I read on that website that really grabbed me. I had no idea what was backing them up, but I loved their attitude.

Let me list what they believe, 'cause I believe the same things. Then I'll clue you in to who's behind some of it.

Here they are:

- Every inmate has the potential to become a law-abiding and contributing member of society.
- Quality education bestows knowledge which unlocks human potential.
- Every inmate should have access to quality education regardless of ability to pay.
- Those most affected by a problem should have the chief hand in its solution.
- We believe in second chances and self-improvement.
- We believe that stripping a person of an education is nothing less than an assault on his or her potential and dignity as a human being, and as a contributing member of society.
- We hope that punishment by educational deprivation will eventually be recognized not only as punishment, but also as a particularly unacceptable form of punishment, one that is literally both cruel and unusual.
- We act on relevant research, we act with common sense, and we act with compassion.

Here's the deal. For every dollar you can get from the scholarship, I'll match it. Then you can take advantage of the correspondence courses that I know are available to anybody with the cash. (Please don't forget the vow we made on the phone a few months ago: "Anything Hill does for me has to be matched or surpassed by something proactive I do for myself." We're in this together 50/50.)

It wasn't until I went to a page on the same website called "Prison Scholars" that I discovered the Dirk Van Velzen Scholarship, which can be used at any "accredited two/four-year college or university in the U.S., for any undergraduate study." To make it more likely to get that scholarship, you need certain personality characteristics: "motivation," "character," "leadership," and "service to others." Sound familiar? In order to apply, you needed to write three essays;

fill out, sign, and date an application; and provide information about your incarceration. All of that was accompanied by a couple paragraphs of application instructions, as well as more tips for success: "The successful candidate will present a well-articulated application and a coherent plan for the use of scholarship funds to further his or her educational goals. This means that you will need to know what college or university you want to attend, which course(s) you want to take, how much it will cost, etc. You will need to research your plan." You can apply every quarter for this scholarship, and they make their decisions at the end of March, June, September, and December. If they do turn you down, you can apply again and again, quarter after quarter.

I went right back to Google and found an application for the fund. You'll find it in the envelope with this letter. But in case any of your homies want to try the same thing, they can ask for an application by mail:

The Prison Scholar Fund
23517 Orville Road East
Orting, WA 98360

Discovering that scholarship certainly helped my outlook. But I kept wondering who was behind it and where the money for it came from. After some digging, I discovered a lot about it. What I found tells you a lot about not only the person behind this scholarship program but the attitudes of certain people on the outside toward those who've been incarcerated.

The Prison Scholar Fund was started by a prisoner just like you, Dirk Van Velzen, who was in the second year of a ten-year sentence for a series of burglaries. He'd managed to get the money to pay for some college credits from Penn State's World Campus by selling calendars made by other guys who were locked up. But when his pops started helping him out, he decided to redirect the funds to help other prisoners.

I don't know if money is still available from that particular scholarship fund, but it's good to know that this kind of thing is out there.

BACKUP PLANS

We can't, however, put all our eggs in one basket by hoping that any one scholarship fund is still available and also hoping that there will be non-Internet course offerings. Or that you'll get moved to a prison that allows access to a computer. We don't need to rely on a "lucky break." We need to handle it ourselves. So we're going to work on that tech training in auto mechanics you've decided to add to your blueprint as a parallel, temporary plan, and hopefully that skill will carry you along in your first months, or year, on the outside. I think it was a good choice. Maybe none of those college courses are available to you now, but as we've discovered so many times before, lessons in growing new skills are everywhere. No lack of funds or public prejudice can keep us from learning.

> **All education, all knowledge, is cumulative and builds personal power.**

For example, the other day, I was reading about Leo Hayden on the website of the New Orleans newspaper *The Times-Picayune*. I found out he has a maxim he shares with all his incarcerated students: "Living justly in an unjust world."

What he means is that, sure, you may have been dealt a shitty hand. But the key is to stop thinking about who to blame for it and figure out what to do about it. One of Hayden's mantras says that the only way to stay out of prison once you get out is to change "people, places, and things."

Finally, keep in mind that education is also a spiritual transformation. You cannot predict all the ramifications of the knowledge you will obtain. What you learn in one area has a tendency to leak into another totally unexpected field and be of help. All education, all knowledge, is cumulative and builds personal power.

Peace,

Hill

SCHOLARSHIPS

THE LOCKED-UP LIBRARY

Mill,

How you doing? Been tryna reach you on the phone for the past few days but keep getting voicemail. call me when you get this cuz theres some really cool stuff happenin. i did some more research on that con from Angola John Haynes. Dude was in for life without parole but came up with the plan for every con who wants to read to stash books in their personal lockers like each one was a shelf in a library. They would pass books back and forth and even have discussion group. They call it "locker Library". Guess what? Thats what i'm gonna do only its gon be called "The Locked up Library". crazy huh? if this shit pops thought i might start locked up university!

we got one con here who knows all about law got an AA in it his law books too. Another dudes moms sends him psych books and he can't get enough of them. then we got a bunch of atlases in our extra shitty prison library that my buddy Scoop want to use to teach us how to read maps and about the world. ~~The~~ Everybody want to help in and teach what they know like you said each one teach one. i gotta give credit where its due you really turned me on to this education shit and im kinda diggin it.

– your educated brotha

LETTER 31

Grit and Grind

If you really want it, you got to work for it and if you work for it, it will work for you, in its own time.

—Lemon Andersen

Once a musician has enough ability to get into a top music school, the thing that distinguishes one performer from another is how hard he or she works. That's it. And what's more, the people at the very top don't work just harder or even much harder than everyone else. They work much, *much* harder.

—Malcolm Gladwell, *Outliers*

Courage isn't having the strength to go on-it is going on when you don't have the strength.

—Napoléon Bonaparte

My Miracle Brotha,

You're on a roll! Never would it have occurred to me that not only could you organize your own circulating library, you could also organize your own university! That may be a first. I've heard of the University of the Streets, but you just founded a self-started and self-run U of P! The University of Prison run by and for cons. Amazing! What's going to be your mascot? Ha! Progress should be recognized and praised, so great job. Now that you've shown me that, though, it's time to raise the ante a little. I think you're ready and can handle it. Working in Hollywood for more than twenty years, I've realized that so many people want to be on the red carpet at the movie premiere, but they don't want to be on the carpet in years of acting class. So many want to be "rich," but they don't want to do rich work. I don't want that to ever describe you or me. That's what this letter is all about.

Reading your letter describing your own Locked-Up Library reminded me of the incredible Johna Haynes and made me go back and look up that article on him in *The Times-Picayune* by Cindy Chang that said, "Angola inmates are taught life skills, then spend their lives behind bars."[1]

I picked up a few more of Haynes's tips for getting your education in prison by any means necessary:

1. Haynes keeps up with technology without a computer by saving news clippings about social media sites like Facebook and Twitter.
2. He subscribes to a trade magazine for chief financial officers of companies he's interested in. In your case, you could get ahold of some magazines about computer programming language, graphic design, animation, or video game design. Just say the word and I'll look into it, get you a subscription to one of them.
3. He keeps flash cards in all his pockets with the new vocabulary words he wants to learn.
4. Having decided he's interested in learning in general, he's widened his reading tastes enormously. The written word has become one of his greatest pleasures. About reading the Japanese novel *The Makioka Sisters,* he said, "I saw the cherry blossoms from Angola; reading is my escape."[2]

There's another important thing Haynes does, but it doesn't really have a lot to do with getting an education. I debated with myself about mentioning it, because I know it's a sensitive subject. But what the hell, we said we'd be honest with each other. Haynes frequently writes letters to his four children full of good, upbeat advice, carefully checked for grammar, spelling, and handwriting. I know we spoke earlier about your corresponding more often with R. J., and I wanted to remind you to do that.

LOOK, MA, NO COMPUTER!

Hey, it's serendipity time again. While you were organizing your Locked-Up Library and university, I started wondering what you could learn about designing games if you don't have access to a computer. Well, I researched a bit and found a website called StackExchange.com, which bills itself as "a fast-growing network of 105 question and answer sites on diverse topics from software programming to cooking to photography and gaming." On a chat board on that site, some professional computer programmers were discussing the possibilities for learning to program *without* a computer. It didn't take long to find somebody taking part in that discussion who began asking exactly what I wanted to know. "I have a friend in prison who wants to learn programming," the post said. "He's got no access to a computer, so I was wondering if people could recommend books that would be a good introduction to programming without requiring a computer."[3] Bingo!

Let me put it this way: In order to design games, you'll have to know quite a bit about programming. And it's important to blueprint your approach to this because all the information could be overwhelming. Start simple and get more and more complex as you learn more and more. Also, it would be ideal if you could get "jump-started" by somebody who already knows some basic stuff about this. According to the discussion I read, even thirty minutes of "jump-starting" might be enough.

To figure out the best way for you to start, I had to wade through a lot of information based on stuff I don't know jack shit about. It brought me to the conclusion that the very best way for you to begin might be by trying some of the activities on another site called Computer Science Unplugged (CSUnplugged.org). Computer Science Unplugged has a very cool collection of free learning activities that teach computer science through games and puzzles that use cards, string, crayons, and lots of running around to simulate actual programming. The activities are meant to introduce students to basic programming concepts like binary numbers, algorithms, and data compression—without too many technical details to distract them. CSUnplugged.org even features a book called *Computer Science Unplugged,* containing twelve of the most-used activities.[4] I had the people in my office print it out for me so that I could check it out. Although it's written from the point of view of a teacher of these activities, even I could understand every word. And I can assure you, Brotha, I'm no mathematical or computer genius!

Anyway, that's why the envelope with this letter is so thick. I stuck the whole 105-page book in there! If there's any grief about the number of books you can have at one time, like there was in the other facility, well, you just tell them it's a long letter! Ha ha.

If you get through that book and want to keep going, check out the puzzles from TopCoder, a company that administers computer-programming contests. Somebody else in the discussion on StackExchange.com recommended them as well for learning programming without a computer. To get hold of some of those puzzles, I had to call up a homie who's a programmer and is registered with the TopCoder.com website, which runs competitive coding "tournaments" with cash prizes. He went to the high school section of the site and downloaded some of the best puzzles. I stuck those in the envelope, too, though I couldn't make head or tails out of 'em. I know this sounds like a lot of work, but that's exactly what I want to talk to you about next.

AMBITION —→ GRIT —→ NEVER QUIT

If opportunity doesn't knock, build a door.

—Milton Berle

Now let's have some fun. Ever watch the Memphis Grizzlies play basketball? My boy, Dana "DD" Davis (RIP) used to work for them. He would have me come to as many of their games as I could and I even met with the players to talk about a lot of the things you and I have been writing about. The Grizzlies got a saying about their approach to things: "Grit and Grind!" With that in mind, I've included a little test for you to take. Don't panic. This test isn't about what you *know*. It's a measure of your grit and grind. The test below is my own creation, but it's inspired by a short scale meant to measure "grit" that a professor, Angela Duckworth, developed with a few other students when she was still getting her doctorate.[5]

I hope this little assessment test will prep you for the hard work ahead and help you set goals and figure out which mental "muscles" need the most work. Take the test, and then ask one of the dudes inside who you feel you can trust to answer the *same* questions about you. Tell him to be completely honest in his assessment, not "try to be harsh" or "try to be nice," just real and honest. Keep the scores a secret until both of you have had a chance to complete the assessment. If both your scores are close—within a couple of points of each other—you have a pretty clear sense of yourself. If there are wide differences, you need to both take a critical look at how you answered the questions and discuss why the perceptions were so different. Just answer each of these ten questions as honestly as possible, keeping in mind that there are no right or wrong answers. They are simply diagnostic questions that will help you shape how you approach the future. Don't judge your answers; just be honest about how *you* access yourself. It is from this honest assessment that we will build a plan for success. So the more honest and open you are the better.

Are you ready? Good. Remember to choose only one answer for each question, and keep in mind that the answers are not always arranged in the same order. So read them carefully. When you're done, add up all the points and divide by 10. The maximum score on this scale is 5 ("BUSTIN' WITH GRIT!"), and the lowest score on this scale is 1 ("GET A GRIP!").

1. I get totally into a new project at first, but usually chuck it in favor of another.
   1. That's me to a T.
   2. I'm mostly like that, but not always.
   3. That's kind of like me.
   4. I'm just a little bit like that.
   5. No way! That's not me at all!
2. Criticize me while I'm trying to accomplish something, and I'll toss it in your lap and say, "You do it!"
   1. That's me to a T.
   2. I'm mostly like that, but not always.
   3. That's kind of like me.
   4. I'm just a little bit like that.
   5. No way! That's not me at all!
3. I've acquired several valuable skills that took months to perfect.
   1. You must be thinking of somebody else.
   2. Maybe one.
   3. I've done that two or three times in my life.
   4. I've got several skills like that.
   5. That describes me to a T.
4. I've left a lot of unfinished stuff behind me.
   1. That's me to a T.
   2. I'm mostly like that, but not always.
   3. That's kind of like me.

    4. I'm just a little bit like that.

    5. No way! That's not me at all!

5. When I want to accomplish something, I really dig in, focus, and work at it.

    1. You must be thinking of somebody else.

    2. Maybe one or two times in my life.

    3. I've been known to do that several times in my life.

    4. Most of the time, that's true.

    5. That describes me to a T.

6. When the going gets rough, I bail. (Have you ever quit something when it got hard?)

    1. That's me to a T.

    2. I'm mostly like that, but not always.

    3. That's kind of like me.

    4. I'm just a little bit like that.

    5. No way! That's not me at all!

7. No matter how into a project I am in the beginning, it often gets boring as time passes.

    1. That's me to a T.

    2. I'm mostly like that, but not always.

    3. That's kind of like me.

    4. I'm just a little bit like that.

    5. No way! That's not me at all!

8. I choose my tasks by favoring those that take the shortest time to complete.

    1. That's me to a T.

    2. I'm mostly like that, but not always.

    3. That's kind of like me.

    4. I'm just a little bit like that.

    5. No way! That's not me at all!

9. I consider myself a hard worker. (I got a fire in my belly and I work hard like that.)

    1. You must be thinking of somebody else.

    2. Not usually.

    3. Sometimes.

    4. Most of the time.

    5. That describes me to a T.

10. When I set a goal for myself, no difficulty can make me give it up.
    1. You must be thinking of somebody else.
    2. Not usually.
    3. Sometimes that's the case.
    4. Most of the time.
    5. That describes me to a T.

Now, add up all the numbers that correspond with your answers and then divide that number by 10 (or another way to do it is to just move a decimal point over—so if the total added-up score was 27, then your Grit and Grind scale score would be 2.7). Make sense?

Now that you've established where you fall in terms of grit and grind, it's time to get to work and shore up those areas where you're weak and build on those areas in which you show strength. I want you to use this score to help figure out how much work you have to do in building up your muscles of resolve, determination, and sustained effort in the face of obstacles. We know that throughout our lives we will always hit obstacles; the most important thing is how we react to them. Studies show that hard work, especially in the face of obstacles, has been the primary factor that separates those who tend to win consistently versus those who tend to lose, or worse still, quit. Having "Grit" and being able to "Grind" are two of the most useful skills you can add to your toolkit of success for the rest of your life. So how do we build them up? How can we get to a 5 on the scale?

Just like any muscle, the way we build up our grit and grind is that we have to exercise it daily. The harder we work in planning out each day and sticking to that plan, no matter what distractions or obstacles come up, the more we are building our grit and grind muscle. If we add a few more minutes of reading, meditation, exercise, prayer, or homework of any kind, we are exercising our grit and grind muscle. If we work on our mind-set/attitude and begin to channel any anger or fear into just focusing more on the task at hand and working harder on completing a given task, we are building our grit and grind muscle. Every time we complete a task that "we really don't feel like doing," we are increasing our grit and grind muscle.

I want your grit and grind muscles to be so big that you become a damn grit and grind bodybuilder. I want people to consider you a grit and grind Olympic champion. But I'll be honest, man, sometimes I'm not sure whether *you* want it.

I hope it's not the case that I want you to be a king, but you want to remain a foot soldier. Because to be a king it takes king-level grit and grind. And you can do it. And, by far, the most beautiful thing about grit and grind is that it's available to everyone and anyone. It's not about how much money you had growing up, what race, what gender, what quality school, family life or anything—grit and grind is an equal opportunity employer. It's open to anyone who is willing to put in the work! And the question I have is—are you? Are you willing to put in a level of hard work and perseverance through obstacles that the next time you or anyone fills out that assessment about you, it comes back a 5 all the way? Come on. For the rest of our lives—let's Grit! Let's Grind!

Much love,

Hill

P.S. Do you like boxing? As I was about to send off this letter I heard a quote from the Greatest of All Time, Muhammad Ali, that I think has a particular relevance to our situation:

> Champions are made from something they have deep inside them, a desire, a dream, a vision. They have to have last-minute stamina, they have to be a little faster, they have to have the skill and the will. But the will must be stronger than the skill.

Ali was not the champion, but an 8-to-1 underdog against Sonny Liston when he said this, and people thought he was crazy. You know the rest.

Let's choose to be champions, Brotha.

```
AMBITION
AND GRIT
```

LETTER 32

FEAR

Over you is the greatest enemy a man can have and that is fear.
I know some of you are afraid to listen to the truth—you have
been raised on fear and lies. But I am going to preach to you the
truth until you are free of that fear.

—Malcolm X

Dear Brotha,
    You surprised me again. Everything was going so well. Your blue-
print is in shape, you got weekly meetings of your "U of P" going on, and your
library is growing. I'm proud of you. But on the phone you said some things
that took me aback a little. A lot of times right before we are going to have a
breakthrough, our fears and doubts pop up, trying to drag us back to our old
lives—just like old friends often try to drag us back to our old way of doing
things.

    Change always brings about fear, but our job is to acknowledge it
and move on. In a completely different way, I'm experiencing the fear and
uncertainty of change myself. For the past nine years, I've had the security
of playing Dr. Sheldon Hawkes on *CSI: NY.* It's been a great job and one that

I'm proud of. But as this season ended, a voice inside me said, "It's time to move on."

The idea of leaving my "safe job" scared me. What if no one else would hire me? A voice of fear and doubt ran through my head. But I acknowledged it and decided to move on anyway. Am I afraid? Yes. Do I still have my bills and employees to pay? Yes. Am I going to move through the fear? Yes. But now you're telling me that you're "tired as fuck" and that you're quitting the auto mechanic technical training course because you want a straight path to your dream of being a video game designer.

I don't get it. What led up to this? You're not a quitter. Level with me. What kinds of frustration have you been dealing with? Does it have anything to do with those

> **Change always brings about fear, but our job is to acknowledge it and move on.**

programming/design puzzles and activities I sent you? Whatever it is, you haven't been sharing it with me, and that sign of distrust saddens me. You can tell me anything, man. That's what a real friend is for.

MICRO-QUITS

There's a term I made up called *micro-quitting*. It refers to the fact that most of us don't make huge decisions all at once that take us off our path. No, most of us make all these little debilitating decisions that ultimately lead us to a place we never wanted to be. Every time we fail to do whatever we can to keep us in the race, to keep us chasing our dreams, we are micro-quitting.

Micro-quits are the small surrenders, the little ways in which we whisper, "No more." Taken individually, they don't seem like much. But over time, these micro-quits add up, and they impact both how you see yourself and how others see you. In some cases, micro-quitting is a skill that we've developed for our own protection. If we didn't quit, we might have to deal with things that subconsciously we don't want to face, so we take the easy way out and walk away. Often this reaction occurs because the challenge we face is an old one, and we just can't believe it's raised its ugly head again. The truth is, most big issues recur. Even the small problems come back in different forms.

The big issue that recurs for me is my fear of losing my acting job and not getting a new one. But in this case, I have some good news: I'll be going away for a bit to start a new job. Yes, overcoming the fear and leaving *CSI: NY* made me available to join another successful show called *Covert Affairs*. I'll be heading down to Medellín, Colombia, to being shooting season four. Yes, God is good, and stepping out on faith works! (When you combine it with a good audition! Ha ha.)

While I'm away, keep maintaining your Locked-Up Library, your technical training, and your programming puzzles. You're embarking on a great journey. It will be hard; it takes a lot of reflection and difficult work, but it will lead to a fuller, happier you. Don't forget that I love you, fam.

Peace,

Hill

P.S. The Honorable Michael Steele, a politician, political analyst, and former chairman of the Republican National Committee, has something to say about taking responsibility for ourselves and not quitting on ourselves. Here's his letter.

Dear Brother,

Young Black men are often told that because of their current circumstances and the difficulties they experience, the outcome of their lives is already predetermined. That their choices are far fewer than those of any other group of men in this country. You will either go the way of drugs and crime, or you'll go through the local cemetery. I heard that a lot as a young man growing up in Washington, DC, and I had to reconcile that against what my heart was saying and what I felt to be true for me.

The first words that I want to say are, "Don't let this one mistake define the rest of your life." We all make mistakes; we all stumble, we all fall, and every experience is a teaching moment in which you realize you have choices that you can make going forward. If you listen to people who tell you that your choices are fewer and fewer with each mistake you make—that your opportunities decrease every time you fall—then you'll never be incentivized to get up. You'll never be motivated to turn that corner in your life that sets you in a new direction and puts you on a different course.

As lieutenant governor of Maryland, often I visited the Baltimore City Detention Center and looked into the eyes of thirteen-to-seventeen-year-old African-American males. I wanted them to know that this mistake, whatever landed them in these circumstances for however much time they had to spend there, would not define the rest of their lives. You are more powerful and empowered than you are made to believe. You have opportunities that you can and should explore for yourself. These are not just words; it's not a pipe dream; it's real. But oftentimes our society and sometimes our own community puts blinders on us that lessen our ability to see those opportunities. And you can fall into the trap of believing that your options are fewer and your opportunities are less important, therefore condemning you to a life in prison, a life on drugs, a life of poor education, before you're thirteen, fourteen, fifteen years old.

My words to you, as you sit here contemplating the clock on the wall and looking at the time passing, are "Take control of that time. Find ways to improve your life, even in this dark circumstance of being in prison." So when the next minute is about to tick by, you'll realize, "That is one more minute I have to do something for me." The next hour is getting ready to tick by, and you realize, "That's one more hour that I have to do something that will change my circumstances. While I'm here in prison, I will work to improve and put myself in a better position."

Freedom is an interesting thing. It's not necessarily having the ability to move from one place to another. Our people learned that in slavery. We were enslaved, and yet in many ways we were free. We were free in our minds to find ways to improve and teach ourselves, and to learn to read and write, even though we were prohibited from doing the things that were of value to us. So when that moment of freedom (as defined by society) occurred, we were ready and prepared. My hope, prayer, and wish would be that you take advantage of this opportunity to free yourself, so when that moment comes and society says, "You're now free," you are truly free and do not fall back into the stereotypes and traps and lowered expectations that have been laid out for you. If you realize that, then just imagine what you can do!

As Black people and as a community, we need to wake up and recognize that sometimes the enemy of our progress and our opportunities can be us. We cede too much control to others. We have to realize that when you look at white America and majority communities around this country, they have no obligation to help us. They have no incentive to do that, especially when they see that we aren't living up to our own expectations for ourselves. We need to wake up and see that the failure of a young Black man is a statement about us as a community. His failure is our failure. We can't put that off on someone else. That's why the way we raise our sons and daughters is so important.

I see a big rise in the number of young Black women who are now being incarcerated. In my first year of visiting the detention center in Baltimore, there were one hundred Black males and three young women in the system. My last year in office, there were still one hundred Black males but also fifteen young women. The number increased fivefold in the course of four years. That says something about us and is a reflection of our community. If we allow that to persist and accelerate the way it has, why should we expect anyone else to intervene on our behalf?

What made civil rights matter was that our community said it mattered, and we pressed the point politically and socially. But in the last forty or so years, we've stopped pressing the point. Oh yes, we have a protest here or there, and that's great. But when it's all said and done, what are we doing systemically to turn around that narrative about us? How do we put pressure on ourselves to define the agenda for this generation in this century, so we don't fall into the same traps and make the same mistakes? So that we're actually making progress in ways that we haven't up until now?

Our parents and grandparents created a pathway for us. My mom had a fifth-grade education; I graduated from Johns Hopkins undergrad and Georgetown law school. What does that say? And now I have two young sons, and it's incumbent on me to make sure their pathway is greater than the one my parent gave to me. Yet that has not been the story consistently across the community. We need to begin to take these issues seriously when you're looking at a million-plus young men incarcerated and over a million on probation of some form. The drug addiction, the AIDS infection rate, the lack of even baseline educational opportunity—that's on us. We need to look at our political and educational leadership—at all those who hold themselves out as leaders—and say to them, "Enough is enough." And bring the pressure to turn this narrative around.

Sincerely,
Michael Steele

NO MICRO-QUITS

MY SON

Hill,

You crazy sonofabitch why didnt you tell me was sending RJ to see me! Your the man and i will never forget what you did for me. That lil lady Lynn is a prize man. imagine going through all that red tape and travel bullshit just so i could see my lil man. i hope she understands how much i appreciate it. She kinda hot too. Anyways i think the visit went really good. RJ was so happy to see me and him hugging me was the best feeling ever. Even writin this now makes get a bit emotional. A few minutes after i was sittin there it hit me who was behind making this happen and it made me feel so bad for the way bugged out on you. i really gotta work on my trust factor. so im gonna go out on a limb and tell you gotta keep between just you and me. cool? i had the weirdest dream the night after i see RJ it was more like a intense memory. i was a youngin maybe 5 or 6 and my pops took me to the circus. i dont know why vern wasnt with us. The thing about it was the feeling i had sitting next to my pops it was powerful and comforting like everything in the world was going to be ok. it was the same feeling me and RJ shared. i miss not having those kind of moments with my pops.

—Your friend and dear brotha

LETTER 33

Allies

No man is whole of himself. His friends are the rest of him.

—Unknown

And even if we are occupied with important things, if we attain honor or fall into misfortune, still let us remember how good it was once here, when we were all together, united by a good-time feeling, which made us better than perhaps we are.

—Fyodor Dostoevsky

Hey, man,

I'm back from South America. Bet you barely noticed the time passing. I figured your reaction to my "surprise" would be waiting for me in the mail pile when I got home. I gotta admit it, I was as excited as a kid opening a Christmas present—even though I knew the present was just gonna be your reaction to what I've done. I would have loved to see the look in your eyes when you walked into the visitors' hall and spied R. J. What was the word you used? *Ecstatic*?

Obviously, you couldn't have been more thrilled. But I'm curious to know how you felt about my making it a surprise without any advance warning. I'll be honest, because we've talked about these problems I'm gonna mention. My reason for keeping it secret and making it a surprise was my fear that your insecurities—those negative voices—would try to take over if you knew about the visit in advance. I figured you'd run around worrying about whether you knew how to act with him, if he'd treat you like his father or even recognize you after more than three years. If you yourself even *knew* how you wanted to act as a father and whether he'd act ashamed when he understood your situation and where you were. That's why I didn't say anything.

From your letter, looks like we both handled it the right way. I'm so proud of you. You've never sounded as happy as you did in that letter! On that note, why don't we take this to another level. Tomorrow, on my landline, I'm going to see if I can rig up one of those recording devices reporters use to do phone interviews. I can't do this too often, but Lynn told me R. J.'s birthday is coming up in six weeks. Maybe you could record a spoken message for R. J., even sing "Happy Birthday." Whatever . . . I'm just feeling good about your being reunited with your son. But the recording will just be a backup, if for some reason they won't let you get on the phone with him live on his actual birthday.

And thanks for slipping your new blueprint into the envelope with that letter. I see you added a door to that blueprint, too, and look who came running through it! You know what you gotta do now, don't you? Write your boy a letter about how much you dug seeing him. Since you're such a good artist, maybe you can slip one of those drawings you do into the envelope for

Your past with your father does not have to be your future with your son.

him. I bet he'll be proud of it. Probably ask the group-home people if he can tape it to the wall or tack it up on the bulletin board.

Follow-up is what I'm talking about. That's something that's not just important in business. You gotta follow up with your family and friends also. Don't you think?

As for the dream, the best thing is for us to talk on the phone about it, unless you don't want to. I know you're a little depressed by the contrast between the dream and real life. But I see that dream as a positive sign about a next step with *your* son. Your past with your father does not have to be your future with your son. You're building a whole new life, remember, and that includes a new relationship with your son and family. That's all I'll say for now.

Can't wait to hear your voice on the phone, Brotha. Will you call me Thursday evening around eight?

Love,

Hill

HILL'S LETTER FOR THE PAROLE BOARD

From: Hill Harper
To: Parole Board

Re: Incarcerated Brother

To Whom It May Concern:

I have known the inmate who appears before you for nearly twelve years. Over the past five years in particular, we have communicated regularly by mail and by telephone. I wouldn't be exaggerating to say that I'm astonished by the many ways he's transformed his mentality and improved his education during our friendship.

You may or may not know that I'm a motivational speaker and author who has written several books containing advice for youth and adults. I'm also the founder of the MANifest Your Destiny Foundation, whose mission is to provide underserved youth a path to empowerment and educational excellence through academic programming, college access skills, and personal development. I think these activities and involvements provide me with the experience needed to evaluate certain key aspects of this inmate's development. Over the period of our acquaintance, he has become an avid reader with a curious mind. He has even mastered the rudiments of computer programming and video game design *without* a computer, using exercises and books that I've sent him. He has been assiduous in attending the automotive technology training course you offer.

He has also developed a plan for a life of success according to certain guidelines I've been sharing with him. These involve developing a detailed "blueprint" containing the steps he'll need to avoid recidivism and become financially independent after his release.

Finally, he has evolved considerably on an emotional and psychological level. He has reestablished contact with his son, currently in a group home, and is planning the steps necessary to resume responsibility for him and, if possible, to live with him.

All in all, I have seen this individual slowly turn away from the destructive values of the street and reform many of the attitudes that led to his incarceration. For the first time in his life, he appears optimistic about his future. For all these reasons, I am asking that you strongly consider granting him an early release so that he may begin living that future in the outside world as soon as possible. I want to do anything and everything in my power to assist him in living a life full of love, happiness, and success. Please don't hesitate to call me with any questions you may have.

Sincerely,
Hill Harper

LETTER 34

Changing Your Tune

In order to break the cycle of incarceration, you've got to go inside yourself and take an honest, unflinching look at the things that sent you to jail. How you built your house. In preparation for curing self-pity, you have to divide the social conditions of your birth and background—which you cannot change—from things you could have changed and still have a chance to. You got to go inside your house, take inventory, and plan its rebuilding.[1]

—Mark Pincus, businessman and billionaire

Change is the end result of all true learning.

—Leo Buscaglia

Dear Brotha,

Man, I know. It's a huge disappointment. You hadn't missed one day of your mechanic's course. You got half the cons in your pod reading and talking about books. I take my hat off to you. The parole board knew about your son's visit, too, and how positive it was for both of you. Then why did you get turned down by parole review?

It's hard to believe that it was just for those three minor infractions. I don't think that sour-faced hack who supervises your porter duties and had the nerve to snitch on you is totally responsible for this. But listen to me: Whatever you do, *do not* seek revenge. Don't even give that hack a sign you know what he did. I doubt that he's the only thing that caused the denial. His word ain't got that much power with those people. If anything, he just helped reinforce what they were going to probably do anyway the first time you ever went up.

I called the warden to ask what I could do that would be more effective. He said a letter of character from me might help a lot. I don't know if they mentioned my sending it. Probably not. So I've put it in with this letter for you to read. Every word of it was sincere, man.

Also, I got on the phone with the head of the parole board and expressed my heartfelt support for you, but he seemed totally unreceptive to what I was trying to tell him. He tried to tell me that releasing you now would be too far ahead of schedule, and it would set a bad precedent for his board. I wanted to say, "Bullshit, you should release more non-violent drug offenders right now." But I didn't; I kept my mouth shut and then I just expressed my confidence in you. I thought they made a mistake and should reconsider. I told him that you're more than ready to be out. I was hoping like hell that your sentence

> **"The temptation to quit will be greatest just before you are about to succeed."**

would be shortened, but it looks like you'll have to serve the remainder of your term. I'm sorry. I know how discouraging that is, but you gotta persist and not give up.

Even though you didn't make parole, the biggest chunk of your sentence is behind you. Just a bit longer and you'll be out. You can use your time to maximize your potential, but you have to make up your mind to keep up the good work. Keep reading, keep taking your correspondence courses, and stay away from the gangs, man! According to an old Chinese proverb, "The temptation to quit will be greatest just before you are about to succeed." Try to keep that in mind when things get rough.

In your last letter, you said that you weren't sure how you were going to be able to find any more courses. So I did a little research. Here are some tips on getting funding for correspondence courses: You can write to the school requesting a scholarship. Or write to local associations, churches, and civic clubs, such as Rotary or Kiwanis, to inquire about scholarships for incarcerated individuals. Many churches have prison ministries and outreach programs, and you can write the pastors a letter requesting a special collection to be made one particular Sunday specifically for your classes. It is also important to try to get good grades in your courses, because those awarding future scholarships want to see that a real effort has been made. Many people change for the better while they are incarcerated, and a big part of that is self-education. The great thing about getting an education while you're in prison is that you're *using* your time instead of just *doing* your time!

> **The great thing about getting an education while you're in prison is that you're *using* your time instead of just *doing* your time!**

DEALING WITH THE PAROLE BOARD

I hope you remember that a week after you got transferred to this farm, you signed a document giving me the right to discuss your situation with any member of the administration—as if I were family. Thanks to that, I had quite a conversation with the warden. I'll tell you about it in a minute, but first I want to make sure you understand how the parole board works.

The warden told me that every state has different procedures, but the general approach is basically the same. Every state has a parole board (or board of corrections), a panel whose job is to conduct parole reviews, or parole hearings. And in a lot of states, including yours, all the panel members must be "qualified professionals"—judges, psychiatrists, criminologists, etc.

However, there's essentially just one consideration that outweighs all the others in choosing the parole review panel. All of them have to have good "moral standing" in their community. They're people who, at least officially, are considered ethical and objective by their peers—people with good public reputations. That said, we both know many governmental appointments can be political in nature. Yet another reason voting is important.

They have a lot of power over you, my man. In fact, from the day you went to prison, all power to determine the length of your sentence and the conditions of your release became the sole responsibility of that panel. The board can make the determination to release an offender on parole, and they can even end the sentence short of the statutory limit or require full service of the sentence—in your case, ten years. The board uses guidelines in making their decision. But they're not bound by those guidelines or any recommendations psychologists, clergy, or anybody else makes. Even the warden. It's all up to them.

I know you started preparing for your parole review six months before the actual hearing, which is the minimum in your state. The warden told me it takes that long to prepare and process the information file that the voting board will use to make their decisions. Sometimes they call what the parole board gets a "parole packet" or "parole plan." Included in it are things that work on your behalf, like my letter in favor of your release, any certificates or degrees you might have earned, evaluations by the prison counselor or from a member of the clergy if you see one and any social workers you might have been in contact with, and a short report from your teacher of automobile technology. (By the way, I felt like a fool when I kept asking the warden about the prison's "mechanic's" training, until he realized what I was talking about and said they call it "automobile technology.")

Your record of arrests is part of it, too, of course, but in your prison, so is your record of "inmate conduct." Apparently, every time you infringe on a rule or break your prison's code of inmate conduct, it's written up on your record as a violation and sometimes accompanied by a disciplinary report. They keep a record of the disciplinary actions you receive for any infringement, whether it was just a reprimand, or a fine, or having some of your privileges suspended (exercise in the yard, visits to the commissary or library, for example). Or most important of all, if you were sent to the Hole.

I won't ask you why you didn't tell me about all this, because I think I know why. But during my talk with the warden, I found out, almost by accident, that the reason you still have to do two hours of janitor duty a day is because of several incidents of hostile behavior against other prisoners in the mess hall and with that hack you hate in the corridor. At least, that was *their* version of it.

It got me down that you don't trust me enough to tell me about stuff like that. Please don't think you have to "look good" in my eyes, to the point of lying or concealing stuff. Don't you get it, man? I'm not going to judge you. Our relationship is way deeper than that. That doesn't mean we can't disappoint each other, though. To that point, if the attitude that says "good behavior" is not authentic, that's one of the primary reasons that people end up back in prison!

Anyway, now I know why the library they have where you are seemed so incredibly shitty to me. It's not shitty for everybody, but it is for you. The warden told me that in that prison, permission to use the library is adjusted to your privilege level. Your privilege level is based on how many violations you racked up for conduct. Seems that a year ago your library privileges were reduced to half, and then reduced to half of that this year. That means you're only getting the right to visit the library 25 percent of the time you would have been able to without any violations.

No, man, I'm not going to play "angry mentor" and scold you. You're a grown-ass man who is perfectly capable of making his own choices. I don't believe in punishment; people always punish themselves. But I do believe in imposing *responsibility*. That's why I expect you to start putting aside some of your commissary money to pay me back for those two books on video game design I bought and sent to you. I found out they ended up in this prison library because you lost privileges to keep them.

Like I already explained, man, it's not what you do that gets under my skin and fucks me up, it's your lack of trust in me and inability to confide in me about the troubles you're having.

SECOND CHANCE

Let's move on. You probably know this: You were convicted for a second-degree felony, because the amount of stuff found on you was over six grams but under twenty-five (it's different in every state, but that's the way it goes where you were arrested). People serving time for a second-degree felony can only apply for parole every six months after they finish the equivalent of a minimum sentence (which was five years in your case). So you'll be applying again almost immediately, since you need to start the process about six months in advance. Since you're restarting now, the more *positive* stuff you've begun the better, right? Here's what I think you should do:

Keep up the training: Keep up that training in auto technology. If you finish that course and there's time, sign up for a second skill: plumbing, construction, drywalling, machining—even office technologies. I didn't even know they had that last one until I found it out from the warden. Apparently, it involves some computer training—Word, Excel, PowerPoint. It ain't programming or video game design, but that's okay. At least if you took that class, it would give you a chance to get your hands on a real computer, reacquaint yourself with it. . . . And from what I understand, PowerPoint is a very basic design program. You could start with creating some simple designs and go from there. And **read. Read. Read. Read!**

Develop your social communications: Try to keep in contact with R. J., and improve your communication with me and anyone else who can/will support you at your next hearing.

Keep your blueprint going: You know this already, but you've got to constantly revise your blueprint as you acquire new skills, new research, and new connections. I guess the reason you didn't submit one of your blueprint versions to the parole board was because you felt it was too personal, but maybe you should have.

Take the financial literacy course in your prison: This course is mostly about how to figure out a budget. And I know you say you're "no good at math," but that's no reason not to take a math-based course that could have real-world applications for you when you get out. Keep in mind, in order to raise R. J., you will need to know how to manage your money so you can buy groceries, pay bills, and more.

Take the anger management course: I didn't know you were exploding all over the place at hacks and other prisoners, man. I didn't know that your temper had become hair-trigger. Listen. It makes sense. You're on the verge of a new life, you've been dealing with all my challenges, you've reconnected with your son and even dreamed about your father.

Things get tense for everybody from time to time. However, probably more than anything else except drug and alcohol use, you're going to need to keep that in check when you get on the outside. You'll be trying to win back trust from certain people, and that won't help. The parole board knows this, and they're going to take your ability to control negative emotions into account. So take that little course, would you? The warden said it only lasts four and a half weeks.

Start going to Narcotics Anonymous: I'm not saying you're doing drugs. But you're in there on a drug charge. Parole boards need tangible proof, not just a promise. Whether you need to go to NA or not, show 'em that you're willing— willing to go the extra mile. NA teaches good techniques for how to remain conscious of our choices, things that apply to other aspects of your life. Remember, we are on a lifelong *learning* journey! And we can expose ourselves and learn new things everywhere. They may even make NA one of the conditions of your parole, so beat them to it and demonstrate your willingness.

And now, just to release some of your attitude about the fact that I just gave you a bunch of assignments, count to three, and repeat after me:

"You fucking suck, Hill! This is bullshit! But I'm gonna do it."

Feel better?

TALKING LIKE THEM

You know, Brotha, all the research about parole I looked into made the point that parole is a privilege rather than a right. I'm not sure how I feel about that point of view, but at least it clues me in to the mentality of those who'll be judging you once again. And that's something we can't change, whether we like it or not.

Am I putting this first parole denial all on your shoulders? No. A good deal of it has to do with the personality of the people who were on that parole board, even the mood each of them was in that day. I've already mentioned some of the things *you* can do to make them react differently the second time around, but there's more. This may sound stupid, but in many ways, all they want you to do is act and talk like *them*. That even holds true for future job interviews, etc.

I'm not only talking about your clothes or your hair or teeth at that hearing— although they count, too. Unfortunately, in the world we live in, impressions are used to determine too many things. It's superficial, isn't it, that the way a guy looks can determine his fate?

You know what's more important than that in creating a first impression? The way a guy *acts*. Our bodies have a kind of language that we unthinkingly manipulate to show off our background, our mood, even our moral sense. If you strutted into that parole board with the jail walk you learned to ensure your survival on the street or in prison, they'd react to it. They'd be seeing gestures and rhythms of movement they associate with their stereotypical ideas of a "gangsta." We obviously don't want that, do we?

And you know what's even more important than grooming or how you move? *Speech, language!* Throughout my life, I've noticed what a strong (in so many ways false, but yet also real) marker it is for social status, intelligence, economic class, identity, and treatment by others. I never mentioned it, but it's one of the reasons I've been urging you to read, read, read! The more books you read, the more you get into the habit of thinking the kinds of thoughts people who write have. And your language is always considered a reflection of the thoughts running through your brain.

I'll prove it. There was a skinny little personal assistant, a PA, to one of the actors on my old show who'd grown up dirt poor on the streets of East L.A. His father worked in a factory. He himself wore a kind of hip-hop look. Hadn't even finished high school. But during every free moment he had on set, he never took his nose out of a book. He was reading the classics—Shakespeare, Melville, Dickens, you name it.

I used to like to converse with the dude because he knew so much and understood so much. But as I did, I always chuckled a bit to myself. He'd spent so much time living in great literature that even when he spoke spontaneously his speech sounded like literary speech, almost like a book.

Don't get me wrong. I don't see anything wrong with that, and I admired the guy. And he wasn't putting on an act. Even though he'd never gone to "formal school," he was more intelligent and learned than most people I went to Harvard with. And the amazing thing is, people treated him that way. They assumed he went to a top university. He was repeatedly offered different job opportunities and invited to events and gallery openings because he was not only a nice person, he was interesting to speak with because he educated himself and carried himself accordingly. Oftentimes perception creates our reality.

I wanted to tell you about that because this little PA in his thug threads impressed everybody and won their trust immediately just because of his *voice*. They called him "Li'l Professor." He now is a successful film, TV, and music video producer.

The voice is a powerful instrument, Brotha. And parole panels as well as employers want you to sound like *them,* like somebody who never knew the streets or went to jail. That's just how it is.

BRILLIANT MISTAKES

Here's what you need to understand about being turned down by the parole board the first time: Mistakes will be made, trial and error will happen, forging a new path is likely to result in hitting several dead ends before success is met. Don't let that get you down! Planning provides a framework for success, not a direct line. Shit happens, obstacles always come, and we need to be aware (even anticipate) that setbacks will occur. And there's often a pretty valuable "tortoise vs. hare prize" for a guy who makes all of his mistakes early on.

I have another quantification exercise for you to add to your activities: recording progress in your daily journal. You can even make your quantifying calendar part of this one. Just evaluate your performance in a paragraph or list every day, and give that day a score 1 to 10 as to how effective it was in getting you closer to your goals. No need to show your journal to me. You might enjoy adding very personal stuff, as well. Go ahead; take a peek into your own brain. You might be surprised at what you see!

Mistakes will be made, trial and error will happen, forging a new path is likely to result in hitting several dead ends before success is met.

Tracking behaviors is a part of this process; it's the technical side of the conversation with yourself. Information is power. Knowledge is power. The more we know about ourselves, the more powerful we become. And powerful people do not give up. So I don't want to hear any more bullshit about selling drugs when you get out, all right? Be a winner, not a quitter!

Yours,
Hill

GROWTH
MIND-SET

LETTER 35

Unequal Just Us

I've learned that people will forget what you said, people will forget what you did, but people will never forget how you made them feel.

—Maya Angelou

Hey,

Yes, Brotha. All right, I'm not going to argue with you. If you think there's some loophole for overturning the parole board's decision, and you want to spend part of what might be your last six months locked up trying to find it, then go for it. I say that not because I think it's a particularly good idea, but because there are side benefits. It doesn't hurt anybody to get a bird's-eye view of our legal system and the people and organizations making efforts to change it. What you can learn about law and the courts can be useful any time in your life. That's true for everyone, not just those who've been locked up. Also, there might be others locked up with you who'd benefit as well. Didn't you say one of them was studying law? Well, with all that in mind, here's what I could find out.

CHALLENGING THE JUSTICE SYSTEM

There are various ways of petitioning the legal system while you're in prison and some very well-meaning organizations that might help. Some of them only operate within their own states, but there are a few with a national focus. When it comes to those, however, seems like all of them are interested in prison injustice's of national significance. Though I'm not saying it wouldn't hurt all of us to learn more about them, they usually don't take first-time parole denials.

The Equal Justice Initiative is a private, nonprofit organization that offers legal representation to defendants or prisoners who can't afford their own lawyers but think they've been treated unfairly and unjustly by the system.[1] They do a lot of activism in Alabama, where they're located. Good thing, since Alabama's the only state in this country that doesn't provide government-funded legal assistance to prisoners on death row!

I started rummaging around on their site and discovered something that shocked me. Our country had three thousand children age seventeen or younger who've been sentenced to life without parole, and some of them are as young as thirteen. Two different rulings, one in 2010 and one in 2012, are beginning to change all that, thanks partly to the efforts of the Equal Justice Initiative. That doesn't mean that a lot of these kids aren't still being held. They need legal representation to file their cases and offer proof that these laws pertain to them before they can be released. The Equal Justice Initiative is helping with that, too.

Anyway, I called them for you, and they told me I should go see what I could dig up by calling the Center for Constitutional Rights. They're even more global. It's amazing how many issues they focus on. It's almost like they're trying to take on the entire prison industrial complex.

For one thing, they want to abolish long-term solitary confinement that deprives people of health care, human contact, and even the benefits of sunlight. They've filed a lawsuit against the state of California for its use of solitary confinement in Pelican Bay prison. What's the sense of such punishment anyway? Being stuck inside a windowless cell between twenty-two and twenty-four hours a day, having your food slipped through a slot in the door, being denied telephone calls and visits, being taken outside handcuffed to pace around in a circle to fulfill your "recreation" requirement. How does it help anybody?

Anyway, some good soul there reminded me of the book *Jailhouse Lawyer's Handbook: How to Bring a Federal Lawsuit to Challenge Violations of Your*

Rights in Prison. I went to their site at JailhouseLaw.org, and what d'ya know? I found the entire book for free download by anybody. My office will print it out. The book is written in a plain, easily understandable style. I've never seen anything on the subject with so much valuable information. The best parts are all the appendices at the end. They have several kinds of legal forms you can copy, including a sample complaint form. You can read the Universal Declaration of Human Rights and find out about constitutional amendments. There's also a great list of lots of other organizations that offer legal support to prisoners. They clue you in to books and newsletters with information about prisoners' rights. They even have a list of magazines you can try if you want to get publicity for your case.

Another appendix has free book programs I didn't know about. I already told you about Books Through Bars, the place in Philadelphia. Well, there are more than twenty others on that list. Just check out the ones that look promising to you. All the addresses are there, but let me know if I can help once you find something interesting.

What I want to know is, can I send you a book like *Jailhouse Lawyer's Handbook*? Are there any regulations against it? Allowed or not, we have to do everything by the book as we approach the next hearing. I've even heard some bad things about administrative vengeance in prison against prisoners who "get too smart" about the law. The *Handbook* states that,

> A terrible but common consequence of prisoner activism is harassment by prison officials. Officials have been known to block the preparation and filing of lawsuits, refuse to mail legal papers, take away legal research materials, and deny access to law books, all in an attempt to stop the public and the courts from learning about prisoner issues and complaints. Officials in these situations are worried about any actions that threaten to change conditions within the prison walls or limit their power. . . . Prisoners with legal skills can be particularly threatening to prison management who would like to limit the education and political training of prisoners. . . . With this in mind, it is very important for those of you who are interested in both legal and political activism to keep in contact with people in the outside world. . . . It is always possible that organizing from the outside aimed at the correct pressure points within prison management can have a dramatic effect on conditions for you on the inside.[2]

If you were locked away for life without parole, I'd probably encourage you to try every legal strategy you could find. But that's not your situation.

HAVE A PIECE OF THE PI

We need you to get your tech game up by any means necessary. Most any job you take in the future, video game designer, graphic designer, or otherwise, will require some level of technological proficiency. As of this year there are more mobile tech devices in the world than people. I once asked you if you would be allowed to have a programmable calculator where you are? There's a lot you can learn by fooling around with one. I never heard back from you about it, so finally, I talked the warden into allowing me to send one to you. Also, I do have help for one thing. I've been asking around, and I found out you're not going to have to worry too much about finding a computer to practice programming on when you get out. I found a sophisticated one that only costs $35.

No, that wasn't a bad joke. It's called a Raspberry Pi computer, and it's smaller than a pack of cigarettes. The Raspberry Pi Foundation, a charity in the UK, developed it to use for teaching basic computer science to kids in school. The whole idea was so ingenious that a million people have ordered them, hobbyists, professional programmers, everybody. It's a single-board computer with an operating system that can be put on a camera memory card. The new model—I mean the second one to come out—has 512 MB of RAM. You can boot up the amazing little thing on some form of Linux or Debian and even using Google Chrome or the Android "Ice Cream Sandwich" OS (whatever the hell that means, 'cause I copied it from Wikipedia.org, figuring you'd want to know). By the time you get out, it'll probably support Python as the main programming language but will also allow a form of BASIC and Perl.

Keep up the good work!
Hill

LEARNING

LETTER 36

Out There

The worst thing about doing a bid in prison is going home.

—Lemon Andersen

Dear Brother,

You're about to be separated from the prison world. My heart leaps with joy as you prepare to leave these walls and bars behind you and move along your path toward your own version of success and freedom. I'm excited to bear witness to the impact and legacy you will create. I fully expect you to lead an unreasonably happy life. You leave in thirty days. It'll be right after your second tech course, the one on office technology, ends, right? Congrats!

You're probably wondering why I waited awhile with my congratulations the day you wrote me about the panel approving your parole. The answer to that is simple. Both you and I know that the decision of the parole board is just a recommendation. That decision could have been reversed after it was reviewed.

I'm so glad that your prison believes in what I'd call "gradual release." I don't like the idea of their keeping you locked up and in the same prison routine you always had until you walk out of there and start blinking at all that sunlight. If I understood you right, while you wait for release, you must still stay on prison property, but you're also allowed to go outside on supervised work assignments. What was it like walking into that garage on the outside for the first time?

Listen, I'm in touch with other guys who are in prison and confused about the parole process. I jotted down what you said on the phone about the conditions of your parole, and I just want to check my list with you. Don't worry; I'm not doing this to "police" you, but just to learn more about the process. Also, I know it differs from state to state. But if I understood what you explained, these are the conditions you'll be under out there. If they're deemed violated, you get sent back to finish more of your sentence:

- You can't commit another crime of any kind.
- You can't be found with illegal controlled substances on your person or in your home or car.
- You have to attend a treatment-center program related to drug abuse; your social worker on the inside and then your parole officer will give you details. It will include random drug testing.
- At least until your parole officer revises the decision, you must stay home or wherever you are being lodged after working hours.
- You'll start out at a halfway house.
- You'll have six months to get established in a job and get your own living conditions, or you may be sent back to prison.
- You must live within fifty miles of your hometown.
- You must get permission before marrying, moving, changing jobs, or traveling out of state.

WALKING PAPERS

You're going to need a lot of documents, man. So I asked my prison "guru" Cindy Franz to send me a list of documents you'll need along with copies of forms. Maybe that'll be easier than you digging all that up yourself. Although things might be partly different in your state, here's what she says you'll need:

- Birth certificate.
- Release papers (given upon release).

- Proof of education (GED, apprenticeship certifications, or college course transcripts).
- Certificate of Good Conduct (Apparently, if you have one of these, a licensing agency or employer must consider it as evidence that you are "rehabilitated." (Yeah, I don't like that word, either. Isn't the stuff of red tape magical? Ha ha.)
- Résumé.
- Letters of reference (you'll have one from me, one from Cindy, and one from my office assistant Lynn; three should do it).
- Record of arrest and prosecution (rap sheet).

Cindy also sent me this incredible pamphlet from the New York City Bar's Reentry Law Project. It's called the "Small Business Toolkit." I copied down a few things for you:

> You must have acceptable forms of identification to conduct all kinds of public and private business. Also, you will need photo ID just to enter many public and private buildings. The following forms of ID issued by the government are important and, in some cases, necessary to have.[1]

Here they are:

- Social Security card: You can find out how to get it by going online to www.ssa.gov/online/ss-5.html or calling (800) 772-1213 for your local office and information.
- Driver's license or nondriver photo ID: The applications for a license or learner's permit are usually online, or you can call your local Department of Motor Vehicles.
- U.S. Passport Card (with photo): This is a U.S. government ID card that's not the same as a passport and costs less to get. You can't use it for international air travel, but you can use it for border crossings with Mexico and Canada and for entering U.S. ports from the Caribbean. Of course, if you have a regular U.S. passport, that's even better. (I don't think you'll necessarily need both the motor vehicles license or ID card

and the passport or passport card in most situations. One or
the other should be acceptable identification.)

After Cindy told me about the toolkit, I went online and found out you can
download it for free. This is what it claims to be about:

> The toolkit starts with an explanation of the laws that prohibit employ-
> ment discrimination based on criminal records and provides tips for
> getting necessary identification documents and applying for certifi-
> cates of rehabilitation, both of which can be very helpful when starting
> a new business or trying to get a job.[2]

Yeah, I know, it's for people who were released from New York State prisons and who want to start a small business. But it has fantastic information for
any ex-con from any state who wants to work as soon as possible after he gets
out. I'll leave it to you to do some research in the prison library or ask a counselor if your state follows all these procedures and regulations. But check out the
pamphlet. It's in this envelope.

Cindy also tipped me off on how you can clean up your rap sheet. That's all
about expunging, or erasing, certain records of infractions that are either plainly
incorrect or that don't need to be there anymore. Anybody who's been arrested
and fingerprinted has a rap sheet.

Where Cindy lives, in New York State, you just write the Legal Action Center to see it. They publish a pamphlet about it that explains the steps.[3] I checked
several other states I could find on the Internet, and every state seemed to have
a way of doing it. For example, in California, you can get a request form here:
http://caag.state.ca.us/fingerprints/forms/AOCSSCHR.pdf. And if you don't
have the Internet, you can write to:

California Department of Justice
PO Box 903417
Sacramento, CA 94203-4170
Attn: Record Review Unit
(916) 227-3835

I'm sure the librarian or your social worker knows how to find yours. Get
proactive about it and ask, okay? Apparently, there are controls preventing an

employer from seeing your rap sheet without your permission in most states, *unless* it's a certain type of employer, such as government employers (federal, state, and local government agencies) and all law enforcement agencies, child care agencies, hospitals, museums, home health care agencies, financial institutions, schools, and companies hiring school bus drivers and school bus attendants. But then they also added that "hundreds of jobs (including barber, real estate broker, doctor, nurse, and taxi driver) require a state or municipal license." And often, the agency that issues that special occupational license won't let you have it unless you can show that you possess "good moral character."

There are a few licenses that people with criminal records can't apply for—"good moral character" or not. Finally, they explain that even if a prospective employer isn't entitled by law to see your rap sheet without your permission, they can still use a service that does criminal background checks and get some of that info anyway. No, it's not gonna be easy, man. But hey, we never expected or even wanted it to be, right?

BANKS

The toolkit has a chapter on becoming "financially literate."[4] They recommend you open a bank account as soon as you can. Here are the reasons they give:

- Bank accounts are insured by the FDIC (Federal Deposit Insurance Corporation) so your money is safe—up to $250,000.
- Banks make it easy for you to keep separate accounts for personal and business expenses.
- Checking accounts let you take out money by writing a check or using a debit or ATM card.
- When you pay with a check, the check becomes an automatic record that you made that payment.
- Your bank statements can help you keep better track of your money and expenses.
- Banks offer easy twenty-four-hour access to your money with ATMs.
- If you put money into a savings account, you can usually earn interest on that money. It's a good, easy way to save money.

Don't just hand the bank your money, though. Before you open an account with a bank, there are a few questions you should ask first, like whether you need to keep a minimum amount in your account not to get charged, whether there are monthly fees and how much, and whether the account will have overdraft protection. Overdraft protection keeps a check from bouncing temporarily if there's not enough money in your account. But *beware*: A friend of mine racked up a small overdraft, never paid it back, and it mushroomed to five times the amount through interest. He ultimately couldn't pay it and it ruined his credit score.

There's a hell of a lot to think about, isn't there? We can handle it, though. To do that, we want to start working on it now. One thing we should get to immediately is figuring out how you're going to create and use a résumé when you first get out, and how it will change several months into your freedom—when you've had more experience.

Listen, Brotha, you never mentioned it, but you must have some kind of pre-release unit inside that helps you plan your reentry, including where you're going to live. Most of those units have specially trained staff for doing just that. The unit should have updated listings of agencies in the community that'll help you find a job, deal with a drug program, solve a medical issue, whatever.

Before you get out, we need to talk about looking for a job in more detail. Finally, I want to give you some tips about job interviews, too. But since I'm excited—real excited—I'd rather end on that up note. Don't forget to call me tomorrow. I'll be home by eight P.M.

Peace and love,
Hill

P.S. Now that you're just about to be released and I know you're sick and tired of hearing from me, I asked a buddy of mine, Kevin Hagan, who did twenty-eight years in Cali prisons, to write to you about what to do once you're out. I hope you find this helpful.

Dear Brother,

At one time I was a "lifer," and most of the guys I was locked up with were lifers, too. The first thing you have to do when you get to prison is forgive yourself for whatever reason you're in there. You have to look at yourself and do a lot of self-evaluation. Why did I get to this point, why did I do what I did, and what wrong turns did I take? Prison gives you a lot of time to evaluate yourself, but you have to want to do it. You have to get involved in a lot of self-help groups, from anger management to NA and AA to self-esteem groups. Education is one of the biggest keys. If you educate yourself while you're there, you will not only fare better inside, but you can learn to think. I have a philosophy: If you can't think, you can't win.

In the job that I do now, working with youth, that's one of the main things that I try to teach: the importance of changing your way of thinking and building a new culture within yourself. It's important that we keep our family ties strong. Some guys have burned bridges, but that doesn't matter, because if there's love, there is forgiveness. You have to respect your-self, too. That's another thing that is really important. You have to know your triggers: the things that got you to the point where you are. You have to recognize those triggers when they come and be able to deal with them, whether it's by sitting down and reading a book, going outside, working out, or talking to somebody. And try to surround yourself with people who are positive. Even though you're in prison, there are positive people around you. There are a lot of volunteers, as well as people who work there, who are willing to help you.

> **If you can't think, you can't win.**

You also have to feed your spirit. You're going to feel like an empty shell at times; there will always be that little voice inside you asking, "What am I missing?" You need to fulfill the spiritual part of your makeup. It's important that we do that. Learn how to be positive, no matter what the circumstances are. Right now you're in a box, but that's okay. Think outside the walls. See yourself out there in the community; imagine yourself out there with a job and living life. A lot of times I'd put my music on and think about going to the beach, walking in the sand, going to the mountains, spending time with my family, my nephews, my son, my grandson, my sisters and brothers, and things like that. It's very important to do that.

It's also important for a guy to understand himself. That's one of the biggest keys: to know yourself again. Most guys who have gone to jail have lost themselves somewhere along the way, and they need to find themselves again. Inherently, people are not bad. Maybe it was learned behavior, or the people you hung around with influenced you. You need to find that person within yourself who says, "You know what? I'm done with this! Apparently I wasn't too good at what I was doing, because I got caught. So now it's time to turn over a new leaf and find something different to do with my life."

You have to stay positive no matter how many times you go before the parole board. I went to the board twelve times and I was told no eleven times, until they saw that I had a true understanding of what I had done. You have to have remorse and empathy for the people you've hurt—not just for your victim, but for your family as well. Because your family does time *with* you, and they suffer. So it's a matter of getting your priorities straight, getting your mind straight. Your heart and soul have to be in good condition, too. If you don't have those things together, you're walking around in a haze and you're never going to get to the point where you're ready to step from behind those walls.

You have to prepare yourself before you get out; you have to put the work in. Then when you are released, be sure to surround yourself with family and good people. Jobs are hard to find for a guy like me; I'm fifty-some years old, and I committed a felony. But there are people who care about me. I have a nice part-time job; three days a week, I go in and work with youth. At some point I hope to have a full-time job, but you just keep trying, and you never give up. That's my whole philosophy in life: Never quit. I quit on myself once, and I paid the ultimate cost for it, which was twenty-eight years of my life. And I learned from that.

When I was released, it took about three and a half months before I felt comfortable. Now, after two years of being out, sometimes I still have a little residue if I'm in certain situations that remind me of prison, but my therapy is going back into a correctional facility and working in it. That has really helped me to evolve and know that I never want to be in that situation again.

The hardest thing when I got out was dealing with large groups of people who were moving too fast. My sister took me to a store, and I had an anxiety attack because there were so many people bumping into me and crowding; I had to step outside for a little while and regain my composure. And I had to relearn how to live in society again as far as the financial aspects—how to use the ATM, for instance. But it was fun for me because it was new, and I took it as a learning experience. You pay your bills, establish credit, get a car, and just live your life. You have to make those adjustments, and you can't have the prison mentality when you're out here, because it doesn't work.

Be sure to surround yourself with people who help you along. If you don't know something, then ask questions. Get out of that "man box," what we call "Mr. BS." A lot of men are brought up with a faulty belief system: "Men don't cry," "Men don't share their feelings." We have to learn that stuff all over again. It's okay to cry; it's okay to share your feelings. It's okay to talk about it if you're overwhelmed. Don't stay stuck in that mentality, in that box.

If something difficult comes up, there are people I can sit down and talk with about it. You have to learn to enjoy your life and leave prison in prison. Leave that mentality behind you. Nothing's personal out here; there's a different mind-set and a different set of rules. We were out of societal norms, and that's why we ended up where we did. But now it's a matter of setting your mind and sticking to the course.

If you stay ready, you don't have to get ready.

If you're on parole when you get out, you don't have to worry about the parole officer breathing down your neck as long as he sees that you're doing what you're supposed to be doing. My parole officer is trying to get me off on early discharge. I have three years of parole—we call it a three-year tail—but because of what I'm doing out here, he's trying to get me off early. If it doesn't work, I'll have parole until next year, which is no big deal. I don't worry about it because I'm doing everything I'm supposed to.

You can't make up for what you lost, but you can live your life to the fullest, regardless of where you've been. I get up every morning and make it to the gym by five thirty A.M. Then I go to the park and drink my coffee and listen to the birds singing. Life is good.

In closing, I want to say that first and foremost, always be true to yourself. If you stay ready, you don't have to get ready. Treat yourself; don't cheat yourself. Do the programs and have a sense of accomplishment, because there's nothing like the feeling that you've started something and you've finished it. And always finish what you start. Finally, don't let your current situation deter you from being the best person that you can possibly be.

Sincerely,
Kevin Hagan

REENTRY

LETTER 37

A Little Help from My Friends

You get these ideas that, well, ain't nobody going to give me a chance because of my criminal background and my criminal record. It upsets you and it puts you in a bad place in your mind, and you get to thinking, maybe I should do this, or maybe I could pick up a bag and start working at it again. If you try to do it by yourself with a background like mine, it's depressing. It's not good, and you've got to take a lot of no's. But, if you can get networking with a group of people, whether it be churches, organizations that offer reentry programs, you've got a base of people that's trying to work at the same goal, trying to help you. So, that would be a better shot.

—Frank (age at release: forty-four)

Hey, Brotha,

I'm up in Colorado visiting my mom. She lives up here in the mountains and man, is it beautiful. Aspen trees and snow everywhere. I'll be back a week before you get out, though. It's warm and toasty by the fire in the lodge here, but outside, it's blustery and heavily snowing. I've been trying to get the energy to get off the comfortable couch in the lodge, throw on some snowshoes, and hike up Independence Pass. I need to get the exercise I planned on. Instead, I keep sitting here with my eyes moving back and forth between that cozy fire and the door leading outside.

It's causing some musings about what a door can symbolize in a person's life. What it reminds me of the most is the fact that you'll need some doors out there in the world, and some passageways leading in and out of them. You'll need to get more focused than you've ever been in your life on creating strategies and resources for a job search and working up some ideas for setting up a living situation. Have you planned on how you will handle the job prospects that will inevitably come? I know you'll be at the halfway house for a maximum of three months—less if you find a job more quickly. But that doesn't mean you shouldn't be blueprinting and acting on that blueprint right now.

If I sound like I'm kind of in a shitty mood, I'm gonna admit that part of the reason is because I really hated something you were joking about during out last phone call. Unless you *weren't* kidding, and that would be ten times worse. Your homie Benny doesn't seem like the kind of connection who's gonna be very much help to you on the outside. As a matter of fact, hearing about his MO gave me a sick feeling in my stomach.

DEFYING ALL ODDS

It must have just been a bad joke on your part. People do that when they're tense or worried about stuff. You know, you made that remark just as I was about to tell you about much better kinds of connections you can set up for the outside.

When I left to see my mom, I knew time was wastin' and there was a lot to do before you got out. I also realized that so many of the services you need are locally based. Sure, I could have tried looking them up on the Internet until I finally found one in your community. But that didn't seem to be the best use of time in helping you at this point. I'm not going to do any finger-pointing, but I should mention that we're in such a hurry now partly because you've been dragging your feet half the time.

So I put together a pretty daring plan. It came to me when I was reading an article in *The Christian Science Monitor* about Catherine Rohr, an ex-venture capitalist who founded a nonprofit group called Defy Ventures.[1] They run a heavy-duty internship program to help ex-cons succeed as income earners, fathers, and even entrepreneurs and role models in their communities. She's a real game-changer. Belief was crucial to bringing Defy together.

Well, Rohr and her banker and fund-managing buddies managed to raise eight hundred grand and she kicked in sixty thousand of her own bucks to pay the $15,000 annual tuition for these ex-cons, although the article I read in the *Monitor* pointed out that even such a large amount—fifteen grand— is only half the cost of keeping a guy in prison.[2] We live in a crazy world, don't we?

Anyway, what got my noggin ticking was reading that Defy thinks it's *obvious* that a lot of skills you need on Wall Street—like risk-taking, creating networks of information, and managing money—are very similar to what drug dealers and gang members do on the street. Defy wants to educate and encourage them to define and channel those skills into something with a better future.

I know you're not ready to immediately start your own business, but I want you to seriously consider being an entrepreneur. I could absolutely see you running your own businesses—being your own boss. Not beholden to others' whims about hiring, firing, and promotions. But to do it successfully will take more education, planning, focus, and practice than you've ever had to exhibit in your life. Are you willing to make that commitment? If so, like all things, let's begin with the educational phase.

I contacted four well-known organizations that help newly released people avoid recidivism and get on with their lives and talked to them about you. I networked through each organization by asking the guy I was talking to who in the organization he or she thought I should contact next about this or that. It took a little digging, but I made contact with a dozen or so people in all four of those groups via e-mail or phone.

I want you to have the opportunity to learn from professionals who are intimately familiar with postrelease problems and strategies.

So, get ready for some heavy-duty postrelease counseling and information, man. One of the ladies told me that even though your state isn't in her sphere of activity, she knows a lot about what's going on there, too. But as soon as you get access to e-mail and a phone, I need you to take over and reach out to all of them directly. This also counts as a way to hone your own interpersonal skills and friendly social manner. They already know what they need to know about you, but they also don't know quite what to expect. Knock their socks off with your politeness, communication skills, positive attitude, and gentle manner. This is who you'll be reaching out to:

1. Ryan Holly, manager of marketing and recruiting from **Defy Ventures**. You already know who they are.

2. A publicist from the **Delancey Street Foundation**. I believe on the phone you said that you know something about them, too. They're based in San Francisco but have six other locations nationwide. One of them is in your state but farther than fifty miles from your town. Not that much farther, though. It would be so good if you could get your parole transferred nearer and start your life outside with them, 'cause they're legendary. For forty years they've been helping ex-cons with job-skill training in the context of a residency—in other words, they also provide a place to live.

3. An employment counselor from the **Safer Foundation**. In their own words, "For more than 40 years, Safer Foundation's mission has focused on reducing recidivism by supporting, through a full spectrum of services, the efforts of people with criminal records to become employed, law-abiding members of the community." They're located in Chicago. With four thousand job starts in 2011, the Safer Foundation saved the state 152 million dollars. The clients who go to them have a recidivism rate of only 13 percent, whereas the state's recidivism rate is 52 percent.

4. And finally, a manager from the **Prison Entrepreneurship Program (PEP)**, which links people in prison to business and academic talent by using an MBA-level curriculum and fostering mentor relationships. I know they're good, because that's where Catherine Rohr first cut her teeth before she did Defy. In fact, she started PEP. What's more, they can boast 100 percent employment within ninety days, and their recidivism rate is less than 5 percent.

JOB HUNT

Remember Nick Higgins? He's the "correctional services librarian" from the New York Public Library who has been doing so much work to help prisoners. He and a whole bunch of others put together a guide for ex-cons called *The Job Search*[3] and bundled it with their other publication *Connections,* which is "a guide for formerly incarcerated people."[4] It costs $15 by mail, but you can see it free at www.nypl.org/help/community-outreach/correctional-services-program. Lots of it's relevant wherever you are. I love their twenty or so pages on finding a job, because they're packed with practical information that can help you immediately.

One of the coolest resources mentioned in Nick's book is called Huntsy (Huntsy.com), an organizational tool for job hunters. It's an extension you can add really easily to your Internet browser, and then it will guide you step by step once you tell it what job you're looking for. You can even use it to create a time-line of tasks to manage your "job hunt work flow," as they call it. The thing is so simple, but it does so much. It keeps track of interviews you schedule, lets you save more than one version of your résumé, helps you find new contacts, and keeps you in the know about the ones you already have.

First go to a site like CareerBuilder.com or one of the many other job-hunting sites. When you find something you like, you can click on a button on your browser and paste the page's URL into a Huntsy box that comes up. Once you do that, it adds the job to your search folder, which can get bigger and bigger.

I picked up other job-search tips on Huntsy, too. Look for and apply to new jobs every day if you can, and put them in your folder. Add lists of to-dos based on your job search, as well as timed reminders and stuff like that. Keep your search organized and on schedule.

Don't forget to become involved with social networks, either, especially Facebook and LinkedIn. Network with the people there for leads. Huntsy will automatically check them for you if you want. And, remember, it's always easiest to get help from people when you offer help to them as well. If someone is help-ful to you, or even if they're not, find out what you may be able to do to help them.

Here's another tip. If you want to search a lot of job sites at the same time, you don't necessarily have to go to each site. Just go to Indeed.com. You type in the job you're looking for and where, and it automatically searches for it on a whole bunch of sites at once.

RÉSUMÉS

I almost forgot to talk about good ol' résumés. Yours will need to look and sound as good as you really are, because, to a potential employer, it's a written repre-sentation of your skills and even your character. I won't say you're not at a disadvantage. They've done controlled studies about the difference in looking for a job with and without a prison record, and there's a big difference between the two situations. However, as we discussed, we know that going in, so we can plan for those obstacles.

One of the strategies you'll have to learn is how to take the spotlight off the fact that you were incarcerated, without anyone being able to say that you're lying on your résumé. There's a whole load of information in *The Job Search* about that, too. As it says about the incarceration issue, "Show that while in prison, you've done constructive things with your time, not just 'done' time. Mention any educational achievements, for example, or work experience you've had while incarcerated. If you've been involved in any organized prison activities or programs, list them. They help indicate to a prospective employer what you may have experienced while away in terms of personal growth and development."

That's good, sound advice. I'm having my office photocopy that part of the booklet for you. When you know where you are on the outside, I'll have them send it to you. But at the end of the day, the best way to take the spotlight off your former incarceration is your attitude, presentation, preparedness, and patience.

Okay, my man. I don't want all this to make you anxious. I'm just excited you're getting out soon! I know you will make it. Make sure I hear from you as soon as you get out. Just know that I'm behind you and backing you up at every moment.

Much love,

Hill

LIBERATION

P.S.   Since I mentioned Ms. Catherine Rohr from Defy Ventures, which trains former prisoners to run their own businesses, I wanted to include a letter from her addressed to you, below.

Dear Brother,

Most people I've met in prison dream of one day starting a business. It doesn't need to be just a dream. I'm the founder and CEO of Defy Ventures, a New York City–based nonprofit that equips men and women with criminal histories to build profitable, sustainable (and legal!) businesses. When I got started in this work nine years ago, people told me I was crazy to attempt it. One prison ministry "veteran" said to me, "These guys in prison aren't even capable of writing home to their mamas." His comment added extra fuel for me to get out there and disprove the stereotypes. We're showing the world that individuals with criminal histories absolutely can defy the odds, transform their lives, and become home-run entrepreneurs, employers, parents, and community leaders.

I know what it takes to succeed as an entrepreneur, and I've seen firsthand that many people with felonies have exactly the skills it takes to run successful businesses. When you get out of prison, pursuing entrepreneurship is a great option. Unlike a potential employer when you apply for a job, it's unlikely that your customers will ask you if you have a felony. In most industries, you won't face discrimination for your past. No one can take away your right to start a business and achieve the American dream.

There are a lot of misconceptions about starting a business. For example, sometimes people think you have to have a lot of money to launch a business. Not true: Nearly every single one of the one hundred business started by Defy grads was launched on $500 or less in start-up capital.

Another myth: You might think that because you've never had a "normal job" on your résumé that you're lacking the right experience to start a business. Now, having worked with more than one thousand people who were in prison or were formerly incarcerated, I can say with confidence that this definitely isn't true. If you've led a drug ring or gang or participated in other criminal activity, you likely have many of the characteristics needed to succeed as an entrepreneur: charisma that can turn a no into a yes, scrappiness and resilience, a profit mentality, the willingness to take calculated risks, the ability to lead and manage others, and strong customer service and execution skills. By redirecting your skill set to a legal venture, you can still be your own boss and create a legacy for your family and loved ones that you're proud of—and you'll no longer have your life on the line or have another prison sentence hanging over your head.

You, too, can *defy* the odds. You can start building your entrepreneurial dreams now by getting your hands on Steve Mariotti's book *Entrepreneurship and Small Business Management,* as well as *Inc.* magazine and *Entrepreneur* magazine. I also recommend that you separate yourself from the crowds in prison. Work on building your character and taking the high road in the face of conflict.

My main advice to you, though, is to never quit on yourself. Many people who get out of prison and get shot down by ten potential employers just give up—not just on a legal job, but on life. The mark of successful entrepreneurs is that they don't get paralyzed by the fear of failure, and when they do fail or face rejection, they create another possibility and keep trying until they find a solution. As someone who faced serious public failure several years ago and nearly gave up on her own life, I consider myself a seasoned expert in the "field of failure." I know what it means to get knocked down and get back up—even when it feels impossible. I like to pretend that I'm a daddy longlegs spider—go ahead and cut my legs off; I'll keep wiggling, somehow.

If you have that spirit about you, too, you ought to thrive in the pursuit of legal entrepreneurship. Go get it!

Catherine Rohr
Founder and CEO,
Defy Ventures

FROM A FREE MAN

From: IB246@gmail.com
Subject: What up?
Date: November 12, 2015, 11:51 PM
To: Hill@manifestyourdestiny.org

Hey, man, what's up? Check it out. Got my own e-mail. How long since we talked? I think twice that first week I was out and staying at the fucking halfway house. Then I ducked outta sight for a while. Not that I didn't wanna be in touch, I was just too bushed. Hope you weren't bugged out about it.

They wake you up at six A.M. like you're still in jail or something. By eight every day you're at NA for two hours. Then by ten, I would be pounding pavement with the list I made with that Huntsy app you told me about. Then back to the library for more job research, back home, etc. Yawn . . . Watch TV at the halfway with red eyes (not from weed, from weariness and fallout).

But that was only three times a week. The other two days of the work week, I still had to get up at six, and this time, after NA, go do that underpaid work at the garage they was still making me hang on to till I could move out of there. Well, I'm outta there! It ain't exactly what I thought "freedom" was gonna be, but hell, it's only been a month and a half, and I got me a job. I'm a stock boy at the supermarket, minimum wage and all. But I bet I can convince the manager to make me a cashier after a while, and they get $2 more per hour. He just has to get to trust me.

My room is wack. Sixth floor of a rooming house, a converted S.R.O. The dickhead across the hall is into heavy metal, and some nights I want to bust his door down and go in and let the dude catch the fade! But then—and this is probably thanks to you—this voice comes in and says, "Is it worth fucking everything up for that? Stick to your plan!" So far, I have. Oh, you probably wondering where I can be e-mailing you so late, 'cause the library obviously isn't open. Remember that Raspberry Pi? One of the homies at the halfway gives me a keyboard he don't want when he leaves. I was able to buy a mouse, and I rigged up a monitor from an old cell phone screen. It's tiny and slow, but I got it! Oh yeah, the connection. Well, so happens I can pick up a free connection over here from this café cross the street, and they leave it on all the time. Anyway, this machine is slow for Internet shit, and I'd like to get me a real laptop. But it can wait.

Listen, Hill. Just a little bit a bad shit going on and I wanted your take on it. I had this fucking argument today. Nothing serious, just shouting, but it bummed me out, and I don't know how to deal with it when that happens. Yvette come into the supermarket when I was stocking the soup section. First she's acting all surprised and friendly, like "Oh, I didn't know you were out. How you doin'!?" And that kind a bullshit. But suddenly she remembers you gettin' R. J. out of there to come and visit me, and for some reason, she lost it. Shit came out of her mouth even I wouldn't say. Says she was gonna get custody of him no matter what! When I came back with, "Fat chance!" she starts cussing more and calling me a goddamn jailbird. Says to me, "You think they're gonna let a loser like you get anywhere near R. J.?" Then she comes out with some half-assed threat that she'll come up the fire escape at night and carry him away from the group home.

I hadda laugh when I heard that. R. J.'s almost ten now. She couldn't even lift him, much less deal with any fire escape. She could hardly stand up straight right there on flat ground. Worst was, everybody was looking. Thankfully, the manager was on lunch break. But I'll tell you, I don't want her type around me. She had these pinhole eyes, totally high. Hot pants like some whore, too, though I guess that's her business.

I calmed down after she left. But just a little while ago, I was trying to fall asleep, and I started thinking, what would happen if that skank gets her hands on R. J. again? Over my dead body! I don't want to say it, but I think I'd even do a crime to protect him from her if I had to. I just don't want her messing him up, know what I mean?

So, that's really why I'm e-mailing you. I could call, I thought. But then I remembered you were away for a few days filming *Covert Affairs* again in Colombia. You told me that and I put it on my calendar when

I was at the halfway. I'm organized now. Anyway, it's buggin' me out. What should I do, bruh? I mean, she can't do nothin', can she?

Your homie,
IB

P.S. Haven't seen R. J. yet, but that's almost all I think about before I doze off. Parole officer says something like I need a year to "demonstrate stability," or something like that. All right, I know I got to establish trust again, and I damn well will. Just tell me what to do about this bitch. Sorry for the word choice. I'm pissed.

LETTER 38

Childhood Eyes

I watch people coming in out of prison with the prison face, the prison attitude, the prison fears—their fear of society, of not making it, not having the stuff. Then seeing them in The Castle, our living facility that's supportive and safe . . . well, if you remember those time-lapsed high school biology class movies showing flowers that slowly blossom, that's what you see with these people who come in. They're angry and dislocated from their community, but now they're in an environment that's safe, and they suddenly have a chance in their lives.

—David Rothenberg, founder of the Fortune Society, with a mission to support successful reentry from prison into the community

First days you face after prison may be worse than the sentence.

—Demico Boothe

Hey, Brotha,

    I am so wired right now it's insane. I can't sleep, so, although I just saw you, I decided to write. I'm still buzzed off the fact that after five years of exchanging letters and then calling, we finally met! Feeling like you know someone so well, but meeting them for the first time in person, wow, I hope I didn't seem weird. There are so many thoughts running around in my head. There's so much I want to say and I don't know where to start. I'm so proud of you, man. Shit, I'm proud of us. I feel like I got to walk with you through your prison journey, and today I got to walk with you through the front door of your apartment. Can you imagine that? You're in your own spot. Your place to think, your place to meditate, your place to work your plan.

After all the fucked-up shit you went through—cellmates trying to get you in the gangs, dudes getting shanked right before your eyes, not being able to get online to research the resources I was sending you—you're finally free. I have to say, I'm really proud that you freed your mind while your body was still behind bars. There were times I thought you weren't going to make it, but it was all about your choices. You chose freedom, and now you have it.

You got a nice spot, too. It's small but neat, and you got it pretty hooked up with your drawings on the wall. Have I told you before how talented you are? Have I told you before how much I believe in you? Yeah, I have. I know it's going to take at least three more years to finish your degree, but please, don't quit. Please, man, I'm telling you. The few graphics, games, and web design clients you have are just the beginning. Just think, if you're able to book small jobs now, there's no limit to what you can do once you finish your degree.

As I sit here writing, I'm thinking about several moments throughout the day. You know what really got me? When R. J. came over. I have to be honest, fam, sitting there watching you two read from the comic book you designed for him made me get a little, you know, *verklempt* (that's Yiddish for choked up . . . and no, I didn't cry, so don't try to tease me). Did you see R. J.'s eyes? Did you see the way he looked up at you? Later, when we were playing video games at Chuck E. Cheese, I had to stop for a minute and ask myself, "Isn't this moment, right here, right now, exactly what we had planned?" Yes, blueprints can turn into reality. Plans can become structures.

I know you're a little frustrated that you don't have custody of R. J. yet, but it's a big deal that you do have unsupervised visits. Be patient because the more responsibility you show, the closer you're going to get to that dream. The good news is you're in his life now. You're one man who's going to be there to leave a thumbprint on *his* son's future. You're one man who's breaking a generational cycle.

I want to say this and I want to make sure you hear me—I believe in you.

You have a strong framework and a clear blueprint and I know you can do this, bruh. That's what you have to keep in mind. If you do, you won't be fazed by scenes like poor Yvette caused. That's a powerless person talking, Brotha, and she was pouring out her pain. That's all. I'm sorry it had to be poured on you. But deep down, I think she can see that you're moving toward a surer place of responsibility for R. J., and unfortunately she isn't. I think that's why she's so pissed. She's feeling shame. But you can still love her even if you two aren't meant to be together. Just always remain calm and loving with her. The last thing R. J. needs to see is his parents going at it.

I'm not a complete stranger to that kind of tension, you know. My parents went through a breakup, and as it was happening, the arguments I witnessed as I grew up made me start blaming myself. That's one thing to keep R. J. from going through. He mustn't feel like he's between you and Yvette in that fight. Or, worse, feel like he's the reason for the fighting. The best thing to remember is not to let guilt make you take the rap for anybody. That doesn't lessen the responsibility you should feel for your son. It should only alleviate the guilt. You got a plan to take care of your son. Hold on to your belief in it.

To me, belief seems like the most important thing in the world right now— for both of us. I recently was cleaning out old boxes my mom had kept in storage. She was moving to a smaller place and wanted to get rid of old things. She asked me to come help her and check a few of my childhood boxes to see if I wanted anything. Most of the things I just threw out because they held no sentimental value. But just as I opened the last dusty box, I saw an old notepad and scrawled on the front in my own childhood handwriting was the word "PO-ETRY." The stiff, old notebook almost cracked as I opened it, and I turned to the third page. And in the middle was written a simple poem that ended with this line:

Goals and dreams are one in the same. Just say you *believe* and both you will attain.

I felt that same verklempt feeling and looked at the date in the upper corner. I wrote that poem when I was about the same age R. J. is now. If *you* don't believe, he never will learn to, either. This is the time. This is your moment, for you and your son. I'm so happy to be a small part of it. Let's both believe and move on to write the next great chapters of our lives. Love you, man.

I'm writing all this as a way of saying that whether it's my belief that the young man who wrote that poem, way back when, is still somewhere inside me or the belief in your feelings for R. J. and the possibilities for your future, let's never let the naysayers, haters, and obstacles get us down. They will always be there but we have to hold on to that inner child who believes that *anything* is possible and sees wonderment everywhere. Hold on to your belief tight and never let go! And if you can do that, you give me permission to do the same. All right?

I believe in you,

Hill

BELIEF

LETTER 39

Six Months Later

One Day at a Time

Sooner or later, all peoples experience this transformation. It is through some kind of radical moral conversion that a people finally become fully aware of, and assume total responsibility for, themselves—for everything about themselves, including their past, however racked with subjection; and their present, however constrained by circumstances; and their future, however bleak.

—Orlando Patterson, PhD, quoted in *African American Core Values: A Guide for Everyone*, by Richard Rosenfield

Hey, Brotha,

Happy Easter! I'm back in L.A. I stuck those financial charts that you asked me for in with this letter. Okay? Glad you asked me for 'em. Know why? Because I'm hoping your financial sense will improve a little. Things have changed, haven't they? I'm *so* glad you were able to get into that upholstery course and that you're making pretty good money now. Your crib sounds cool, man. A flat-screen, huh? And a laptop instead of the good old Raspberry Pi? Bet you can't keep the ladies out, ha! But the best thing is that you've managed to save enough money to take two night courses in programming at the junior college. You're on the path!

Also, I'm glad to hear Yvette is in residential treatment for her habit. No, that doesn't mean I think you should try to get back with her. Just that she deserves to heal like anybody does. See how it goes. . . .

Just one thing: No, I do *not* think you should let that dude who works at the upholsterer's with you sell you that living room set. Do you realize what you could do with that $500 dollars? You've got to sock it away, man. When you get R. J. back in a couple of years, think of what you'll need: clothes, food for him, probably transportation to his school, a sitter for the nights you're at the college. You should forget about new furniture for the time being, don't you think?

> **You never reach the end of your accomplishments while you're alive.**

You know, I get the idea you think there's an end point to life's journey. That once you get there, everything is taken care of. You'll have all you want, and there'll be no more struggling. Well, I don't want to disappoint you, but you never reach the end of your accomplishments while you're alive. That's what's so exciting about life.

And you won't have everything in life figured out by the time you turn forty. Nobody does! Just keep making decisions with a pure heart, a clear mind, and a prayerful spirit, and God or the universe will give you all the information you need to have at just the right times. Things will take care of themselves.

WIDER

My Brotha, I think I should tell you about what I see as the next big step. Ever since I've known you, we've been talking about taking responsibility for yourself, envisioning your goal of becoming unreasonably happy, which is cool. But there is a big step beyond that, which I think is even more fulfilling. I'm talking about a wider sense of responsibility, the feeling of serving your community. I learned that after I became well-known enough to realize that people were somehow looking to me to define certain aspects of life. Every one of us media types must be completely aware of that influence—whether positive or negative. For a celebrity to walk around and say, "I'm no one's role model," is asinine and crazy.

Having published those books I did, one thing that's been proven to me is that young people are watching everything we do on the screen and off the screen. They model their behavior after public figures. If we are given this platform as celebrities, how are we using it? Are we using it to do good? Are we using it to do negative things?

I'm not saying that you're a celebrity or that you have to be one. *That's* no measure of value—by any means. We all have value. But for everybody, including you, responsibility for others is arranged around you in concentric circles. The nearest circle of responsibility, of course, is your family; the next circle includes friends; then the people you work with; then your entire community; and finally, your entire people, whose fates are inextricably bound up with yours, and not only in the present, but for all of history.

I gotta run, man. . . . Call me.

Love,

Hill

RESPONSIBILITY

P.S. I'm enclosing a letter from formerly incarcerated fellow actor Charles "Roc" Dutton. I did Spike Lee's film *Get on the Bus* with him. I told him about our friendship, and he said he had some advice he wanted to share with you.

Dear Brother,

I've been out of prison for almost forty years, since 1976. The difference between my outlaw days, when I was in and out of penal institutions from age twelve to twenty-six, and yours is that mine were in the 1960s and '70s. At that time, most states were spending tens of millions of dollars on rehabilitation, but the recidivism rate was just as high as it is now. The problem was that when those people were finally released or went out on parole, they went back into the same communities they came from, and those communities were now a thousand times worse off. A lot of guys came home with a degree or a trade and were enthusiastic about being a productive member of society, but when they went back, they faced a worse environment, peer pressure, and their friends wanting them to get back into the life. Not everyone can withstand the pressure that you have to deal with upon release. You have to become a leader, at least in your own life, to be able to deal with what you'll be facing.

Before you're released, making a change in prison doesn't have anything to do with getting your GED or a skill for a job. Real change has to do with your rediscovering your own humanity. If you haven't done that, no matter how many degrees or skills you get, it won't do you any good once you get out. Because if you haven't touched on your own humanity, then killing someone again, getting involved in the drug game, or committing armed robbery is still easy to do. But if you rediscover your own humanity, your psychology starts to transform because you're now a human

> **People who manage to stay out of prison are those who have really rediscovered their own humanity.**

being who's concerned about other people—not just in your community, but people in other countries who are undergoing hardships, as well. You open up your mind and start caring about other people. That is real rehabilitation.

People who manage to stay out of prison are those who have really rediscovered their own humanity. They may not become rich; they may be bricklayers, truck drivers, or sanitation workers. However, they are taking care of their kids; they're well respected; they're not living the criminal life. They're relaxed and happy now.

Once you're incarcerated, it's easy to become conditioned by prison life, particularly if you start out as a juvenile. You see the same friends you were in juvenile prisons with when you were twelve or thirteen, and now you're all in your midtwenties or early thirties and are still in prison together; you have been conditioned. Whether you admit it or not, you *like* that shit. It takes a lot of mental toughness to break that conditioning. But you have to ask yourself, "Do I really want this life or am I really tired of it?" And if you're not tired of it, then don't bullshit people; don't bother to go to a self-help program. Why bother to get your GED or get a trade? You're just doing all that to make it seem like you're being positive. But in your heart, you still are connected with all that negativity, and you haven't changed. However, once you're tired of it, then you have balls enough to tell your buddies, "I'm sick of this shit. I've been doing this for twenty-five, thirty years, ever since I was a kid—so don't ask me to hook up with you on those drug deals. I want to spend the rest of my life taking care of my family and myself and being a productive citizen. I'm trying to be a better person." As soft as that may sound in that warrior world you're in, if you're a *real* tough guy, you'll be able to say that and still get respect.

My friend Walter Lomax did thirty-nine years in the Maryland state penitentiary for a crime he did not commit. He was finally released when a judge looked at his case and the DNA. I went in and out of prison four times, and every time, Walt was still in there. He could have been bitter about it, but from the minute he was incarcerated, back in 1966, his sole purpose was to try to get out. He bettered himself while he was in there, because he always had the belief he was going to get out one day. He didn't join a program just to make himself look good; instead, he discovered his humanity while he was in prison. And once he was released, he didn't carry a grudge. He went right out and started trying to help incarcerated people throughout the country who were innocent. I'm in awe of his perseverance and discipline.

I understand how difficult it is to stay out of prison. I understand how the forces beat you down, particularly in these times, which are so much worse than they were when I got out in 1976. Recidivism is the same as a drug addict's relapse, although drug addiction is a disease. There is nothing you can do to help a drug addict until he wants to help himself. You can do all the talking and crying and pleading in the world, but until he's ready to get off drugs, there isn't one single god-damn thing you can do for him. It's the same way with the returning prisoner; you can get him a job, an apartment, but if he ain't ready to stay out, then it's all for nothing.

You have to accept that once you have a criminal record, it stays with you for the rest of your life. There's no sense crying about it; just realize that it's going to stay with you for eternity. That's why you have to tell your son, your nephew, the boy next door, not to ever go to prison, because it stays with you for all of your days.

You fought to get out of prison, and now you have to fight to *stay* out.

I believe that there is a four-to-six-month period after a person is released when they're full of enthusiasm, but then they start to get beat down by their old friends who are still engaging in criminal activities. In today's world, if you go for a job interview and say you have a criminal record, they won't hire you. If you go to the interview and *don't* tell them, and they hire you, then two weeks later they find out, they'll fire you. So it's difficult to get a job and take care of your family. When that happens, before you decide to put a gun back in your hand or scheme on a drug deal, you should volunteer your time with an organization, whether it's church, the NAACP, or whatever. The positive karma of helping people when you volunteer will counteract the negative karma. You'll begin to attract people who will come out of the woodwork to help you. You'll start to get rid of the stigma of being an ex-con by being around people who can be of assistance to you. You're not talking to some guy on the street corner; you're talking to the person who can find you a job, help you out, and give you some direction. These are things that are extremely important once you are released.

You fought to get out of prison, and now you have to fight to *stay* out. Unfortunately, once you get a criminal record, it's a struggle from the cradle to the grave. The struggle is gonna be there regardless of how you feel, whether you feel sorry for yourself, depressed, or happy and upbeat. So you might as well fall in love with

The minute you get out, it's about the moment, now, and tomorrow. How do you make tomorrow better for yourself?

the struggle, because you're gonna have to deal with it and fight it. But if you're insincere in your heart, then you're wasting everyone's time. I would prefer for an addict to tell me, "You know what, I *like* this shit. I *like* being a junkie, so don't try to help me, Roc. I *like* getting high." And I'd rather hear an ex-con say, "I liked being in jail. I'm gonna go back to my old ways." I would prefer to hear that instead of "You know, man, I've changed, I'm positive now. I want to be a productive member of society"—but meanwhile they're scheming and plotting to make money illegally.

It may not seem like having been a criminal has hampered me, but I will admit this. Yeah, when I got out of prison I had my GED and a two-year college degree. Then I went to college in Baltimore and got a degree, and wound up going to Yale University. I went from jail to Yale. I became an actor and was nominated for all kinds of awards: Tony, Emmy, NAACP Image, Independent Spirit, SAG, Golden Globe—every award you could name. And I've won many awards. But through all that, I wasn't allowed to vote in my state of Maryland until the year 2007, when they changed the law. The only time I was allowed to vote was in 2008. That's how my criminal record stayed with me, regardless of what I was achieving. So you have to live with your record, but you have to tell yourself, "It's there, it's my past. I'm not gonna be ashamed of it. I wish I could change it, but I can't, so I won't waste a lot of time on it." What you did is between you and God. You can regret it and weep about it in solitude, but you have to try to get redemption and be a better human being. Then your eyes will be opened up in ways you never imagined.

Once you're released, you can't play catch-up. You can't catch up socially or sexually or monetarily. Unfortunately, those years are gone. You'll never have them again. So you shouldn't play catch-up. The minute you get out, it's about the moment, now, and tomorrow. How do you make tomorrow better for yourself?

Sincerely,
Charles "Roc" Dutton

FINANCIAL CHARTS
Fill out the monthly amounts for each category to see where your money is going.

Monthly Bills	JAN	FEB	MAR	APR	MAY	JUN	JUL	AUG	SEP	OCT	NOV	DEC
Rent/Mortgage												
Car Payment												
Car Insurance												
Life Insurance												
Health Insurance												
Student Loans												
Heating Fuel												
Gas												
Electricity												
Water												
Trash Removal												
Telephone												
Cell Phone												
Tuition												
Vacations/Travel												
Child Care												
Cable												
Gym												

Credit Cards	JAN	FEB	MAR	APR	MAY	JUN	JUL	AUG	SEP	OCT	NOV	DEC
American Express												
Visa												
MasterCard												
Discover												
Store Cards												

Daily Expenditures	MON	TUE	WED	THU	FRI	SAT	SUN
Groceries							
Gasoline							
Car Maintenance							
Public Transportation							
Cabs							
Medical Not Covered by Insurance (Doctors, Co-pays, Pharmacy)							
Clothing/Shoes							
Toiletries							
Haircuts							
Entertainment							
Class Fees							
Books/Magazines/Music Downloads/CDs							
Gifts							
Charity							
Other (Housekeeping, Babysitting, Etc.)							
Other							
Other							
Other							
Other							

TRACKING FOR PERSONAL FINANCES

❑   Set up weekly and monthly finance tracking charts

❑   Assess where cuts can be made

❑   Target savings vehicles

❑   Make sure investments are diversified

LETTER 40

Final Judgment

Don't wait for the final judgment. The final judgment is
every day.

—Albert Camus

Dear Brother,

I had a nightmare last night. You called me and told me you *wanted*
to go back to prison. It sent shock waves through my body. It felt so real. I wonder if it's possible to get so used to a thing—even if it's against your own
humanity—that it becomes more comfortable and familiar than the unknown.
I've heard the stories in life and in movies about the guy who isn't ready to go out
into the world. If I am really to call you my brother, then I should admit that the
greatest fear I have for you is that you've been blinded to your own future. That's
why I've asked if you met yourself five years from now, who would that person
be? Thinking and acting on where you want to be is like a muscle that's got to
be used.

When you have a certain level of comfort—a roof, food, friends, the ability to travel and to have options—you kind of fall into a routine because

you know you got the lucky break this go-around. But it doesn't make life easy and all of us have our demons, and we all create many of our own. Sometimes we mistake our demons for our friends. They may seem like familiar figures, but in reality, they are in fact demons that just hold us back. I know I've been guilty of confusing the two. There's an African proverb that says, "Until the lions have their own historian, the hunters will be the heroes." You

You changed the lives of two men.

and I can become our own historians—changing and making history—but neither of us can if we are imprisoned in cells, real or metaphorical. So make a pact that neither of us will ever mistake our demons for friends or imprisonment for home.

I can't wait until you get back to town so we can hang. I miss you, man. And guess what? My brother Harry called me for my birthday last week. First time in years. And when I heard his voice on the other end, I thought of you. Because I knew that he and I wouldn't be talking, if it wasn't for you inspiring me to reach out to him. You see, you're more powerful than you even know. You changed the lives of two men. Two brothers. I love that we have become friends. And I know there will be

Let's do the work every day.

struggles ahead, but we can face them together and look for as many moments along the way to laugh. Here's to you and the freedom you have given me. And I want to make sure we do everything for you to keep your freedom. Let's do the work every day.

Do you hear me? I need you to stay out of prison. I need you to create opportunities in the so-called free world. You and I are now linked. We are brothers. We are connected in a mutual destiny. My success will be measured by yours. *Your success will prove to be revolutionary.* It will strike a direct blow to systems that have set you up to fail. You will cause fundamental systemic change, just as your failure would have perpetuated the status quo.

By succeeding at your new life, you give me permission to fly higher and succeed at my own.

When you succeed you are saying, "I am not a slave. *I am a man!*"

And yes, my friend, my brother, you *are a man*. I am so proud of you, because you represent the *best* of all of us. I can't wait to see how high you will soar!

Your brother who loves you,

Hill

CONTINUE
TO SOAR

PART 5

ADDENDUM

Dear Brother,

This is *your* owner's manual. I call it that because after you stepped through those prison doors, you became the caretaker of your own life. Just as when you drive a car off the dealer's lot, that car becomes your responsibility and you use your owner's manual to learn how it works, as well as how to take care of it. From now on, you are taking ownership of your life!

I want no excuses; no bullshit; no "If only I would've been born into the right family" or "If only I would've known this or that person." This manual is a nuts-and-bolts guide for the rest of your life. And for the purposes of this manual, no excuses are allowed, because there is enough information and guidelines in this manual for you to build a solid foundation for an extremely successful and unreasonably happy life. The only thing that can stand in the way of that is *you*. Are you going to step up and own your life? If you are, here's the manual.

> **After you stepped through those prison doors, you became the caretaker of your own life.**

Now that you have been released from prison, some of the key components of starting life anew are taking care of your health, continuing your education, getting your finances together, and getting a job. I know I've talked a lot about that in earlier letters, but I'm going to say it again: You won't get anywhere without an education. You have your GED, but I want you to continue taking courses at your community college, at the same time that you're working your first job upon release and also planning the business that you're going to start. I know that this might sound like too much at once, but I know that you can do it, and I'll be cheering you on all the way.

Then the manual takes you through some basic health information, including diet, exercise, what to expect at doctors' checkups, and mental health.

So here's your very own owner's manual to get you in the driver's seat of your life and heading in the right direction!

Yours,

Hill

OWNER'S MANUAL

Dear Owner,
   Judging by the life you have now chosen, you are a member of a special breed. By choosing to follow this manual, you are choosing to change your life for the better. Remember, you are unique, so you must follow these instructions according to your unique capabilities. Read this owner's manual very carefully, because the more you know what needs to be done to be successful, the more successful you will be and the more pleasure you will experience!

EDUCATION
This is the most important functional element for building a successful life. Education and training do not always mean formal schooling. Expanding your education and training is foremost in helping you succeed for the long term.

Education Options
Reading: You are already using the reading list at the end of this book, and there are also trade schools and apprenticeships that you can apply for. Education and training are critical, but there are many ways to get both.

Getting Your GED Through Correspondence Courses
- You can write to the school requesting information on scholarships they offer.
- Write to local associations, churches, and civic clubs, such as Rotary or Kiwanis, to inquire about scholarships for incarcerated individuals.

- Many churches have prison ministries and outreach programs. Write the pastor a letter requesting a special collection to be made one particular Sunday specifically for your classes.
- It is important to get good grades in your courses because those who may award you scholarships in the future will want to see that you have made a real effort.

Trade apprenticeships: A lot of people don't recognize the real value and opportunities that apprenticeships provide. P. Diddy had an apprenticeship/internship with Andre Harrell at Uptown Records, and so can you. Usually, getting an apprenticeship training program means finding a job first. Speak with employers in your chosen trade and find out if they train apprentices.

- For apprenticeships in construction, contact the local joint apprenticeship committee (JAC) of the trade that interests you. A JAC is a volunteer committee that shares information about a specific trade and usually directs people to a technical school where you can obtain applications and information.
- For apprenticeships in manufacturing and service industries, contact employers directly. Talk to someone in each firm's personnel office to find out their procedure for choosing apprenticeship candidates. Sometimes these apprenticeship programs are listed with a job service, with a technical school, or in newspaper ads.
- In large industrial plants, apprenticeships are often open only to workers already employed in the plant. In these situations, you must first be employed by the firm and then seek an apprenticeship.
- Looking for an apprenticeship is like seeking a job. Don't be discouraged if you have to wait to get into an apprenticeship program. Continue your educa-

tion through courses at technical or trade schools. Employers will be impressed by this. Most importantly, be both relentless and patient. If you persist and really try to uncover every opportunity, eventually you can and will land an apprenticeship.

Display your qualifications: Courses taken in school, grades, and any related experience you have had regarding the trade you have chosen should be on the application/résumé.

Go to the library: Check online for free at your local public library or the telephone directory yellow pages for the appropriate trade union and ask about their joint apprenticeship committee application procedure. Nonunion or open-shop construction employers also train apprentices.

YOUR FIRST JOB INTERVIEW

In *How to Make People Like You in 90 Seconds or Less,* author Nicholas Boothman shows that when you first meet someone, your greeting should reflect an open attitude and body language. Here are some tips.

- Be the first to make eye contact and the first to smile.
- Have a firm yet respectful handshake.
- Establish a rapport by giving the person your attention and warmth.
- Synchronize your body language and tone of voice with theirs.
- Have a useful attitude (be cheerful, interested, curious, and warm).

ACCESSORIES, SPARE PARTS, AND MODIFICATIONS TO YOUR VEHICLE

Be sure to dress appropriately when going on interviews. Be neatly shaven and have clean, neat hair. Do not overdo it with colognes, perfumes, or scented oils. A subtle, fresh, and clean scent is always best. And most importantly, *smile*! Even if your teeth are jacked up, smiling is the number one way to put other people at ease and to position yourself for that job or apprenticeship. (You can get that grill fixed with braces after you get the job.)

YOUR PERSONAL BOARD OF DIRECTORS

You need to make new personal connections that will help you in your goal of moving up. You may meet people at your new job or while volunteering at a soup kitchen or community center. Do not rely on other people to make the introduction.

No one succeeds in a vacuum: You must take advantage of the wisdom, experience, and different perspectives of a trusted group of individuals, or your *personal board of directors*. You are building a new life, so you need new information and positive influences.

Set your goals and do research: Bring in your personal board of directors. Use their insights as you get to know them. Engage them in the process of reaching your goals. And this is important—if they tell you something that goes against your instincts or you are faced with hard questions about the process and goal, don't take that as a signal that it's time to quit. Attacking the hard questions at the outset makes dealing with challenges much easier when they arise. Obstacles will always come, so the better we are at anticipating them, the more efficiently we'll overcome them.

Building the board: Choosing your personal board of directors takes some thought, but do not get bogged down in the process. Here are the key points to building the group:

- **Don't go too big:** Personal boards of directors should have three to five people on them. No more, no less. With fewer than three, you don't get enough diversity of input into your planning process. With more than five, things get unwieldy.
- **Choose a diverse group:** The broader the experience of the board members you are able to assemble, the more types of insight you will get into your

process. Some of the members' talents and abilities will complement yours and some will supplement them.

- **Choose people who are**:
  - Creative
  - Well organized
  - Older
  - Well connected
- **Stay in touch regularly:** The members don't need to know each other—they don't even need to like each other. You need to put together the team that will best serve your own interests. That means being in regular contact through e-mails, phone calls, evening brainstorming sessions, Sunday-morning coffees, etc. You need to talk to each of them *at least* once a month and e-mail even more. If there is an item that needs feedback, make sure each member of the team has a chance to weigh in. It is your responsibility to nurture the relationships.
- **Acknowledgment:** When you build your team, you can be as formal or informal as necessary, as each individual will vary. People are busy—especially successful people—so be mindful of their time. However, when you engage your board of directors, be sure to reinforce your gratitude for their input. Don't be a suck-up, but let them know they are valued and appreciated! And even try to think of ways you could be helpful to them, because *reciprocation* is very important.
- **Build a system:** You need a tracking system for meetings with the members of your personal board of directors, because no plan succeeds if it's not documented. Have a dedicated notebook and log everything. Keep track of names, dates, issues discussed, next steps required, and future appointments.

Below is a sample checklist that you can use to track your progress.

CHECKLIST	DATE COMPLETED
Preliminary research conducted	
Board of directors identified	
Tracking system developed	

FINANCING YOUR VEHICLE

You must create a personal budget. Money buys us options. Options are very valuable. That's why prisons take away your freedom, because they completely limit your options. So our relationship to money and how we use money to maximize our options is critical. You need to *use* money rather than let it use you.

Keep track: Write down the exact amount of *everything* you spend per day, week, and month. Within a few weeks, you'll have a pretty precise account of how much you're spending and on what. You will be much more conscious about how you spend your money.

Analyze: After a month of keeping track of your spending, sit with your chart and figure out what expenses you can cut. Is there somewhere less expensive to buy your groceries? Could you cook more?

Plan a budget for the year: Estimate what you'll *need to spend* month by month. "Need to spend" includes *only the basic costs,* no frills whatsoever.

Emergency stash: Be sure to keep some cash on hand for emergencies.

Be specific: This includes paying attention to mindless spending. The key to a detailed understanding of yourself is to be as specific as possible.

Smart tracking: After tracking your money for a few weeks, you'll have an accurate portrait of where it all goes. You'll have a sense of recurring bills as a proportion of your take-home income as well as a sense of what you spend on those "one-offs."

One-offs: The best way to cut expenses is to eliminate as many one-offs as possible. Did you absolutely need those brand-new sneakers or could you just have kept the ones you had really clean?

Variables: Factor in those recurring annual bills that might not show up in the initial stages of tracking, like health insurance and taxes.

I suggest using the chart below to track your money. You can personalize it any way you want, but it is a starting point.

MONTHLY BILLS	AMOUNT DUE	DATE DUE
Rent		
Electricity (If Not Included in Rent)		
Phone		
Other		

DAILY EXPENDITURES	AMOUNT BUDGETED	AMOUNT SPENT
Groceries		
Meals/Drinks Not Consumed at Home		
Public Transportation		
Clothes		
Shoes		
Other		

Resources and Tools

Personal Finance Tracking Sites: Use a public library computer if you don't have Internet access.

- Mint: www.mint.com
- HelloWallet: www.hellowallet.com
- MoneyStrands: money.strands.com

Personal Finance Books: See reading list on pages 353–354, which includes some personal finance books.

Local Newspaper: Money/Finance section

Local Bank: Free financial/investment consultants

THE BUSINESS PLAN

Now that you've got your personal finances under control, you will want to begin thinking about starting your own business, which I urge any ex-incarcerated individual to do. If you were a street-corner pharmacist before you were incarcerated or entrepreneurial in prison, you already intuitively understand many of these business concepts. Now you just need to transfer them to a legit business using a specific plan.

Figure out your business idea: This can be something you already know how to do and/or something that provides a service to fulfill a need that exists but isn't being met. You can also learn to do something that fits into an existing business model.

Write a business plan: Making a detailed plan is critical for success in business and in life. So many people try to start businesses without a detailed plan and that is one reason many of them fail. Here's how not to fall into that trap.

- **Mission statement:** A mission statement explains what your business is about. This should be about a paragraph in length and should answer the following questions:
  - What are you selling?
  - How will you sell it and how will you make it?

- What is your cost of goods sold (the inventory costs of the goods that a business has sold in a certain period of time)?
- What are your objectives?
- What is your action plan?

- **Business information:** This includes when you will start your business and where it is located. Provide a brief description of your products and/or services. The description of your product or service should include information about its specific benefits from a customer's point of view. Describe your product's ability to meet a need and its competitive advantage. Include information about the life cycle of the product, as well as factors that could influence its cycle in the future.

- **Copyright or patent filings:** If you plan to file for these, list them here. Divulge whether any aspects of your product could be considered a trade secret, and include information on existing legal agreements, including nondisclosure agreements. Will you be using/needing a lawyer? Legal fees for corporate documents (such as those regarding investments and organizational structure) and copyright/patent filings need to be included in the budget if needed.

- **Outline of research and development plans:** Identify your competition in the industry and outline their plans as well. Answer these questions in your outline:
  - How do you plan to market your product or service?
  - What is your competitive advantage?

- **Business structure:** First you will need to figure out if your business is going to be incorporated, and if so, whether it will be a C or S corporation. Or will it be a partnership with someone, and if so, will it be a general or limited partnership? Or instead will you be a sole proprietor? More specifics on how to incorporate are available online, and keep in mind that the rules vary from state to state. If your investment structure is complex, you may need an attorney to help with the documents. Many standard ("boilerplate") documents are available online. Ask someone from your personal board of directors who has knowledge of these things to help. When you draw up plans for your business, include the following information:

- Names of owners and percentages of ownership, as well as the form of ownership (for instance, common or preferred stock). If common stock, is it authorized or issued?
- Extent of each owner's involvement with the business.
- Outstanding equity equivalents (such as warrants or options).
- Key people in your company and their backgrounds, including their résumés. Describe how they support your own skills and how they will contribute to your business's success.
- Advisory board or board of directors: Well-known, successful business owners who advise you. Include their names and positions/titles on the board, how involved they will be, and their backgrounds.
- **How you will sell your product:** Identify the prospective buyers, prioritize them, and choose the leads with the highest potential to buy. Then identify the number of sales calls you'll need to make over a certain period of time, and figure out the average number of calls you'll need to make per sale, the average dollar amount you'll need to make per sale, and also the average you'll need to make per vendor.

- **Communications:** How will you reach your customers? Normally this would include promotions, advertising, personal selling, printed materials, and public relations. Include social networking: Twitter, Facebook, YouTube, LinkedIn.
- **Sales force:** Will you use the Internet or reps? How many people will you need, and how will you recruit them? Will they work for commission, salary, or a combination? How will you train them?
- **Target market:** Who is your target market? In order to determine your target market, narrow it to a manageable size. How big is your audience and how is your product relevant to them? Read industry articles and census information. Include the critical needs of your customers, their demographics, and whether there are seasonal trends that could have an effect on your business.
- **Market analysis:** Identify the forecasted growth for the market and how much market share you can gain. How many customers can you get in your area? Your market analysis should include the following information:
  - Pricing structure
  - Gross margins for profit
  - Discounts
  - Market penetration
- **Competition:** Include as many specifics as possible, like your competition's market share, how strong the competition is, and the barriers (if any) to your entering the market. Identify the window of opportunity for you to enter the market. Is there indirect competition that could affect your entering the market? Are there problems such as changing technology or high start-up costs?
- **Regulatory restrictions:** These include government requirements that will affect your business and

how you will comply with them, as well as the price of compliance.

- **Financial information:** This includes what type of investors you are seeking. How much money will you need to start your business and how much to run it? What are the expected profits?
- **Funding:** If you are looking for investors, you will need to write a request for funding that demonstrates your ability to repay their loans. Create a PowerPoint presentation to present to your potential investors (a PowerPoint lesson should be included in the computer course at your community college), and include the following:
  - The amount of money you are asking for.
  - Any additional funding you might need over the next five years.
  - Detailed description on how you plan to use the funding—is the money going to be used for capital expenditures, working capital, acquisitions, or other purposes?
  - Strategic financial plans for the future, such as being acquired, repaying debt, or selling your business.
  - An estimated time at which investors can expect a return and what interest they can expect to earn on their investment.
- **Financial reports:** Historical financial information (this doesn't apply to you now but will in the future). Include the company's past income statements, balance sheets, and cash-flow statements for every year that you've been in business.
- **Prospective financial information:** Show what your business will do in the next five years. Include forecasts for income statements, balance sheets, cash-flow statements, and capital expenditures. For the first year, include monthly projections, and then

include quarterly and/or yearly projections for years two through five. Make sure your projections match your funding requests. If you make assumptions, describe what they are.

- **Brief financial analysis:** Include a ratio and trend analysis of your statements (both historical and prospective). Graphs are helpful here.
- **Future plans:** Where and how will your business expand? Where would you like to be two, five, ten years from now? Provide strategies for any of the following points that apply to your business:
  - Increasing your human resources
  - Acquisition strategy for buying another business
  - Franchise strategy for branching out
  - Horizontal strategy to provide the same type of products to different users
  - Vertical strategy to offer your product at different levels of the distribution chain
  - Strategy for channels of distribution (this would include the original equipment manufacturers and internal sales force, distributors, or retailers).
- **Appendix:** Here, include your résumé, letters of reference, credit history, and any additional information that could be useful to a prospective lender.

I know this whole business plan can seem a little overwhelming. But it's not something that you have to create in a day. It's something you create over time as you do more and more research into your new business venture. Don't feel overwhelmed. Begin right now by just thinking about business ideas and ask yourself some of the questions described previously. You *can* create a successful video game design business if that is what you want. This is your life, so you are in the driver's seat.

NEW VEHICLE WARRANTY

You and you alone are responsible for maintaining your vehicle. It is the owner's responsibility to make sure that all specified maintenance is performed. This means that you need to have regular doctor, dental, and vision checkups to make sure that everything is in good working order. You can't do anything if you don't have your health.

Maintaining a Healthy Weight

- Calculate your body mass index (BMI). The higher your BMI, the greater the risk for health problems. BMI = [(weight in pounds) ÷ (height in inches × height in inches)] × 703.
  For example, if your weight is 205 pounds and you are 5'11" tall, your BMI is 28.6: [205 ÷ (71 × 71)] × 703 = 28.6.

BMI	WEIGHT STATUS
Below 18.5	Underweight
18.5–24.9	Normal
25.0–29.9	Overweight
30.0 and above	Obese

- Measure around your waist, just above your hip bones, while standing. Health risks increase as waist measurement increases, particularly if the waist circumference is greater than thirty-five inches for women or forty inches for men. Excess abdominal fat may place you at greater risk of health problems, even if your BMI is about right.
- Find out how many other risk factors you have. The more of these risk factors you have, the more you

are likely to benefit from weight loss if you are over-weight.

	YES	NO
Do you have a personal or family history of heart disease?		
Are you a male older than 45 years, or a postmenopausal female?		
Do you smoke cigarettes?		
Do you have a sedentary lifestyle?		

- Has your doctor told you that you have any of the following? If you have any of the conditions below, work with your physician to correct the imbalance.

	YES	NO
Diabetes		
High blood pressure		
Abnormal blood lipids (high LDL cholesterol, low HDL cholesterol, high triglycerides)		

Exercise and Excel-eration

Doctors recommend that we get at least twenty minutes of cardio exercise at least five days a week. On the other two days, it's good to lift weights for at least twenty minutes per day. This helps us to burn our "fuel" (calories) more rapidly and efficiently. If there are no weights available to you, you can do fifty push-ups and one hundred sit-ups every day. Those are free, so there are no excuses!

CARDIO (TYPE OF ACTIVITY:
RUNNING, JOGGING, BASKETBALL, TENNIS, SWIMMING):
List type of activity and minutes per day:

	1	2	3	4	5	6
SUN						
SAT						
FRI						
THU						
WED						
TUE						
MON						
WEEK						

RESISTANCE TRAINING/WEIGHT LIFTING
List type of activity and minutes per day:

WEEK	MON	TUE	WED	THU	FRI	SAT	SUN
1							
2							
3							
4							
5							
6							

Checking your fuel (nutrition): The following suggestions will help you to get the proper nutrition.

- Choose a variety of grains daily, especially whole grains.
- Choose a variety of vegetables and fruits daily.
- Choose a diet that is low in saturated fat and cholesterol and moderate in total fat.
- Choose low- or no-sugar beverages and foods to limit your intake of sugars.
- Limit intake of sodas and alcohol.
- Water is the best beverage to drink most of the time.
- Choose and prepare foods with less salt.
- Control your portion size. If you're eating out, choose small portion sizes or share an entrée with a friend. You can also take half of your food home. Be especially careful to limit portion size of foods high in calories such as sweets, french fries, and other greasy foods. An easy way to control portion size is to make the shape of a cup with one hand and don't have a portion of any one food group bigger than what you can fit in your palm.
- Check product labels to learn how much food is considered to be a serving and how many calories, grams of fat, and so forth are in the food.

Below is a chart for food groups and servings per day, based on the daily calorie needs for most men and active women (about 2,200 calories).

FOOD GROUP	SERVINGS PER DAY
Bread, cereal, rice, and pasta group, preferably whole grain	9
Vegetable group	4
Fruit group	3

| Milk, yogurt, and cheese group, preferably fat free or low fat | 2–3 |
| Meat, poultry, fish, dry beans, eggs, and nuts group, preferably lean or low fat | 2, for a total of 6 ounces |

*Adapted from U.S. Department of Agriculture, Center for Nutrition Policy and Promotion

Sources of calcium: Yogurt; milk; natural cheeses such as mozzarella, cheddar, Swiss, and Parmesan; soy-based beverages with added calcium; tofu, if made with calcium sulfate (read ingredient list); breakfast cereal with added calcium; canned fish with soft bones such as salmon and sardines; fruit juice with added calcium; soups made with milk; dark-green leafy vegetables such as collards and turnip greens.

Sources of iron: Shellfish like shrimp, clams, mussels, and oysters; lean meats like beef, liver, and other organ meats; ready-to-eat cereals with added iron; turkey dark meat (remove skin to reduce fat); sardines; green leafy vegetables such as spinach, collards, and turnip greens; cooked dry beans (such as kidney beans and pinto beans), peas, and lentils; enriched and whole-grain breads.

LIMIT FAT CALORIES CONSUMED PER DAY

TOTAL CALORIES SATURATED FAT	TOTAL FAT PER DAY IN GRAMS
1,600 cal/day	18 or less
2,000 cal/day	20 or less
2,200 cal/day	24 or less
2,500 cal/day	25 or less
2,800 cal/day	31 or less

Cutting back on sodium: Salt contains sodium. Sodium is a substance that affects blood pressure. High blood pressure and heart disease are our biggest killers. The best way to cut back on sodium is to reduce your intake of salty foods and seasonings. When reading a nutrition facts label, look for the sodium content. Foods that are low in sodium (less than 5 percent of your daily value for sodium) are low in salt. Just get into the habit of never buying salt or adding it to anything. Salt is used so much in everything we buy anyway, you won't even miss it, I promise.

DAILY CALORIE AND FOOD PORTION CHART
Fill in boxes below with types of food/calories/fat/sodium content

TIME	Breakfast	Lunch	Snack	Dinner	Snack	Other
MON						
TUE						
WED						
THU						
FRI						
SAT						
SUN						

Fill in boxes below with types of beverage/calories:

TIME	MON	TUE	WED	THU	FRI	SAT	SUN
Breakfast							
Lunch							
Snack							
Dinner							
Snack							
Other							

Overview of instruments and controls: Too many African-American men are being diagnosed with testicular cancer, diabetes, and other preventable diseases, and all because they don't see a doctor regularly. Make sure you get an annual physical. Below is a list of things that your physician will check at your annual physical. Review your health history with your doctor. He/she will ask you about smoking, alcohol use, diet, and exercise. He/she will also check your vaccination status and update your medical history.

IGNITION SYSTEM AND TRANSMISSION

Things your doctor will check:

- Your blood pressure should be less than 120 over 80. High blood pressure (hypertension) is 140 over 90 or higher.
- Your respiration rate should be around 16; if it's over 20, it can suggest a lung or heart problem.
- Your temperature should be 98.6 degrees.
- Your heart rate should be between 50 and 100.
- Your doctor will check your general appearance, your memory, and the condition of your skin and nails. She will listen to your heart and lungs with a stethoscope. She will check your head and neck, teeth and gums, ears, nose, eyes, sinuses, lymph nodes, and carotid arteries. She may tap your abdomen to determine liver size and listen for bowel sounds with a stethoscope. She will check the pulse in your arms and legs.
- Nerves, muscle strength, reflexes, balance, and mental state may be assessed.
- A doctor can check each testicle for lumps, tenderness, or changes in size. A hernia exam and/or penis/prostate exam will be conducted.
- Some doctors will order these tests: complete blood count, chemistry panel, and urinalysis. Unless symptoms already suggest a problem, however, these tests are unlikely to provide useful information.

- A cholesterol test is recommended every five years. At age sixty, you should begin regular screening for colorectal cancer. People with immediate family members with colorectal cancer may need to be screened before age fifty.

Headlights: Have your vision checked regularly by an ophthalmologist or an optometrist. He will check your sight and also check for eye diseases such as glaucoma.

Audio system: Have your hearing checked by an ear specialist once a year. Try not to listen to really loud music on earbuds or headphones to avoid future hearing problems.

Other scheduled maintenance: Go to the dentist every six months. For healthy gums and teeth, between meals, eat few foods or beverages containing sugars or starches. If you do eat them, brush your teeth afterward to reduce the risk of tooth decay. Brush at least twice a day and floss daily, and use fluoride toothpaste and mouthwash.

Breaking debilitating habits: In *The Power of Habit,* Charles Duhigg states that to break a bad habit, you have to *create a new habit.* "A new habit is created by putting together a cue, a routine, and a reward, and then cultivating a craving that drives the loop." For example, if you want to start going walking in the morning, you have to begin with an easy cue, like putting on your sneakers first thing, and a clear reward, such as the good feeling of being more fit. Yet as Duhigg points out, only when your brain starts expecting the reward will it become automatic to lace up your shoes each morning. The cue must also trigger a craving for the reward that is coming. Duhigg also notes that AA works for alcohol addiction because the program forces people to identify the cues and rewards that encourage their addiction and then helps them create new alternative behaviors. It's helpful to work through the steps for not only alcohol but any debilitating habits that you want to eliminate, such as smoking. And as with AA, it's great to have a "sponsor" who helps you toe the line, particularly if it's someone who has been through the same problems you're dealing with.

- **Smoking and drinking:** The best way to avoid a medical crisis is to prevent it! So take care of yourself. There are many measures you can take to help ensure that you will have a long, healthy life. Giving up smoking is one of the biggest things you can do to improve your overall well-being. Keep in mind that 50 percent of all long-term smokers will die of tobacco-related causes. About five million people die every year from tobacco use, and smoking will claim 500 million lives this century unless something happens to stop it. If you smoke, you really need to quit *right now.* Here is a checklist to help you quit.

GOAL	DONE
Think through each level of plan to quit	
Research connections/organizations to help me quit smoking	
Make a contract with myself	
Set the stakes for failure	
Bring in referees to monitor my progress	
Quit smoking	

- **Alcoholic beverages:** Use only in moderation. Moderation is defined as no more than one drink per day for women and no more than two drinks per day for men. As a rule though, don't drink every day. Choose three days a week you'll have a drink; the other four, drink something besides alcohol.

Count as a drink:

- ❑ 12 ounces of regular beer (150 calories)
- ❑ 5 ounces of wine (100 calories)
- ❑ 1.5 ounces of 80-proof distilled spirits (100 calories)

ALCOHOL CONSUMPTION

TYPE	MON	TUE	WED	THU	FRI	SAT	SUN
Drinks/ Ounces Consumed							

Life insurance policy: Every person needs life insurance so that if something happens, their loved ones are not hit with funeral costs. Think of R. J. What would happen to him if anything should happen to you? You have to be sure to get a basic life insurance policy. Life insurance is the number one way to transfer wealth from one generation to the next. Most people from low-income communities view life insurance as unimportant, while they think that getting a home is the best way to transfer wealth to the next generation. Not true! Dollar for dollar, life insurance is a better investment. If something happens to you, your children need some financial stability. Life insurance can help with that.

Vehicle registration: Don't take it at face value that being convicted of a felony makes you unable to vote. Be sure to research the local and state laws for voter registration for the formerly incarcerated. Voting is important. You need to work to elect people who will represent your interests. What makes this country the greatest country in the world is that it is a participatory democracy. But that only works when we **participate**. Too few ex-felons vote, even when they *can* vote. Seeing systemic change requires all of us to use the power of the ballot. Every time you don't vote, you give away some of your power.

Warning lights: Insomnia is a warning that something is out of whack. According to the National Sleep Foundation, getting a good night's rest is a key to being healthy and alert. Lack of sleep can lead to obesity, drug and alcohol abuse, and even psychological problems, so it's good to nip an insomnia trend in the bud. Exercise can be an aid to sleep, so do get out and move around. Try to go to sleep at the same time every night if possible, and maybe even a little earlier than you're used to doing, to make up for lack of sleep.

Gauges, meters, and service-reminder indicators: When your body sends you a signal that something isn't working properly, think of that as a service-reminder indicator. For instance, if your knee gives out when you walk, you need to check it out with your doctor. Most people wait too long, till the problem becomes much worse or unbearable. We are living a new proactive life now, which means if you get a warning signal, you go to the free clinic immediately and get it checked out.

OTHER WARNING SIGNALS

Warning Signs of a Heart Attack

- **Chest discomfort:** Most heart attacks involve pain or discomfort in the center of the chest that lasts more than a few minutes or that goes away and comes back. It can feel like fullness, pain, uncomfortable pressure, or squeezing. If you feel this, immediately chew an aspirin (it helps thin your blood) and seek medical attention.
- **Other discomfort in the upper body:** Pain or discomfort in one or both arms, the back, the neck, the jaw, or the stomach.
- **Shortness of breath:** This may be with or without chest pain.
- **Other indicators:** Breaking out in a cold sweat, nausea, or feeling light-headed.

Symptoms of Stress

- A rapid heartbeat or breathing
- Sweating
- Cold hands and feet
- Feeling sick to your stomach
- Dry mouth
- Tight muscles
- Feeling anxious, frustrated, or angry
- Difficulty in concentrating
- Not feeling happy or relaxed
- Loss of appetite
- Lack of sleep
- Skin problems and getting sick more often (colds, flu)
- Feeling tired and exhausted
- Sex life is affected

CHECKLIST FOR STRESS

Note how often you feel stressed during the day and what your symptoms are. If you are feeling stressed often or every day, you should seek professional counseling or therapy.

	Times I Felt Stressed	Symptoms
SUN		
SAT		
FRI		
THU		
WED		
TUE		
MON		

Air-conditioning system: If you are feeling angry, here are some ways to "cool down."

- Don't lash out. Try to do nothing or divert your attention.
- Leave the area if at all possible. Suggest taking a breather or talking about the issue at a later time.
- Count to ten.
- Visualize a relaxing place or image.
- Repeat calming mantras or phrases to yourself.

Track your angry reactions and what triggered them

	Why I Felt Angry	Time of Day
SUN		
SAT		
FRI		
THU		
WED		
TUE		
MON		

DO-IT-YOURSELF MAINTENANCE

Tune-ups: Mental health is just as important as physical health. If something goes wrong, seek out help through therapy and support groups. Below are some ways to manage stress and other psychological issues.

- Jon Kabat-Zinn's books *Full Catastrophe Living* and *Wherever You Go, There You Are* are both good resources for information about mind-body stress-reduction techniques and meditation. He shows the reader how to do a "body scan," mentally going over every muscle and paying attention to where you are tense. If you want to be calmer, have more inner balance, and have a clear perception of your everyday life, mindful meditation can really help.

- Dr. Suzanne Kobasa of the City University of New York studied how people handle stressful events in their lives. She found that psychological hardiness resulted from three things: the person's belief that he could influence his surroundings, being fully engaged in daily activities, and seeing change as a natural part of life that allows further development. These "hardy" people saw change as an opportunity, as opposed to a threat. You can increase your level of hardiness by asking yourself how your life is going right now and how it could be enriched in these three areas.

Journaling: Write down a statement that reflects a desire. How does that make you feel? How can you attain that desire? Try this with three different desires. Frame your goals in a positive manner to be more effective. Instead of saying, "I don't want to do _____," say, "I *do* want to _____." Be specific in your goals, and think in terms of one small step at a time.

DESIRES AND GOALS
1.
2.
3.

Mistakes: Make a list of decisions that you have control over, versus things you do not. List how you handled these things in the past and how you plan to handle them in the future.

DECISION	HOW I HANDLED IT IN THE PAST	HOW I WILL HANDLE IT IN THE FUTURE

Write in a journal: Over the next several days, take a piece of paper and write about your worst trauma, how you felt about it, and why you feel that way. Try to be completely open, honest, and vulnerable. Know that what you write is for your eyes only, so you can be totally honest. Be sure to write about why you think it happened and what good you might get out of the traumatic event. This kind of journaling can have lasting effects on both your physical and mental health and your outlook.

MY WORST TRAUMA WAS:

More writing: Write down your upsetting thoughts and feelings and the negative events that triggered them to help you analyze why you are feeling this way.

UPSETTING THOUGHT/FEELING	TRIGGER

Visual or sense-memory exercise: This can help when you are feeling blue. List three pleasant sense memories and recall them in vivid detail. Recall and use an experience you have had before through one of your five senses. Think about what it tasted like, looked like, smelled like, felt like, and sounded like. This activates multiple brain regions simultaneously.

PLEASANT SENSE MEMORIES
1.
2.
3.

Affirmations: Another approach to overall mental well-being is through affirmations, which are simply statements made today about how we see ourselves being tomorrow. The theory behind affirmations is that we can affect our subconscious by repeating positive attributes or goals. Some people repeat a word to themselves throughout the day, like *confident* or *productive*. Others say entire sentences every morning as they look into a mirror, such as, "I am confident that I will reach my goals. I am a creator of joy, happiness, possibility, and inspiration everywhere I go."

THREE AFFIRMATIONS I WILL REPEAT EACH DAY:
1.
2.
3.

Other Ways to Ease Stress and Avoid Feeling Depressed

- Eating healthy: This will promote a better overall mood
- Getting bright light or sunshine
- Avoiding alcohol and drugs
- Meditation
- Listening to relaxation CDs or music
- Getting regular physical exercise

Track stress-reducing activities and the time spent doing each activity below.

	MON	TUE	WED	THU	FRI	SAT	SUN
Week 1	Meditated 30 minutes						
Week 2							
Week 3							
Week 4							

Be the change: Another way we can get stuck in negativity is by not believing that we can change. In *Mindset: The New Psychology of Success*, author Carol Dweck talks about the difference between a growth mind-set and a fixed mind-set.[1] The first step, she says, is to **"learn to hear your fixed mindset 'voice.'"** She suggests that you write down these thoughts and then write down thoughts with a growth mind-set that can counteract the fixed-mind-set thoughts.

FIXED-MIND-SET THOUGHTS
1.
2.
3.

GROWTH-MIND-SET THOUGHTS
1.
2.
3.

Believe you can change: One way to change negative behaviors is to believe that you can change, according to *Changing for Good* by James O. Prochaska, John C. Norcross, and Carlo C. DiClemente. The authors advise readers to seek out people who want to help them to change and social situations that will enable them to change. It is also important to take credit for your success when you do succeed, instead of attributing it to others or outside influences.

Another good book about making permanent positive changes is *Do One Thing Different: Ten Simple Ways to Change Your Life.* In it, author Bill O'Hanlon advises people to pay attention to patterns in their life and change what they can. He also says that we should notice what we're doing when things are going well and do more of it, and whenever you find yourself doing a behavior that's problematic, force yourself to also do something positive for yourself that you really don't like to do.

PROBLEMATIC BEHAVIORS	WAYS I CAN CHANGE THE BEHAVIOR
1.	1.
2.	2.
3.	3.
4.	4.
5.	5.

Be optimistic: Martin Seligman, the author of *Learned Optimism: How to Change Your Mind and Your Life,* spent years studying why optimists seemed better able to thrive, even in the face of failure. He showed that people can actually learn to be more optimistic and that an optimistic attitude allows people to get over hurdles. According to Seligman, it helps to dispute your belief that you are doomed to failure, and also you must not blame yourself for things that are out of your control. Finally, write down the thoughts that you have right before you feel sad or angry, so that you recognize them the next time they occur and fend off the unhappy feelings.

THOUGHTS THAT OCCUR BEFORE I BECOME SAD OR ANGRY
1.
2.
3.
4.
5.

LIST THREE PEOPLE YOU CAN RELY ON WHEN YOU ARE FEELING DISCOURAGED OR JUST NEED A HELPING HAND
1.
2.
3.

Getting your driver's license: Following this owner's manual is a suggested reading list. I would like for you to read every single book on this list, and to track your progress, here's a checklist for your reading plan. Make a copy for each month of the year, and try to read at least one book a week. Once you have read all the books on the list, you will have passed your "road test" and will be an expert on living fully and well.

MONTH: _____

	TITLE OF BOOK	DATE COMPLETED	WHAT I THOUGHT
Week 1			
Week 2			
Week 3			
Week 4			

SUGGESTED READING

Wrongful Conviction: Law, Science, and Policy by James R. Acker and Allison D. Redlich

The New Jim Crow by Michelle Alexander

I Know Why the Caged Bird Sings by Maya Angelou

Mandela's Children by Oscar A. Barbarin and Linda M. Richter

The Diving Bell and the Butterfly by Jean-Dominique Bauby

The Bible

Doing Time on the Outside: Incarceration and Family Life in Urban America by Donald Braman

Wrongful Convictions: Cases and Materials by Justin Brooks

Manchild in the Promised Land by Claude Brown

Bear by Paul W. Bryant

Chicken Soup for the Prisoner's Soul by Jack Canfield, Mark Victor Hansen, and Tom Lagana

The Seven Spiritual Laws of Success: A Practical Guide to the Fulfillment of Your Dreams by Deepak Chopra

Spiritual Solutions: Answers to Life's Great Challenges by Deepak Chopra

Innocent: Inside Wrongful Conviction Cases by Scott Christianson

Soul on Ice by Eldridge Cleaver

The Alchemist by Paulo Coelho

By the River Piedra I Sat Down and Wept by Paulo Coelho

Manuscript Found in Accra by Paulo Coelho

Cage Your Rage: An Inmate's Guide to Anger Control by Murray Cullen

An Autobiography by Angela Davis

Post Traumatic Slave Syndrome: America's Legacy of Enduring Injury and Healing by Dr. Joy DeGruy Leary

The Power of Habit: Why We Do What We Do in Life and Business by Charles Duhigg

The Name of the Rose by Umberto Eco

Invisible Man by Ralph Ellison

The Autobiography of Benjamin Franklin by Benjamin Franklin

Autobiography: The Story of My Experiments with Truth by Mohandas Gandhi

Convicting the Innocent: Where Criminal Prosecutions Go Wrong by Brandon L. Garrett

Creative Visualization by Shakti Gawain

Outliers: The Story of Success by Malcolm Gladwell

You Can Make It Happen: A Nine-Step Plan for Success by Stedman Graham

The 50th Law by 50 Cent and Robert Greene

The Innocent Man: Murder and Injustice in a Small Town by John Grisham

No Death, No Fear by Thich Nhat Hanh

The Conversation: How Men and Women Can Build Loving, Trusting Relationships by Hill Harper

The Wealth Cure: Putting Money in Its Place by Hill Harper

Switch: How to Change Things When Change Is Hard by Chip Heath and Dan Heath

Fragments by Heraclitus

Teaching Critical Thinking by bell hooks

Soledad Brother: The Prison Letters of George Jackson by George Jackson

Steve Jobs: His Own Words and Wisdom by Steve Jobs

Fear and Trembling by Søren Kierkegaard

"Letter from Birmingham Jail" by Dr. Martin Luther King Jr.

The Power of Negative Thinking by Bob Knight

The Koran

The Way of Life by Lao Tzu

The Worry Cure: Seven Steps to Stop Worry from Stopping You by Robert L. Leahy

Freakonomics: A Rogue Economist Explores the Hidden Side of Everything by Steven D. Levitt and Stephen J. Dubner

The Man Who Outgrew His Prison Cell: Confessions of a Bank Robber by Joe Loya

Chronicle of a Death Foretold by Gabriel García Márquez

The Courage to Create by Rollo May

The Way of the Peaceful Warrior: A Book that Changes Lives by Dan Millman

The Other Wes Moore: One Name, Two Fates by Wes Moore

Between Earth and Sky: Our Intimate Connections to Trees by Nalini Nadkarni

Within Prison Walls by Thomas Mott Osborne

15 to Life: How I Painted My Way to Freedom by Anthony Papa with Jennifer Wynn

Freeing the Innocent: How We Did It—A Handbook for the Wrongly Convicted by Michael and Becky Pardue

False Justice: Eight Myths That Convict the Innocent by Jim Petro and Nancy Petro

The Measure of a Man: A Spiritual Autobiography by Sidney Poitier

In the Place of Justice: A Story of Punishment and Deliverance by Wilbert Rideau

Here I Stand by Paul Robeson

Counting the Years: Real-Life Stories About Waiting for Loved Ones to Return Home from Prison, edited by Sheila R. Rule and Marsha R. Rule

For Colored Girls Who Have Considered Suicide/When the Rainbow Is Enuf by Ntozake Shange

The Gift of Acceptance by Janine Shepherd

Fail Up: 20 Lessons on Building Success from Failure by Tavis Smiley

The Game of Life and How to Play It by Florence Scovel Shinn

Super Brain: Unleashing the Explosive Power of Your Mind to Maximize Health, Happiness, and Spiritual Well-Being by Dr. Rudolph E. Tanzi and Deepak Chopra

Prisoners' Guerrilla Handbook to Correspondence Programs in the United States and Canada by Jon Marc Taylor

The Power of Now: A Guide to Spiritual Enlightenment by Eckhart Tolle

How Children Succeed: Grit, Curiosity, and the Hidden Power of Character by Paul Tough

The Upanishads

Waiting for God by Simone Weil

Muzzled: The Assault on Honest Debate by Juan Williams

Blue Rage, Black Redemption by Stanley Tookie Williams

Native Son by Richard Wright

Autobiography of Malcolm X by Malcolm X

Conversations of Socrates by Xenophon

The Lucifer Effect: Understanding How Good People Turn Evil by Philip Zimbardo

Education Behind Bars: A Win-Win Strategy for Maximum Security by Christopher Zoukis

RESOURCES

Alcoholics Anonymous: www.aa.org

Alternatives to Violence Project: www.avpusa.org

Bard Prison Initiative (for New York State only): www.bpi.bard.edu

Books Through Bars: www.booksthroughbars.org

Connections 2012: A Guide for Formerly Incarcerated People to Information Sources in New York City and The Job Search, published by the New York Public Library: www.nypl .org/sites/default/files/11_1_11__connections_2012.pdf

Dr. Carol Dweck's site: www.mindsetonline.com

Family and Corrections Network: fcnetwork.org

The Innocence Project: www.innocenceproject.org

International Network of Prison Ministries: www.prisonministry.net

Job Corps: www.jobcorps.gov

Longtermers Responsibility Project: www.osborneny.org

Mrs. GE-6309 Time, Reesy Floyd-Thompson's blog: pwgp.org/ mrs-ge-6309-time-the-blog

Narcotics Anonymous: www.na.org

Office of Correctional Education: www2.ed.gov/about/offices/list/ovae/pi/AdultEd/correctional -education.html

Prison Fellowship: www.prisonfellowship.org

The Quantified Self: www.quantifiedself.com

TED conference talks: www.ted.com/talks

Think Outside the Cell Foundation: www.thinkoutsidethecell.org

The Voice from Inside, John Wannamaker's blog: www.thevoicefrominside.blogspot.com

STATE CORRECTIONAL EDUCATION COORDINATOR BY STATE

ALABAMA
Correctional Education Division
J. F. Ingram State Technical College
PO Box 220350
Deatsville, AL 36022-0350
Phone: (334) 285-5177
Fax: (334) 285-2521
E-mail: dchambers@ingram.cc.al.us or jmerk@ingram.cc.al.us
Website: www.ingram.cc.al.us

ALASKA
Inmate Programs
State Department of Corrections
Suite 601
550 West Seventh Avenue
Anchorage, AK 99501
Phone: (907) 269-7434
Fax: (907) 269-7420
Email: annaherzberger@alaska.gov
Website: www.correct.state.ak.us /corrections/index.jsf

ARIZONA
Correctional Education Bureau
State Department of Corrections
Third Floor
1601 West Jefferson
Phoenix, AZ 85007
Phone: (602) 542-5620
Fax: (602) 364-0550
E-mail: bganz@azcorrections.gov or lkrause@azcorrections.gov
Website: www.azcorrections.gov /adc/divisions/newsuppdiv /newsupp_Workforce.aspx ?

ARKANSAS
Arkansas Correctional School
Correctional School System
8000 Correction Circle
Pine Bluff, AR 71603
Phone: (870) 267-6725
Fax: (870) 267-6731
E-mail: dubs.byers@arkansas.gov
Website: arkcs.arkansas.gov

CALIFORNIA
Correctional Education Division
State Department of Corrections and Rehabilitation
PO Box 942883
Sacramento, CA 94283-0001
Phone: (916) 445-8035
Fax: (916) 324-1416

E-mail: doug.mckeever@cdcr.ca.gov
Website: http://www.cdcr.ca.gov
/OCE/index.html

COLORADO
Correctional Education Division
State Department of Corrections
2862 South Circle Drive
Colorado Springs, CO 80906-
4195
Phone: (719) 226-4417
Fax: (719) 226-4424
E-mail: tony.romero@doc.state
.co.us or bill.zalman@doc.state
.co.us
Website: www.doc.state.co.us

CONNECTICUT
Correctional Education Division
State Department of Correction
Unified School District #1
24 Wolcott Hill Road
Wethersfield, CT 06109-1152
Phone: (860) 692-7537
Fax: (860) 692-7538
Email: doc.pio@po.state.ct.us or
angela.jalbert@po.state.ct.us
Website: www.ct.gov/doc/cwp
/view.asp?a=1503&q=265554

DELAWARE
Correctional Education Division
State Department of Correction
Bureau of Prisons
245 McKee Road
Dover, DE 19904
Phone: (302) 857-5276
Fax: (302) 739-7215
E-mail: johnj.ryan@state.de.us
Website: doc.delaware.gov

FLORIDA
Office of Education and Initiatives
State Department of Corrections
Building B, Room 300
2601 Blair Stone Road
Tallahassee, FL 32399-2500
Phone: (850) 922-3621
Fax: (850) 922-2121
E-mail: overstreet.allen@mail.dc
.state.fl.us or crockett.mckin
ley@mail.dc.state.fl.us
Website: www.dc.state.fl.us

HAWAII
Correctional Education Division
State Department of Public Safety
Room 405
919 Ala Moana Boulevard
Honolulu, HI 96814
Phone: (808) 587-1279
Fax: (808) 587-1280
E-mail: maureen.l.tito@hawaii.gov
or mtito14@gmail.com
Website: hawaii.gov/psd/corrections

IDAHO
Correctional Education Division
State Department of Correction
Suite 110
1299 North Orchard Street
Boise, ID 83706
Phone: (208) 658-2066
Fax: (208) 327-7458
E-mail: gcushman@idoc.idaho
.gov or mperien@idoc.idaho.gov
Website: www.idoc.idaho.gov

ILLINOIS
Office of Adult and Vocational
Education
State Department of Corrections
1301 Concordia Court
Springfield, IL 62794

Phone: (217) 558-2200 extension 3601
Fax: (217) 522-9518
E-mail: info@idoc.state.il.us
Website: www.idoc.state.il.us

INDIANA

Correctional Education Division
State Department of Correction
E334 Indiana Government Center South
302 West Washington Street
Indianapolis, IN 46204
Phone: (317) 233-3111
Fax: (317) 234-0956
E-mail: jnally@idoc.in.gov
Website: www.in.gov/idoc

IOWA

Correctional Education Division
State Department of Corrections
Suite Four
510 East 12th Street
Des Moines, IA 50319
Phone: (515) 725-5728
Fax: (515) 725-5798
E-mail: info@doc.state.ia.us or laura.farris@iowa.gov
Website: www.doc.state.ia.us

KANSAS

Correctional Education Division
State Department of Corrections
Landon State Office Building, Fourth Floor
900 SW Jackson Street
Topeka, KS 66612-1284
Phone: (785) 296-3317
Toll-free (KS and MO residents only): (888) 317-8204
Fax: (785) 296-0304
E-mail: kdocpub@doc.ks.gov
Website: www.doc.ks.gov

KENTUCKY

Correctional Education Division
State Department of Corrections
Health Services Building
275 East Main Street, PO Box 2400
Frankfort, KY 40602-2400
Phone: (502) 564-4795, extension 229
Fax: (502) 564-0572
E-mail: martha.slemp@ky.gov
Website: www.corrections.ky.gov

LOUISIANA

Correctional Education Division
State Department of Public Safety and Corrections
PO Box 44314
Baton Rouge, LA 70804-4314
Phone: (225) 342-6633
Fax: (225) 342-5556
E-mail: creed@corrections.state .la.us or webmaster@corrections .state.la.us

MAINE

Adult Correctional Education
State Department of Corrections
State House Station #111
Augusta, ME 04333-0111
Phone: (207) 287-4342
Fax: (207) 287-4370
E-mail: ellis.king@maine.gov
Website: www.state.me.us/corrections

MARYLAND

State Department of Education
200 West Baltimore Street
Baltimore, MD 21201
Phone: (410) 767-0500
Fax: (410) 333-2254
E-mail: mmechlinski@msde.state .md.us

MASSACHUSETTS

Correctional Education Division
State Department of Corrections
PO Box 71, Hodder House
2 Merchant Road
Framingham, MA 01704
Phone: (508) 935-0901
Fax: (508) 935-0907
E-mail: cvicari@doc.state.ma.us
Website: www.state.ma.us/doc

MICHIGAN

Correctional Education Division
State Department of Corrections
Prisoner Education Programs
5656 South Cedar Street, Suite 100
Lansing, MI 48911
Phone: (517) 335-1388
Fax: (517) 241-9717
E-mail: derosejl@michigan.gov
Website: www.michigan.gov
/corrections

MINNESOTA

Correctional Education Division
State Department of Corrections
Facility Services Division—
Education
1450 Energy Park Drive, Suite 200
St. Paul, MN 55108-5210
Phone: (651) 361-7244
Fax: (651) 603-0150
TTY: (651) 643-3589
E-mail: marcie.koetke@state.mn.us
Website: www.doc.state.mn.us
/org/facilityserv/education.htm

MISSISSIPPI

Correctional Education Division
State Department of Corrections
723 North President Street
Jackson, MS 39202
Phone: (601) 359-5304
Fax: (601) 359-6760
E-mail: kstierle@mdoc.state.ms.us
or jnhopkins@mdoc.state.ms.us
Website: www.mdoc.state.ms.us

MISSOURI

Division of Offender Rehabilita-
tive Services/Education
State Department of Corrections
1717 Industrial Drive
PO Box 236
Jefferson City, MO 65102
Phone: (573) 526-6534
Fax: (573) 526-3009
TTY: (573) 751-5984
E-mail: tony.spillers@doc.mo.gov
or ellen.hueste@doc.mo.gov

MONTANA

Correctional Education Division
State Department of Corrections
1539 11th Avenue
PO Box 201301
Helena, MT 59620-1301
Phone: (406) 444-3930
Fax: (406) 444-4920
E-mail: webadmin@mt.gov or
banez@mt.gov
Website: www.cor.mt.gov

NEBRASKA

Correctional Education Division
State Department of Corrections
PO Box 94661
Lincoln, NE 68509
Phone: (402) 479-5723
Fax: (402) 479-5623
E-mail: jpannkuk@dcs.state.ne.us
or lwayne@dcs.state.ne.us

NEVADA

Education and Vocational Training
State Department of Corrections
Building 17
5500 Snyder Avenue
Carson City, NV 89701
Phone: (775) 887-3237
Fax: (775) 887-3253
E-mail: mhall@doc.nv.gov

NEW HAMPSHIRE

Correctional Education Division
State Department of Corrections
Corrections Special School
    District
PO Box 14
Concord, NH 03302-0014
Phone: (603) 271-1855
Fax: (603) 271-0401
E-mail: info@nhdoc.state.nh.us or
    daniel.t.tanguay@nhdoc.state
    .nh.us
Website: www.state.nh.us/nhdoc

NEW JERSEY

Office of Educational Services
State Department of Corrections
PO Box 863
Trenton, NJ 08625-0863
Phone: (609) 292-8054
Fax: (609) 777-4143
E-mail: pubinfo@doc.state.nj.us
    or patty.friend@doc.state.nj.us

NEW MEXICO

Adult Correctional Education
State Corrections Department
Casa Nor Este Building
4101 Pan American Freeway NE
Albuquerque, NM 87107
Phone: (505) 841-4282
Fax: (505) 841-4267
E-mail: johannes.hedrich@state
    .nm.us

NEW YORK

Correctional Education Division
State Department of Correctional
    Services
Harriman State Campus, Building
    Two
1220 Washington Avenue
Albany, NY 12226-2050
Phone: (518) 457-8142
Fax: (518) 457-1914
E-mail: nydocsedu@docs.state
    .ny.us

NORTH CAROLINA

Correctional Education Division
State Department of Correction
Division of Prisons
831 West Morgan Street, 4264
    MSC
Raleigh, NC 27669-4264
Phone: (919) 838-3642
Fax: (919) 838-4764
E-mail: ugm01@doc.state.nc.us
Website: www.doc.state.nc.us
    /DOP/education/index.htm

NORTH DAKOTA

Correctional Education Division
State Penitentiary, Adult Services
    Division
PO Box 5521
3100 Railroad Avenue
Bismarck, ND 58506-5521
Phone: (701) 328-6100
Fax: (701) 328-6640
E-mail: tmbarsta@nd.gov
Website: www.nd.gov/docr

OHIO

Correctional Education Division
Ohio Central School System
PO Box 779
London, OH 43140
Phone: (740) 845-3240

Fax: (740) 845-3387
E-mail: jerry.mcglone@odrc.state
.oh.us
Website: www.drc.state.oh.us
/OCSS/OCSS_home.htm

OKLAHOMA

Correctional Education Division
State Department of Corrections
Suite 200
2901 North Classen
Oklahoma City, OK 73106
Phone: (405) 962-6106
Fax: (405) 962-6171
E-mail: pam.humphrey@doc
.state.ok.us
Website: www.doc.state.ok.us

OREGON

Correctional Education Division
State Department of Corrections
Workforce Development Division
1793 13th Street, SE
Salem, OR 97302-2595
Phone: (503) 934-1003
Fax: (503) 378-5815
E-mail: karen.trembley@doc.state
.or.us
Website: www.doc.state.or.us
/DOC/TRANS/PROGMS/index
.shtml

PENNSYLVANIA

Bureau of Correction Education
State Department of Corrections
Suite 103
75 Utley Drive
Camp Hill, PA 17011
Phone: (717) 731-7823
Fax: (717) 731-7830
E-mail: wkepnerjr@state.pa.us or
chralston@state.pa.us
Website: www.cor.state.pa.us

PUERTO RICO

Correctional Education Division
State Department of Corrections
and Rehabilitation
Call Box 71308
San Juan, PR 00936
Phone: (787) 273-6464 extension
2504
Fax: (787) 277-0695
E-mail: lmorales@ac.gobierno.pr
Website: www.ac.gobierno.pr

RHODE ISLAND

Correctional Education Division
State Department of Corrections
Educational Services, Bernadette
Building
15 Fleming Road
Cranston, RI 02920
Phone: (401) 462-2507
Fax: (401) 462-2509
TTY: (401) 462-5180
E-mail: education@doc.ri.gov or
director@doc.ri.gov
Website: www.doc.ri.gov/rehabili
tative/educational/index.php

SOUTH CAROLINA

Correctional Education Division
SC Department of Corrections
Palmetto Unified School District
4444 Broad River Road
Columbia, SC 29210
Phone: (803) 896-1583
Fax: (803) 896-1513
E-mail: johnson.teresa@doc.state
.sc.us or reagan.randy@doc
.state.sc.us
Website: www.doc.sc.gov/pubweb/
education/pusd.jsp

SOUTH DAKOTA

Correctional Education Division
State Department of Corrections

4904 Quail Run
Sioux Falls, SD 57108
Phone: (605) 773-3478
Fax: (605) 334-3807
E-mail: dianna.miller@state.sd.us
or michael.winder@state.sd.us
Website: www.state.sd.us/correc
tions/corrections.html

TENNESSEE

Correctional Education Division
State Department of Corrections
Rachel Jackson Building, Fifth
Floor
320 Sixth Avenue, North
Nashville, TN 37243-0465
Phone: (615) 741-1000 extension
8176
Fax: (615) 741-1055
E-mail: sharmila.patel@tn.gov
Website: www.state.tn.us
/correction

TEXAS

Correctional Education Division
State Department of Criminal
Justice
Windham School District,
Institutional Division
PO Box 40
Huntsville, TX 77342-0040
Phone: (936) 291-5307
Fax: (936) 436-4031
E-mail: communications@wsdtx
.org or bambi.kiser@wsdtx.org
Website: www.wsdtx.org

UTAH

Correctional Education Division
State Office of Education
250 East 500 South
PO Box 144200
Salt Lake City, UT 84114-4200
Phone: (801) 538-7989

Fax: (801) 538-7868
E-mail: jeff.galli@schools.utah.gov

VERMONT

Correctional Education Division
Community High School of
Vermont
Workforce Development
Partnership
103 South Main Street
Waterbury, VT 05671-1001
Phone: (802) 241-2273
Fax: (802) 241-2377
E-mail: wilhelmina.picard@ahs
.state.vt.us or sheila.commo@
ahs.state.vt.us
Website: www.chsvt.org/wdp.html

VIRGINIA

Virginia Department of Correc-
tional Education
James Monroe Building
Seventh Floor
101 North 14th Street
Richmond, VA 23219-3678
Phone: (804) 225-3314
Fax: (804) 786-7642
E-mail: patricia.ennis@dce
.virginia.gov

WASHINGTON

Correctional Education Division
State Department of Corrections
Educational Services Unit
7345 Linderson Way, MS-41129
Tumwater, WA 98501
Phone: (360) 725-8211
Fax: (360) 586-7273
E-mail: mjparis@doc1.wa.gov
Website: www.doc.wa.gov

WEST VIRGINIA
Office of Institutional Education
   Programs
State Department of Education
Building Six, Room 728
1900 Kanawha Boulevard East
Charleston, WV 25305-0330
Phone: (304) 558-8833
Fax: (304) 558-5042
E-mail: jgreen@access.k12.wv.us
   or fwarsing@access.k12.wv.us
Website: wvde.state.wv.us/institu
   tional/

WISCONSIN
Correctional Education Division
State Department of Corrections,
   Office of Program Services
   Education
PO Box 7925

3099 East Washington Avenue
Madison, WI 53707-7925
Phone: (608) 240-5000
Fax: (608) 240-3310
E-mail: margaret.carpenter@
   wisconsin.gov or ismael
   .ozanne@wisconsin.gov
Website: doc.wi.gov/Home

WYOMING
Correctional Education Division
State Department of Corrections
Suite 100
1934 Wyott Drive
Cheyenne, WY 82002
Phone: (307) 777-6104
Fax: (307) 777-7846
E-mail: babbot@wdoc.state.wy.us
Website: doc.state.wy.us/services/
   education.html

APPENDIX

Educational Opportunities for the Incarcerated

NATIONAL

National Directory of Postsecondary Educational Programs in Prisons, Prison Studies Project

www.prisonstudiesproject.org

The Prison Scholar Fund website contains a map showing postsecondary educational programs inside prisons, state by state: http://www.facebook. com/PrisonScholarFund. You can also write to:

The Prison Scholar Fund
23517 Orville Road
East Orting, WA 98360

Prisoners Guerrilla Handbook to Correspondence Programs in the United States and Canada, 3rd Edition by Jon Marc Taylor and Susan Schwartz-kopf, 221 pages.

For information about the following list of higher education projects in prison, download the PDF booklet at www.universitybeyondbars.org or write to:

University Beyond Bars
PO Box 1267
Poulsbo, WA 98370

HIGHER EDUCATION PROJECTS

1. Prison Arts + Education Project
2. Bard Prison Initiative at Eastern Correctional Facility
3. Changing Lives Through Literature in Dorchester, Massachusetts
4. Georgetown's Prison Outreach Program
5. Hudson Link at Sing Sing Correctional Facility
6. Lipscomb Initiative for Education at Tennessee Prison for Women
7. Marymount Manhattan College at Bedford Hills Correctional Facility
9. Ohio University College Program for the Incarcerated
10. Pathways Program for Incarcerated Students at St. Cloud State University
11. Prison Creative Arts Project
12. Prison Studies Project
13. Prisoners Education Network
14. Prison University Project at San Quentin State Prison
15. Purdue University North Central; Rising Hope
16. University of North Carolina at Chapel Hill's Friday Center for Continuing Education with North Carolina Department for Corrections
17. Wesleyan Center for Prison Education.

HOW TO GET INFORMATION ABOUT EDUCATION IN PRISON FROM THE FEDERAL GOVERNMENT

Office of Correctional Education
U.S. Department of Education
400 Maryland Avenue, SW
MES 4527
Washington, DC 20202-7242

For more information, including legal help for the incarcerated, help for families of the incarcerated, avoiding recidivism, and much more, please visit **www .incarceratedbrother.com** or **www.mydf.org**.

GLOSSARY OF TERMS

Bahando: The cops.

Bid: Your sentence.

Bird: A woman or a kilo of cocaine.

Bitch: This is a huge no-no in prison. If someone calls you a bitch and you don't fight him, everybody feels like you were directly called out and you caught that pussy.

Booty bandit: A male rapist.

Bowling alley: The main walkway of a prison.

Boy: Heroin.

Bubble, the: The area in the center of the cell block encased in impenetrable glass where the COs all hang out and keep watch. Also known as *the sally port*.

Can: A can of tobacco.

Catch the door: Let's fight.

Chicken dinner: A ghetto female.

Clink, the: A name for prison. Also known as *the farm, the joint, the pen,* and *the ranch*.

CO: Correctional officer.

Commissary: The store where you can buy stamps, hygiene, writing instruments, soups, sodas, and chips and other snacks. Usually situated in places not easy to get to. Most prisoners don't have money sent from their people in the world so they can only use their prison job wages and have to hustle to survive.

Count time: When the whole farm freezes and everyone is counted, typically about five times a day.

Dance floor: Visit area. Also called *the club, the stage*, or *visitation*.

Dipdip: A thief or liar.

Dog food: heroin; dope; diesel.

Fishing pole: A device made of tightly bound and spun plastic that inmates use to pass items from cell to cell during a lockdown. One inmate will toss an item out into the dayroom, such as a cigarette, a ramen/soup, or a stamped envelope and another inmate from under the door in his cell will shoot out the line with a lure such as a pen or hard object to try and grab ahold of the item to pull back in his cell. This is called *fishing*.

Flash: A gun.

Getting checked: When someone tests you on your ability and willingness to fight when it comes down to it. Also called a *corta check*.

Girl: Cocaine.

Grit: A cigarette.

Gummy bear: A leech; someone who sticks to you or constantly needs something from you.

Holding jiggers: Watching out for the COs.

Hole: Solitary confinement. Also called *the bucket*.

I'm done talking about it: Say anything else and I will beef for you.

Jill: Pills.

Jodi: Name for the guy your girl is sleeping with while you are incarcerated. Also called a *Sancho*.

Ketchup: Make someone bleed.

Kill: Jacking off.

Kite: A letter.

La ling: Snitch.

Lo lo: Sneaky or dirt-cheap.

Low hate: A schemer.

Off this nastiness: Don't need it or be left alone.

Pardon self: Excuse yourself.

Poppi: A drug dealer.

Prison farms: You have intake farms, minimum security, and maximum security. Texas and California call max units gladiator farms, from the historical gladiator who was ready to live and compete in a constantly violent setting.

Pruno: A beverage inmates create by gathering orange juice and hiding it in their cells until it ferments (aka until it rots), then drink to get drunk.

Rack or Raq: Bed.

Rec yard: The place where guys play basketball and handball and lift weights.

Riot: Three or more people fighting.

Rolley: A cheap brand of roll-up cigarettes.

Scratch: Money. Also known as *scrilla* or *chicken*.

Scurry: Scared.

Setting it off: Kicking off a riot.

Square (Catching the square): The place where people would fight.

S.R.O.: Single Room Occupancy

Stinger: An actually pretty cool contraption made of speaker wire, rubber bands, and nail clippers. When all put together it almost resembles a cord. Goes from the outlet in the cell to a cup of water. Very handy when locked down for long periods of time and you need hot water.

Stomping someone: Kicking a person when he is down.

Woods; peckerwoods: White guys in prison. Nowadays, *wood* is a term describing a white guy who will fight.

That mail: A message from somebody you know.

Zootabang: Found in Texas, Zootabangs are a cheaper brand of cigarettes rolled in the wrappings of a toilet paper roll.

BIBLIOGRAPHY

Adams, Robyn, Jane McKenzie, et al. *Computer Science Unplugged Teachers' Edition, revised and extended.* Computer Science Unplugged (csunplugged.org).

Ahl, David H. *BASIC Computer Games: Microcomputer Edition.* Workman, 1978.

Alexander, Michelle. *The New Jim Crow.* The New Press, 2010.

Americans Bulletin. *Redemption Manual 4.5.* McCutcheons Ink, 2010.

Bauby, Jean-Dominique. *The Diving Bell and the Butterfly: A Memoir of Life in Death.* Translated by Jeremy Leggatt. Vintage, 1998.

Bell, Sandra R. "Dragged Through the Mud." In *Keeping the Faith: Stories of Love, Courage, Healing, and Hope from Black America,* edited by Tavis Smiley. Doubleday, 2002.

Boothe, Demico. *Getting Out and Staying Out: A Black Man's Guide to Success After Prison.* 2nd ed. Full Surface Publishing, 2012.

Braman, Donald. *Doing Time on the Outside: Incarceration and Family Life in Urban America.* University of Michigan Press, 2004.

Brooks, Justin. *Wrongful Convictions: Cases and Materials.* Vandeplas Publishing, 2011.

Brown, Claude. *Manchild in the Promised Land.* Signet, 1995.

Canfield, Jack, Mark Victor Hansen, and Tom Lagana. *Chicken Soup for the Prisoner's Soul: 101 Stories to Open the Heart and Rekindle the Spirit of Hope, Healing and Forgiveness.* Backlist LLC, 2012.

Cent, 50, and Robert Greene. *The 50th Law.* Kindle edition. HarperStudio, 2009.

Center for Constitutional Rights and the National Lawyers' Guild. *Jailhouse Lawyer's Handbook: How to Bring a Federal Lawsuit to Challenge Violations of Your Rights in Prison.* 5th ed. Center for Constitutional Rights, 2010.

Chopra, Deepak. *The Seven Spiritual Laws of Success: A Practical Guide to the Fulfillment of Your Dreams.* New World Library/Amber-Allen Publishing, 1994.

Christianson, Scott. *Innocent: Inside Wrongful Conviction Cases.* NYU Press, 2006.

Cleaver, Eldridge. *Soul on Ice.* Delta Paperback, 1999.

Cullen, Murray. *Cage Your Rage: An Inmate's Guide to Anger Control.* American Correctional Association, 1992.

DeGruy Leary, Joy. *Post Traumatic Slave Syndrome: America's Legacy of Enduring Injury and Healing.* Uptone Press, 2005.

Downey, Allen, Jeffrey Elkner, and Chris Meyers. *How to Think Like a Computer Scientist: Learning with Python.* Green Tea Press, 2002.

Eco, Umberto. *The Name of the Rose.* Translated by William Weaver. Everyman's Library, 2006.

Fisher, Antwone Quenton, and Mim E. Rivas. *Finding Fish: A Memoir.* William Morrow, 2001.

Franklin, H. Bruce. *Prison Writings in 20th-Century America.* Penguin, 1998.

Friedman, Thomas L., and Michael Mandelbaum. *That Used to Be Us: How America Fell Behind in the World It Invented and How We Can Come Back.* Farrar, Straus and Giroux, 2011.

Garrett, Brandon L. *Convicting the Innocent: Where Criminal Prosecutions Go Wrong.* Harvard University Press, 2012.

Graham, Stedman, Stewart Emery, and Russ Hall. *Identity: Your Passport to Success.* FT Press, 2012.

Grisham, John. *The Innocent Man: Murder and Injustice in a Small Town.* Dell, 2012.

Harvey, Brian. *Computer Science Logo Style.* Vol. 1, *Symbolic Computing.* MIT Press, 1997.

Leahy, Robert L. *The Worry Cure: Seven Steps to Stop Worry from Stopping You.* Three Rivers Press, 2006.

Likosky, Stephan, Nick Higgins, et al. *"Connections 2012: A Guide for Formerly Incarcerated People to Information Sources in New York City" and "The Job Search."* New York Public Library Correctional Library Services, 2012.

Loya, Joe. *The Man Who Outgrew His Prison Cell: Confessions of a Bank Robber.* Harper Perennial, 2005.

Milgram, Stanley. *Obedience to Authority: An Experimental View.* Harper Perennial Modern Classics, 2009.

Moore, Wes. *The Other Wes Moore: One Name, Two Fates.* Spiegel & Grau, 2011.

Muller, Jim. *The Great Logo Adventure: Discovering Logo On and Off the Computer.* Doone Publications, 1998.

Nadkarni, Nalini. *Between Earth and Sky: Our Intimate Connections to Trees.* University of California Press, 2009.

Osborne, Thomas Mott. *Within Prison Walls: Being a Narrative During a Week of Voluntary Confinement in the State Prison at Auburn, New York.* Nabu Press, 2010.

Papa, Anthony, and Jennifer Wynn. *15 to Life: How I Painted My Way to Freedom.* Feral House, 2004.

Petro, Jim, and Nancy Petro. *False Justice: Eight Myths That Convict the Innocent.* Kaplan, 2010.

Petzold, Charles. *Code: The Hidden Language of Computer Hardware and Software.* Microsoft Press, 2000.

Pink, Daniel H. *DRIVE: The Surprising Truth About What Motivates Us.* Riverhead Books, 2001.

Poitier, Sidney. *The Measure of a Man.* HarperSanFrancisco, 2007.

Reentry Law Project. *Small Business Toolkit.* City Bar Justice Center, 2009.

Rideau, Wilbert. *In the Place of Justice: A Story of Punishment and Deliverance.* Knopf, 2010.

Robeson, Paul. *Here I Stand.* Beacon Press, 1998.

Rosenfield, Richard M. *African American Core Values: A Guide for Everyone.* iUniverse.com, 2009.

Rule, Shiela R., and Marsha R. Rule. *Counting the Years: Real-Life Stories About Waiting for Loved Ones to Return Home from Prison.* Resilience Multimedia, 2011.

Shange, Ntozake. *For Colored Girls Who Have Considered Suicide/When the Rainbow Is Enuf.* Scribner, 2010.

Tanzi, Rudolph, and Deepak Chopra. *Super Brain: Unleashing the Explosive Power of Your Mind to Maximize Health, Happiness, and Spiritual Well-Being.* Harmony, 2012.

Tolle, Eckhart. *The Power of Now: A Guide to Spiritual Enlightenment.* New World Library, 2004.

Tough, Paul. *How Children Succeed: Grit, Curiosity, and the Hidden Power of Character.* Houghton Mifflin Harcourt, 2012.

Weil, Simone. *Waiting for God.* Harper Perennial Modern Classics, 2009.

Williams, Stanley Tookie. *Blue Rage, Black Redemption.* Touchstone, 2007.

X, Malcolm, and Alex Haley. *The Autobiography of Malcolm X.* Penguin Books by arrangement with Hutchinson, 2001.

ACKNOWLEDGMENTS

In the end, maybe it's wiser to surrender before the miraculous scope of human generosity and to just keep saying thank you, forever and sincerely, for as long as we have voices.

—Elizabeth Gilbert, *Eat, Pray, Love*

Thank you. Thank you. Thank you. I cannot say it enough. To everyone who made this book possible, thank you! As with my previous books, I would like to begin with the most important "thank you"—God is the creator of all things and when it comes to expressing the gratitude in my heart, for me that is where it always begins. Thank you, God, for leading me on a journey toward the completion of this work.

The first letter I received from someone incarcerated was from a sixteen-year-old young man named Brian Dupar. His letter touched my heart deeply. Brian is in his twenties now and will be leaving prison soon. We speak on the phone often. Thank you, Brian. The heartfelt courage in the words of your initial letter inspired this entire book. And upon your release, I look forward to the great contributions you will make to this world!

More than any of my previous books, this book is a true collaboration. So many people offered up their ideas, intellect, and sweat to make this work possible. This project could not have been done without the wisdom, research, and talent of Bruce Benderson. Thank you, Bruce. Thank you, Tommy Oliver, for your time and helping with so many creative elements. Thank you to Leslie Wells for all of her help and expertise. Thanks to Camille Tucker, Meri Nana-Ama Danquah, Enitan Bereola II, Stefan Geordin, Dezil, Tuan Priester, Viliv Studios, Brett Mahoney, Omar Benson Miller,

Dr. Tomekia Strickland, Cynne Simpson, Chivette Burton, Robert Nersesian, Eugene Ray, Richard Fudge, Professor Charles Ogletree, and Jordan Walker Pearlman.

A special thanks to all of you who took the time to write me e-mails, letters, and tweets sharing your stories and solutions. The candid, unfiltered details of your private experiences, ideas, and insights bring an authentic, unscripted depth and magnitude—an unrivaled humanity—to the narrative embodied in this work.

Thank you to all of those who contributed letters for the book: Lemon Andersen, Enitan Bereola II, Dr. Jamal Bryant, Dr. Benjamin Chavis, Charles Dutton, Lupe Fiasco, Chloe Flower, Kevin Hagan, Jeff Johnson, Catherine Rohr, Dr. Rudy Tanzi, Russell Simmons, and Michael Steele.

Thank you, Stephanie Daniels, for your tireless work, as well as everyone else who works in my office—Akello Stone, Parker Delon, and Patricia McNair. Thank you to my mother, Marilyn Hill Harper, for reading so many drafts and offering her wisdom and encouragement.

Heartfelt thanks to Nicholas Higgins of the New York Public Library, whose Correctional Services and Family Literacy programs have brought a wealth of reading materials and literacy skills to the incarcerated and their families. *Connections*, their annual guide for the recently released incarcerated in the New York area, provided valuable information for this book. The Correctional Services programs are constantly in search of books to donate to the incarcerated and would appreciate any you are willing to give.

Thank you to investigator Maureen Kelleher, who pointed me toward several useful resources at the beginning of this project.

Warm thanks also to Signe Nelson and Cindy Franz, whose compassionate and knowledgeable work with the incarcerated has made an enormous difference for the lives of many.

Thank you to everyone at Defy Ventures, who offered their expertise and insight: Jeff Ewell, Corey Henderson, Ryan Holly, Fabian Ruiz, Jose Vasquez, and Louis Kanganis.

Thank you to William Shinker, Lauren Marino, Emily Wunderlich, Lisa Johnson, Lindsay Gordon, and everyone at Gotham/Penguin books. Thank you to my literary agent, David Vigliano, for his support and encouragement.

Henry Ward Beecher said, "Gratitude is the fairest blossom which springs from the soul." For authors, books represent legacy, yet books are not too useful if they go unread. So, finally, with deep gratitude, thank you for reading this work. May all of us find our own peace, happiness, abundant blessings, and freedom. I humbly thank you.

NOTES

INTRODUCTION

1. Lauren E. Glaze, and Erika Parks, *Correctional Populations in the United States*, 2011. (Washington, DC: US Department of Justice, Bureau of Justice Statistics, 2012). In Nicholas Higgins, "Family Literacy on the Inside," *Public Libraries Online*, March 19, 2013. publiclibrariesonline.org/2013/03/family-literacy-on-the-inside.

2. Adam Liptak, "U.S. Prison Population Dwarfs That of Other Nations," *The New York Times*, April 23, 2008. Also in "The Drug War, Mass Incarceration and Race" online from Drug Policy Alliance at www.drugpolicy.org/sites/default/files/FactSheet_Drug%20War,%20Mass%20Incarceration%20and%20Race.pdf.

3. Glaze and Parks, *Correctional Populations in the United States*.

4. The Sentencing Project, www.sentencingproject.org (accessed Dec. 1, 2012). The Incarceration report is at www.sentencingproject.org/template/page.cfm?id=107 (accessed Dec. 1, 2012) and can be found in Higgins, "Family Literacy on the Inside."

5. Michelle Alexander, *The New Jim Crow* (New York: The New Press, 2012), 6.

6. Paul Guerino, Paige M. Harrison, and William J. Sabol, *Prisoners in 2010*, Appendix Table 24: "Reported number of inmates under age 18 held in custody in state and federal prisons, by sex, region, and jurisdiction, June 30, 2009 and 2010," www.bjs.gov/content/pub/pdf/p10.pdf.

7. Allen J. Beck, and Paige M. Harrison, "Prison and Jail Inmates at Midyear 2004," Bureau of Justice Statistics, April 24, 2005; online at http://bjs.ojp.us-doj.gov/index.cfm?ty=pbdetail&iid=843. Also cited in Paul Krugman, "Prisons, Privatization, Patronage," *The New York Times*, June 21, 2012, www.nytimes.com/2012/06/22/opinion/krugman-prisons-privatization-patronage.html. Florida is used as an example of the state level in William D. Bales,

Laura E. Bedard, Susan T. Quinn, David T. Ensley, and Glen P. Holley, "Recidivism of Public And Private State Prison Inmates in Florida," *Criminology & Public Policy* 4, no. 1 (February 2005): 57–82. Found online at http://onlinelibrary.wiley.com/doi/10.1111/j.1745-9133.2005.00006.x/abstract.

8. Vicky Pelaez, "The Prison Industry in the United States: Big Business or a New Form of Slavery?" *El Diario-La Prensa, New York and Global Research* 10 (March 2008), found online at www.globalresearch.ca/the-prison-industry-in-the-united-states-big-business-or-a-new-form-of-slavery/8289. Also in Bryan Stevenson, "We Need to Talk About an Injustice," Filmed March 2012. TED video, 23:41. Posted March 2012. www.ted.com/talks/bryan_stevenson_we_need_to_talk_about_an_injustice.html.

9. Available online at www.ncjrs.gov/App/Publications/abstract.aspx?ID=10865.

10. Sarah Schirmer, Ashley Nellis, and Marc Mauer in *Incarcerated Parents and Their Children*, The Sentencing Project, February 2009, online at http://www.sentencingproject.org/doc/publications/publications/inc_incarcerated parents.pdf.

11. Stephen Kurczy, "Catherine Rohr Helps Ex-cons Return to Society by Learning to Start Businesses," *The Christian Science Monitor*, April 23, 2012, www.csmonitor.com/World/Making-a-difference/2012/0423/Catherine-Rohr-helps-ex-cons-return-to-society-by-learning-to-start-businesses.

12. Howard Husock, "From Prison to a Paycheck," *The Wall Street Journal*, August 3, 2012, online at online.wsj.com/article/SB10000872396390443866404577565170182319412.html.

LETTER 2: THE NATURE OF FREEDOM

1. Sidney Poitier, *The Measure of a Man: A Spiritual Autobiography* (San Francisco: HarperSanFrancisco, 2007).

LETTER 3: LOSING IS LEARNING

1. Jone Johnson Lewis. "About Elizabeth Cady Stanton." About Women's History, womenshistory.about.com/od/stantonelizabeth/a/stanton.htm.

LETTER 4: WHOSE LIFE IS IT?

1. Wes Moore, *The Other Wes Moore: One Name, Two Fates* (New York: Spiegel & Grau, 2011).

LETTER 5: MENTORS AND OPTIONS

1. @DeepakChopra (Deepak Chopra). (2012, June 13). There is no such thing as a thing. There are only relationships #CosmicConsciousness [Twitter post]. Retrieved from twitter.com/DeepakChopra/status/213076976796307456.

NOTES | 381

2. U.S. Department of Education, Education Resource Organizations Directory, State Correctional Education Coordinator, online at http://wdcrobcolp01.ed.gov/programs/EROD/org_list.cfm?category_cd=SCE

LETTER 6: ESCAPE PLAN

1. Books on exoneration include Brandon L. Garrett, *Convicting the Innocent: Where Criminal Prosecutions Go Wrong* (Boston, MA: Harvard University Press, 2012); Scott Christianson, *Innocent: Inside Wrongful Conviction Cases* (New York: New York University Press, 2006); Justin Brooks, *Wrongful Convictions: Cases and Materials* (Lake Mary, FL: Vandeplas Publishing, 2011); Jim Petro and Nancy Petro, *False Justice: Eight Myths That Convict the Innocent* (New York: Kaplan Publishing, 2010); John Grisham, *The Innocent Man: Murder and Injustice in a Small Town* (New York: Dell, 2012); James R. Acker and Allison D. Redlich, *Wrongful Conviction: Law, Science, and Policy* (Durham, NC: Carolina Academic Press, 2011).

2. "The Rich Get Richer and the Poor Get Prison," interview with Anthony Papa in *The Socialist Worker*, August 30, 2002, http://socialistworker.org/2002-2/419/419_06_CorporateCrime.shtml.

3. @DeepakChopra (Deepak Chopra). (2012, March 1). Today consider: If you could jump ahead five years from now and meet yourself, who would you meet? #Choice [Twitter post]. Retrieved from https://twitter.com/DeepakChopra/status/175278678715006976.

LETTER 7: HAVING AN IMPACT

1. Eckhart Tolle, *A New Earth: Awakening to Your Life's Purpose* (New York: Penguin, 2008), 13.

LETTER 8: WHAT IS A SLAVE?

1. Murray C. Cullen, *Cage Your Rage: An Inmate's Guide to Anger Control* (Alexandria, VA: American Correctional Association, 1992) is a workbook that helps you learn how to identify and control anger. *Living on the Outside: A Pre-Release Handbook* gives pointers for figuring out what kind of work you might like to do, getting a job, finding a place to live, figuring out your transportation, managing money, keeping safe and healthy, and finding services on the outside. *Incarcerated Education* contains an outline of training programs and classes in this particular jail: basic office skills, building maintenance, nail technology, plumbing, small engine repair, life management, men's issues, and women's issues. *Chicken Soup for the Prisoner's Soul: 101 Stories to Open the Heart and Rekindle the Spirit of Hope, Healing and Forgiveness* by Jack Canfield, Mark Victor Hansen and Tom Lagana.

LETTER 9: DOING TIME

1. Nalini Nadkarni, *Between Earth and Sky: Our Intimate Connections to Trees* (Berkeley, CA: University of California Press, 2009).

LETTER 10: A LEAP OF FAITH

1. Søren Kierkegaard, *Fear and Trembling*, trans. Alastair Hannay (New York: Penguin Classics, 1986).

LETTER 11: HER POINT OF VIEW

1. Victoria Anisman-Reiner, "Coping When a Loved One Is in Prison," *Suite 101*, March 25, 2013, http://suite101.com/article/coping-when-a-loved-one-is-in-prison-a105398
2. Donald Braman, *Doing Time on the Outside: Incarceration and Family Life in Urban America* (Ann Arbor, MI: University of Michigan Press, 2004).
3. The National Resource Center on Children and Families of the Incarcerated, http://fcnetwork.org/

LETTER 12: HILL'S ASSIGNMENT

1. The National Resource Center on Children and Families of the Incarcerated, http://fcnetwork.org/
2. Ibid.

LETTER 13: SMART ENOUGH

1. Deepak Chopra, and Rudolph E. Tanzi, *Super Brain: Unleashing the Explosive Power of Your Mind to Maximize Health, Happiness, and Spiritual Well-Being* (New York: Harmony Books, 2012).
2. Ibid., 16.

LETTER 14: YOU CAN'T KEEP A GOOD MIND DOWN

1. Janine Shepherd, "A Broken Body Isn't a Broken Person." Filmed October 2012. TED video, 18:58. Posted November 2012. http://www.ted.com/talks/janine_shepherd_a_broken_body_isn_t_a_broken_person.html.
2. Jean-Dominique Bauby, *The Diving Bell and the Butterfly: A Memoir of Life in Death*, trans. Jeremy Leggatt (New York: Vintage, 1998).

LETTER 15: SHOULD I JOIN A GANG?

1. Stanley Tookie Williams, *Blue Rage, Black Redemption: A Memoir* (New York: Touchstone, 2007), xvii.

2. Available online at http://www.fbi.gov/stats-services/publications/2011-national-gang-threat-assessment.

LETTER 16: WHAT MAKES A MAN?

1. Umberto Eco, *The Name of the Rose* (New York: Borzoi Books, 2006).
2. Experiment explained in detail in Stanley Milgram, *Obedience to Authority: An Experimental View* (New York: Harper Perennial Modern Classics, 2009).

LETTER 21: STRAYING

1. Philip K. Dick, *A Scanner Darkly* (New York: Vintage, 1991), 276–77.
2. Cyrus Langhorne, "Becoming Eminem's Hype Man Was Tough, 'That's Always Been Proof,'" *XXL*, February 3, 2011, appearing on SOHH.com at http://www.sohh.com/2011/02/eminem_recruited_mr_porter_for_hype_man.html.

LETTER 22: FORGIVING

1. Simone Weil, *Attente de Dieu*, trans. Brad Jersak, *Clarion Journal*, 2011, 155–57.

LETTER 23: MENTAL HEALTH

1. Available online at http://www.osborneny.org.
2. See a description of the Longtermers Responsibility Project at http://www.osborneny.org/programs.cfm?programID=19.

LETTER 25: FLICKING THE SWITCH

1. Thich Nhat Hanh, *No Death, No Fear: Comforting Wisdom for Life* (New York: Riverhead, 2003), 24, 98.

LETTER 26: END POINTS

1. 50 Cent and Robert Greene, *The 50th Law* (New York: HarperStudio, 2009), 42–43.
2. "Backward Induction," Wikipedia, last modified February 28, 2013, http://en.wikipedia.org/wiki/Backward_induction.

LETTER 27: WARM-UPS

1. Gary Wolf, interview by Brooke Gladstone, "The Personal Data Revolution," *On the Media*, NPR, May 13, 2011, http://www.onthemedia.org/2011/may/13/the-personal-data-revolution/.

LETTER 29: ERASING

1. Cindy Chang, "Prison Re-entry Programs Help Inmates Leave the Criminal Mindset Behind, But Few Have Access to the Classes," *The Times-Picayune*, May 19, 2012, http://www.nola.com/crime/index.ssf/2012/05/prison_re-entry_programs_help.html.

LETTER 30: TRUE ACCESS TO EDUCATION

1. Available online at bpi.bard.edu.
2. Available online at consortium.bard.edu.
3. For more information, contact University Courses for the Incarcerated at Ohio University Correctional Education, 102 Haning Hall, 1 Ohio University, Athens, OH 45701; 1-800-444-2420; or e-mail correctional@ohio.edu.

LETTER 31: GRIT AND GRIND

1. Cindy Chang, "Angola Inmates Are Taught Life Skills, Then Spend Their Lives Behind Bars," *The Times-Picayune*, May 15, 2012, http://www.nola.com/crime/index.ssf/2012/05/angola_inmates_are_taught_life.html.
2. Ibid.
3. Message available at http://programmers.stackexchange.com/questions/119513/learning-to-program-without-a-computer.
4. Available online at http://csunplugged.org/books.
5. An article on the grit scale is at http://www.risk-within-reason.com/2011/12/02/grit-resilience. Longer explanations and discussion of the scale and its purpose can be found in Angela Lee Duckworth and Patrick D. Quinn, "Development and Validation of the Short Grit Scale (Grit-S)," *Journal of Personality Assessment* 91, no. 2 (2009): 166–74, http://www.sas.upenn.edu/~duckwort/images/Duckworth%20and%20Quinn.pdf; and Angela L. Duckworth, Christopher Peterson, Michael D. Matthews, and Dennis R. Kelly, "Grit: Perseverance and Passion for Long-Term Goals," *Journal of Personality and Social Psychology* 92, no. 6 (2007): 1087–1101, http://www.sas.upenn.edu/~duckwort/images/Grit%20JPSP.pdf.

LETTER 34: CHANGING YOUR TUNE

1. A profile on Pincus can be found at http://www.forbes.com/profile/mark-pincus.

LETTER 35: UNEQUAL JUST US

1. Their official website can be found online at http://eji.org.

2. Center for Constitutional Rights and the National Lawyers' Guild, *Jailhouse Lawyer's Handbook: How to Bring a Federal Lawsuit to Challenge Violations of Your Rights in Prison*, 5th edition, (New York: Center for Constitutional Rights, 2010), 43–44.

LETTER 36: OUT THERE

1. City Bar Justice Center, *Reentry Law Project: Small Business Toolkit*, page 5, http://www2.nycbar.org/citybarjusticecenter/pdf/Reentry_Toolkit_April09.pdf.
2. Ibid., 2.
3. *Your New York State Rap Sheet: A Guide to Getting, Understanding and Correcting Your Criminal Record*. Available online at http://www.lac.org/doc_library/lac/publications/YourRapSheet.pdf.
4. *Reentry Law Project*, 13–18.

LETTER 37: A LITTLE HELP FROM MY FRIENDS

1. Stephen Kurczy, "Catherine Rohr Helps Ex-Cons Return to Society by Learning to Start Businesses," *The Christian Science Monitor*, April 23, 2012, http://www.csmonitor.com/World/Making-a-difference/2012/0423/Catherine-Rohr-helps-ex-cons-return-to-society-by-learning-to-start-businesses
2. Ibid.
3. *"Connections 2012" and "the Job Search"* was written by Stephan Likosky, former Correctional Services Librarian for the New York Public Library. It was updated for the 2012 edition by Nick Higgins, current Correctional Services Librarian; Katie Banks; Laurie Drago; Emily Jacobson; Keisha Miller; Mariela Quintana; Madeleine Schwartz; Erica Scott; and Caitlin Wilson.
4. Nick Higgins, ed., *Connections 2012: A Guide for Formerly Incarcerated People to Information Sources in New York City* (New York: The New York Public Library, 2012).

OWNER'S MANUAL

1. Carol Dweck, *Mindset: The New Psychology of Success* (New York: Ballantine Books, 2007).